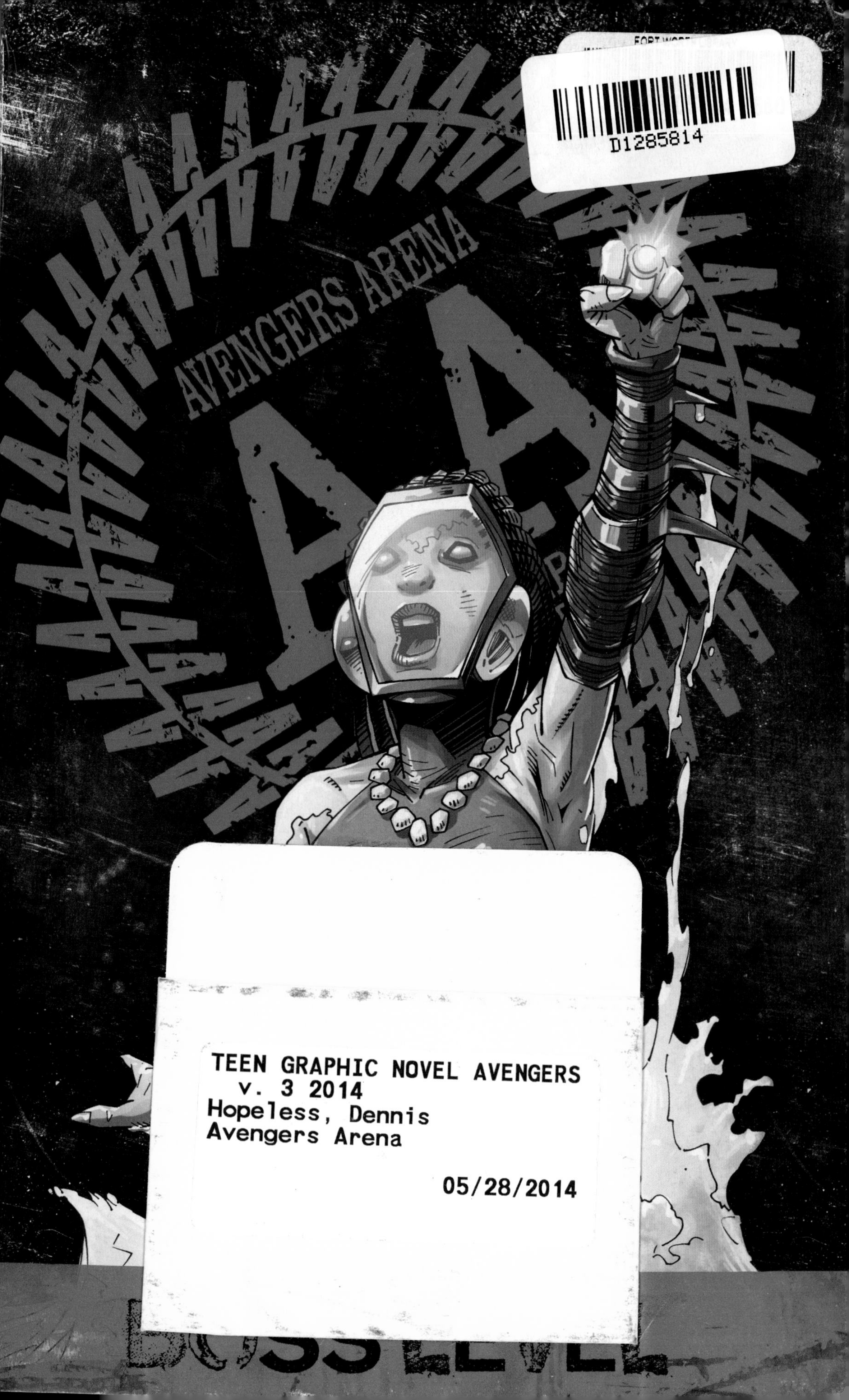
AVENGERS ARENA
BOSS LEVEL

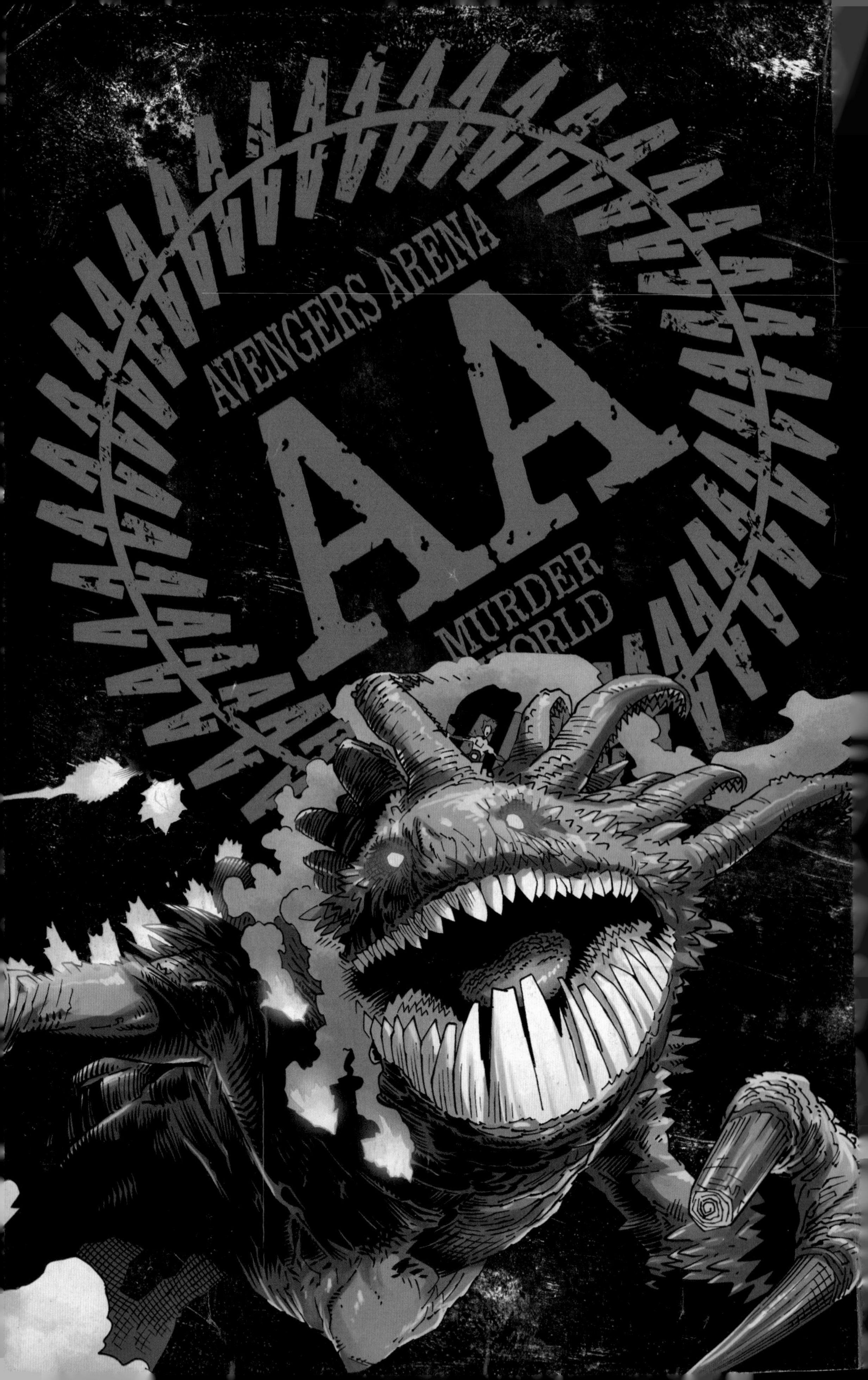
AVENGERS ARENA
AA
MURDER WORLD

BOSS LEVEL

WRITERS
CRISTOS GAGE (#13)
AND DENNIS HOPELESS (#14-18)

PENCILERS
KARL MOLINE (#13 & #16)
AND KEV WALKER (#14-15 & #17-18)

INKERS
MARK PENNINGTON (#13 & #16)
WITH RICK MAGYAR (#16) & KARL MOLINE (#16),
AND KEV WALKER & JASON GORDER (#14-15 & #17-18)

COLOR ARTIST
JEAN-FRANCOIS BEAULIEU

LETTERER
VC'S JOE CARAMAGNA

COVER ART
KALMAN ANDRASOFSZKY (#13), MIKE DEODATO & RAIN BEREDO (#14-15),
FRANCESCO FRANCAVILLA (#16-17) AND DAVE JOHNSON (#18)

ASSISTANT EDITOR
JON MOISAN

EDITOR
BILL ROSEMANN

COLLECTION EDITOR: **JENNIFER GRÜNWALD**
ASSISTANT EDITORS: **ALEX STARBUCK & NELSON RIBEIRO**
EDITOR, SPECIAL PROJECTS: **MARK D. BEAZLEY**
SENIOR EDITOR, SPECIAL PROJECTS: **JEFF YOUNGQUIST**
SVP OF PRINT & DIGITAL PUBLISHING SALES: **DAVID GABRIEL**
BOOK DESIGNER: **RODOLFO MURAGUCHI**

EDITOR IN CHIEF: **AXEL ALONSO**
CHIEF CREATIVE OFFICER: **JOE QUESADA**
PUBLISHER: **DAN BUCKLEY**
EXECUTIVE PRODUCER: **ALAN FINE**

AVENGERS ARENA VOL. 3: BOSS LEVEL. Contains material originally published in magazine form as AVENGERS ARENA #13-18. First printing 2014. ISBN# 978-0-7851-8928-2. Published by MARVEL WORLDWIDE, INC., a subsidiary of MARVEL ENTERTAINMENT, LLC. OFFICE OF PUBLICATION: 135 West 50th Street, New York, NY 10020. Copyright © 2013 and 2014 Marvel Characters, Inc. All rights reserved. All characters featured in this issue and the distinctive names and likenesses thereof, and all related indicia are trademarks of Marvel Characters, Inc. No similarity between any of the names, characters, persons, and/or institutions in this magazine with those of any living or dead person or institution is intended, and any such similarity which may exist is purely coincidental. **Printed in the U.S.A.** ALAN FINE, EVP - Office of the President, Marvel Worldwide, Inc. and EVP & CMO Marvel Characters B.V.; DAN BUCKLEY, Publisher & President - Print, Animation & Digital Divisions; JOE QUESADA, Chief Creative Officer; TOM BREVOORT, SVP of Publishing; DAVID BOGART, SVP of Operations & Procurement, Publishing; C.B. CEBULSKI, SVP of Creator & Content Development; DAVID GABRIEL, SVP of Print & Digital Publishing Sales; JIM O'KEEFE, VP of Operations & Logistics; DAN CARR, Executive Director of Publishing Technology; SUSAN CRESPI, Editorial Operations Manager; ALEX MORALES, Publishing Operations Manager; STAN LEE, Chairman Emeritus. For information regarding advertising in Marvel Comics or on Marvel.com, please contact Niza Disla, Director of Marvel Partnerships, at ndisla@marvel.com. For Marvel subscription inquiries, please call 800-217-9158. **Manufactured between 11/22/2013 and 12/30/2013 by QUAD/**

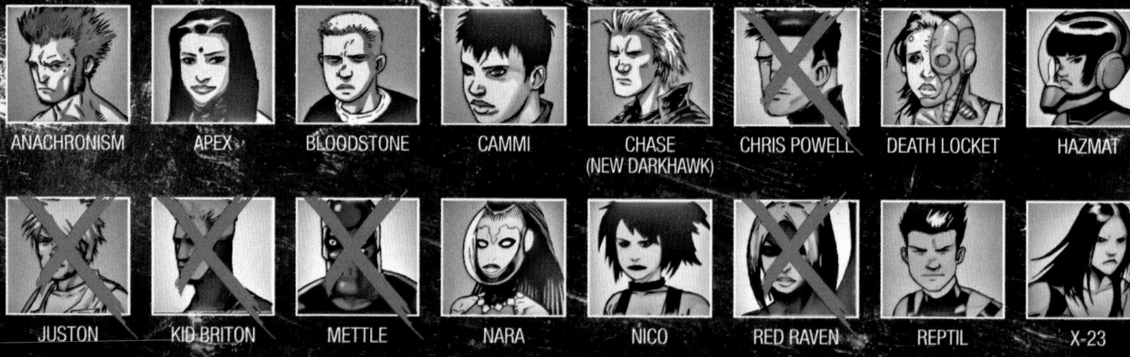
ANACHRONISM
APEX
BLOODSTONE
CAMMI
CHASE (NEW DARKHAWK)
CHRIS POWELL
DEATH LOCKET
HAZMAT
JUSTON
KID BRITON
METTLE
NARA
NICO
RED RAVEN
REPTIL
X-23

PREVIOUSLY

WELCOME TO MURDER WORLD, A MYSTERIOUS ISLAND WHERE A GROUP OF KIDNAPPED TEEN SUPERHUMANS HAVE BEEN FORCED TO BATTLE EACH OTHER FOR THE AMUSEMENT OF THEIR DEMENTED CAPTOR, THE ALL-POWERFUL ARCADE.

APEX RECENTLY REVEALED HER TRUE, MANIPULATIVE NATURE TO THE REST OF THE CONTESTANTS, TAKING CONTROL OF DEATH LOCKET AND DARKHAWK, USING HIM TO CRITICALLY INJURE THE SORCEROUS NICO. HOWEVER, THANKS TO THE NATURE OF NICO'S DARK MAGIC, THE NEAR FATAL SPILLING OF HER BLOOD LED TO HER SHOCKING RESURRECTION. NOW ENHANCED BEYOND HER PREVIOUS POWER LEVELS, NICO RETURNED TO THE BATTLEFIELD AND BURIED KATY AND DEATH LOCKET ALIVE. BUT WHEN DEATH LOCKET WOKE UP, SHE FOUND HERSELF AND APEX IN ARCADE'S UNDERGROUND LAIR — WHICH INCLUDES AN OPERATING ROOM FILLED WITH THE DEAD BODIES OF THE FORMER CONTESTANTS...

MEANWHILE, HAVE THE TEENS' DISAPPEARANCES GONE UNNOTICED BY THE OUTSIDE WORLD?

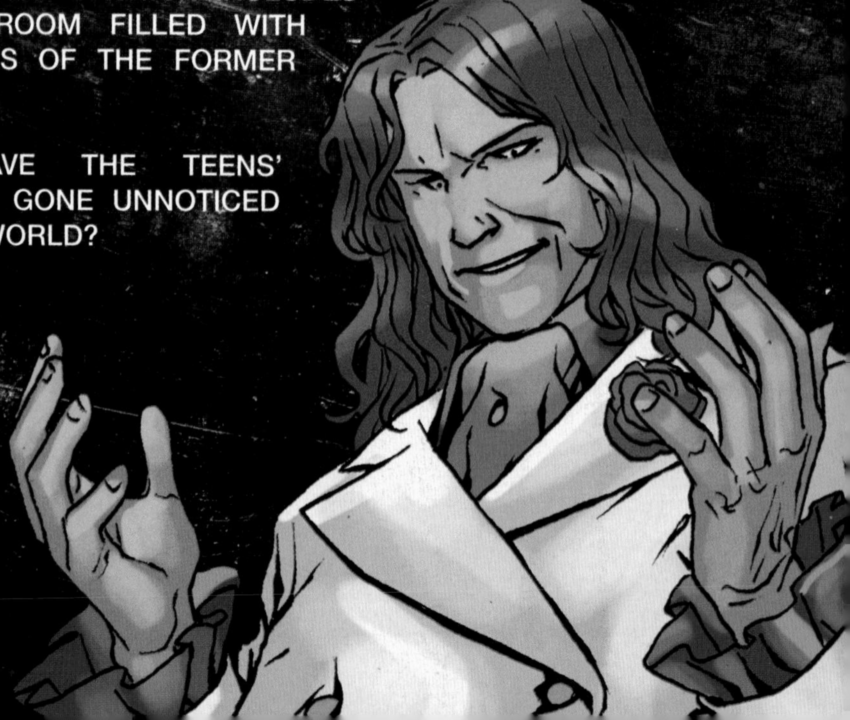

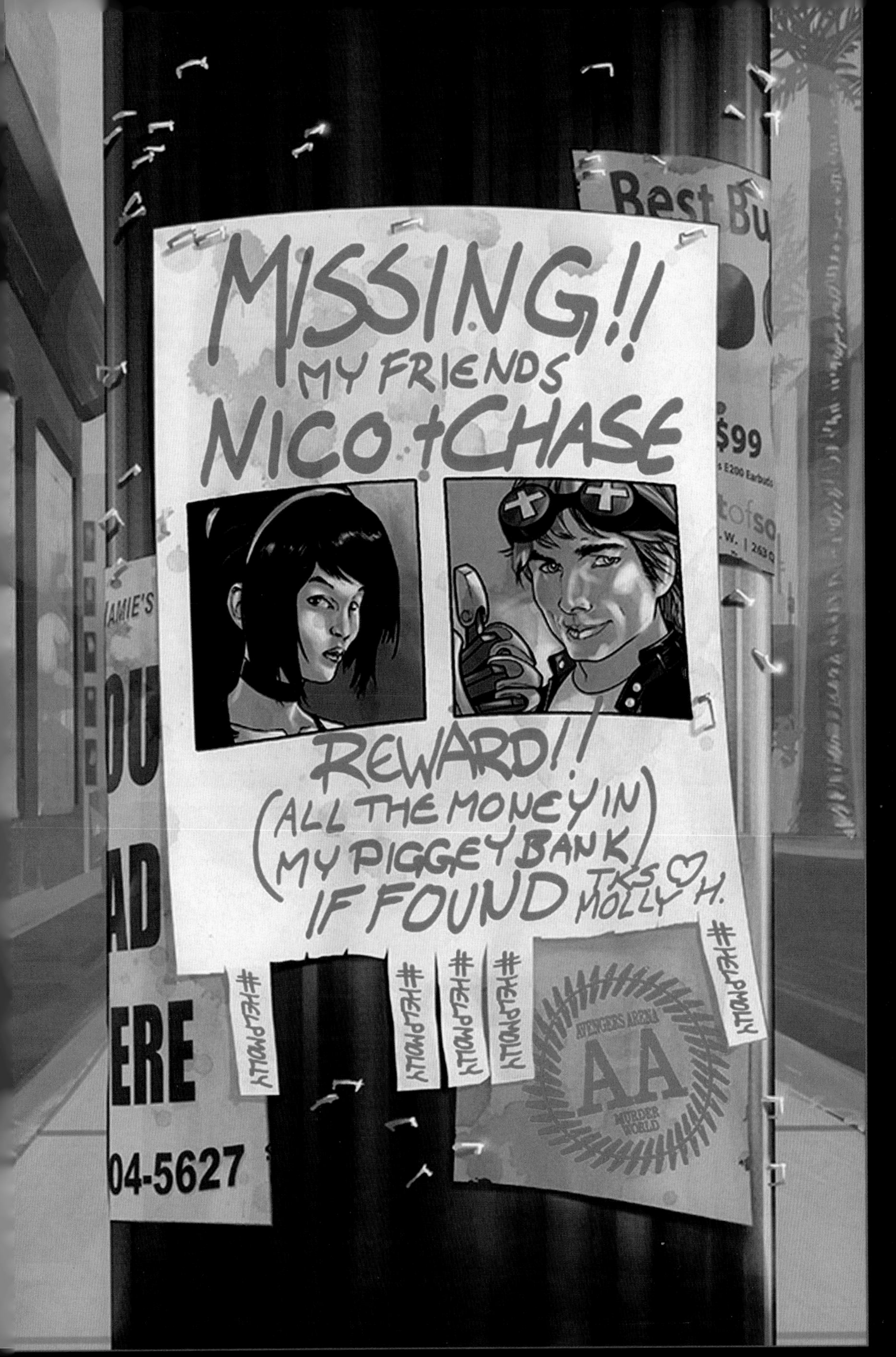
MISSING!!
MY FRIENDS
NICO + CHASE
REWARD!!
(ALL THE MONEY IN MY PIGGEY BANK)
IF FOUND
TKS ♡ MOLLY H.
#HELPMOLLY
#HELPMOLLY
#HELPMOLLY
#HELPMOLLY
#HELPMOLLY
$99
04-5627
AVENGERS ARENA
AA
MURDER WORLD

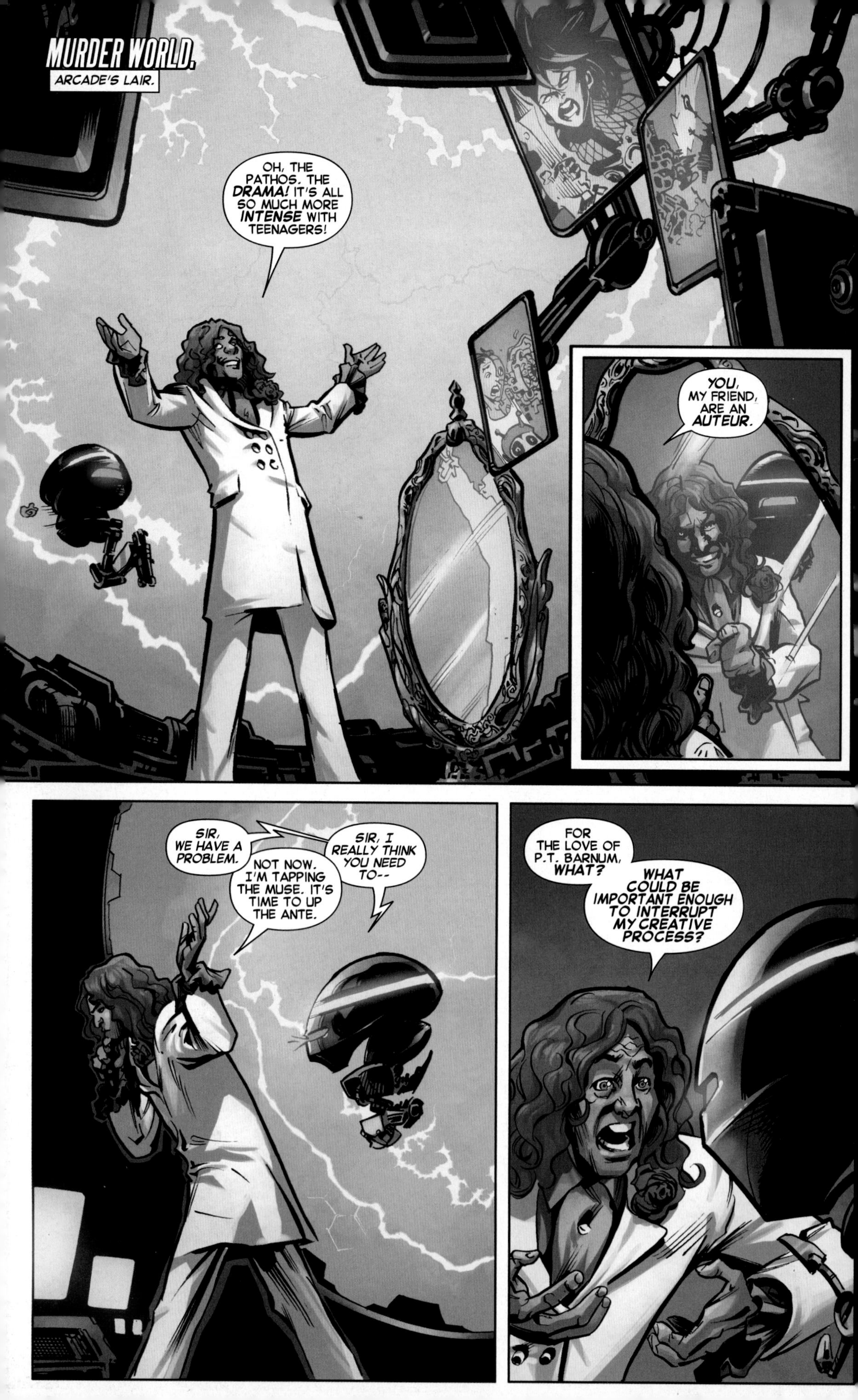
MURDER WORLD.
ARCADE'S LAIR.
OH, THE PATHOS. THE DRAMA! IT'S ALL SO MUCH MORE INTENSE WITH TEENAGERS!
YOU, MY FRIEND, ARE AN AUTEUR.
SIR, WE HAVE A PROBLEM.
NOT NOW. I'M TAPPING THE MUSE. IT'S TIME TO UP THE ANTE.
SIR, I REALLY THINK YOU NEED TO--
FOR THE LOVE OF P.T. BARNUM, WHAT?
WHAT COULD BE IMPORTANT ENOUGH TO INTERRUPT MY CREATIVE PROCESS?

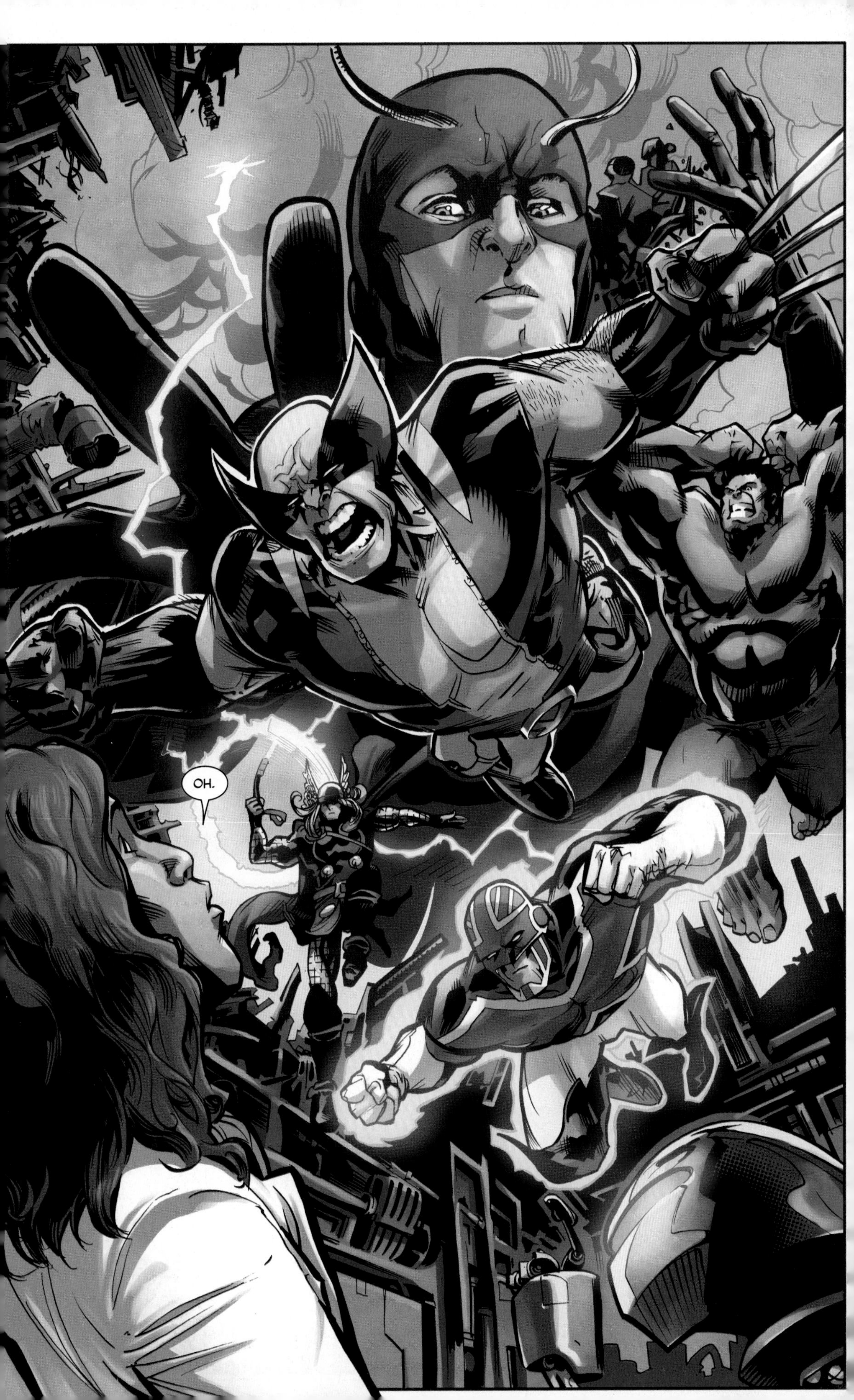
OH.

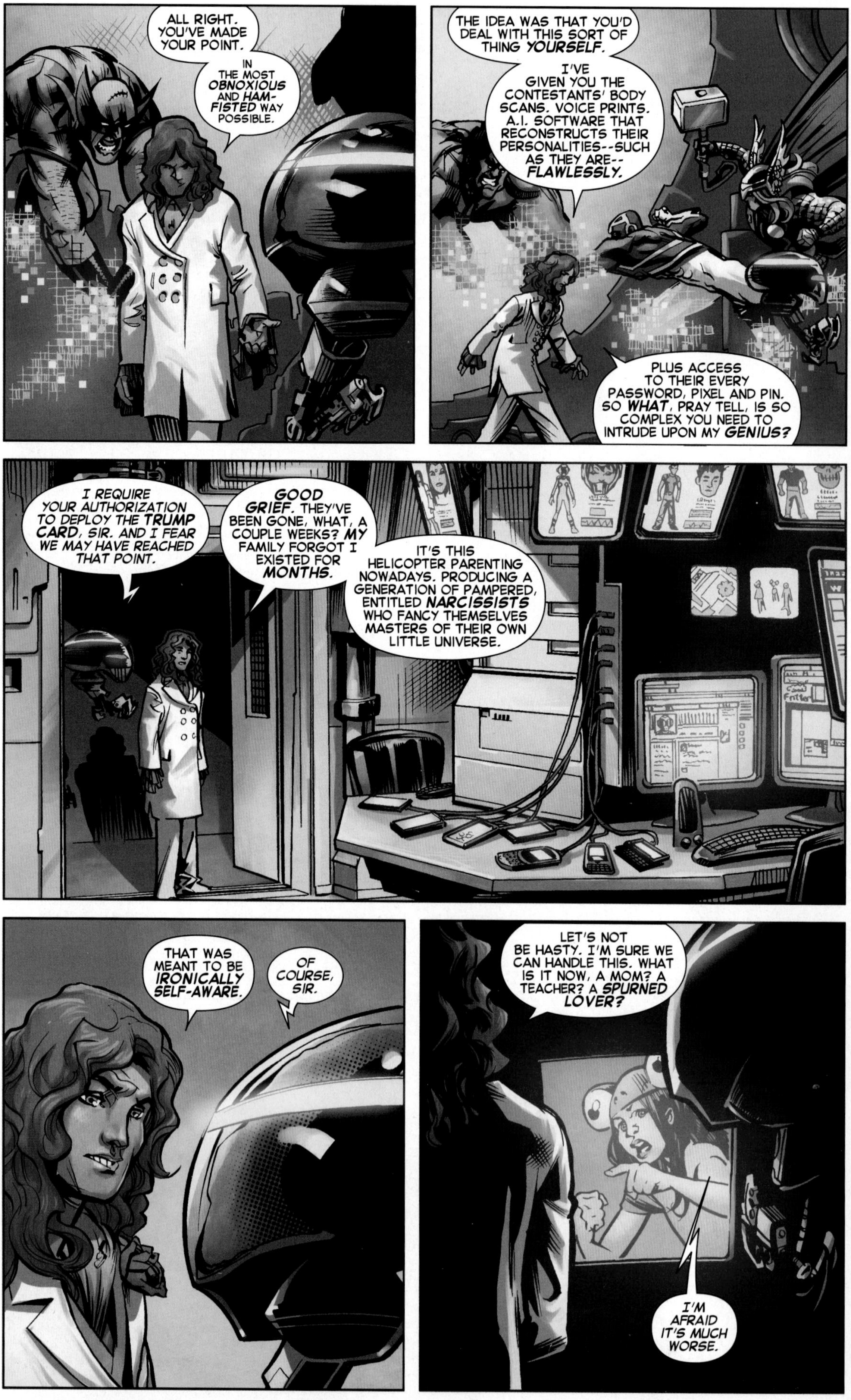
ALL RIGHT. YOU'VE MADE YOUR POINT.
IN THE MOST OBNOXIOUS AND HAM-FISTED WAY POSSIBLE.
THE IDEA WAS THAT YOU'D DEAL WITH THIS SORT OF THING YOURSELF.
I'VE GIVEN YOU THE CONTESTANTS' BODY SCANS. VOICE PRINTS. A.I. SOFTWARE THAT RECONSTRUCTS THEIR PERSONALITIES--SUCH AS THEY ARE--FLAWLESSLY.
PLUS ACCESS TO THEIR EVERY PASSWORD, PIXEL AND PIN. SO WHAT, PRAY TELL, IS SO COMPLEX YOU NEED TO INTRUDE UPON MY GENIUS?
I REQUIRE YOUR AUTHORIZATION TO DEPLOY THE TRUMP CARD, SIR. AND I FEAR WE MAY HAVE REACHED THAT POINT.
GOOD GRIEF. THEY'VE BEEN GONE, WHAT, A COUPLE WEEKS? MY FAMILY FORGOT I EXISTED FOR MONTHS.
IT'S THIS HELICOPTER PARENTING NOWADAYS. PRODUCING A GENERATION OF PAMPERED, ENTITLED NARCISSISTS WHO FANCY THEMSELVES MASTERS OF THEIR OWN LITTLE UNIVERSE.
THAT WAS MEANT TO BE IRONICALLY SELF-AWARE.
OF COURSE, SIR.
LET'S NOT BE HASTY. I'M SURE WE CAN HANDLE THIS. WHAT IS IT NOW, A MOM? A TEACHER? A SPURNED LOVER?
I'M AFRAID IT'S MUCH WORSE.

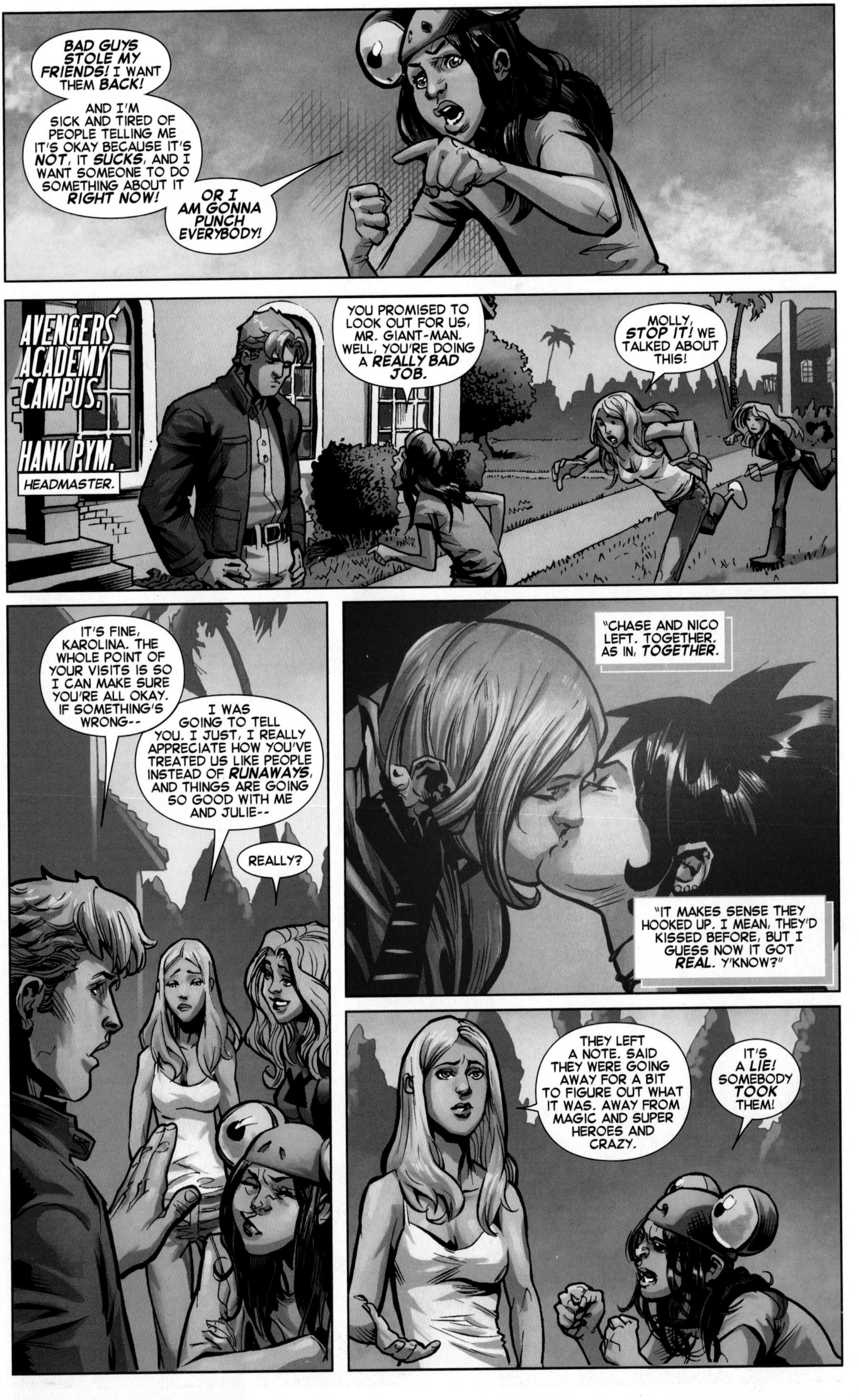

BAD GUYS STOLE MY FRIENDS! I WANT THEM BACK!
AND I'M SICK AND TIRED OF PEOPLE TELLING ME IT'S OKAY BECAUSE IT'S NOT, IT SUCKS, AND I WANT SOMEONE TO DO SOMETHING ABOUT IT RIGHT NOW!
OR I AM GONNA PUNCH EVERYBODY!
AVENGERS ACADEMY CAMPUS.
HANK PYM.
HEADMASTER.
YOU PROMISED TO LOOK OUT FOR US, MR. GIANT-MAN. WELL, YOU'RE DOING A REALLY BAD JOB.
MOLLY, STOP IT! WE TALKED ABOUT THIS!
IT'S FINE, KAROLINA. THE WHOLE POINT OF YOUR VISITS IS SO I CAN MAKE SURE YOU'RE ALL OKAY. IF SOMETHING'S WRONG--
I WAS GOING TO TELL YOU. I JUST, I REALLY APPRECIATE HOW YOU'VE TREATED US LIKE PEOPLE INSTEAD OF RUNAWAYS, AND THINGS ARE GOING SO GOOD WITH ME AND JULIE--
REALLY?
"CHASE AND NICO LEFT. TOGETHER. AS IN, TOGETHER.
"IT MAKES SENSE THEY HOOKED UP. I MEAN, THEY'D KISSED BEFORE, BUT I GUESS NOW IT GOT REAL. Y'KNOW?"
THEY LEFT A NOTE. SAID THEY WERE GOING AWAY FOR A BIT TO FIGURE OUT WHAT IT WAS. AWAY FROM MAGIC AND SUPER HEROES AND CRAZY.
IT'S A LIE! SOMEBODY TOOK THEM!

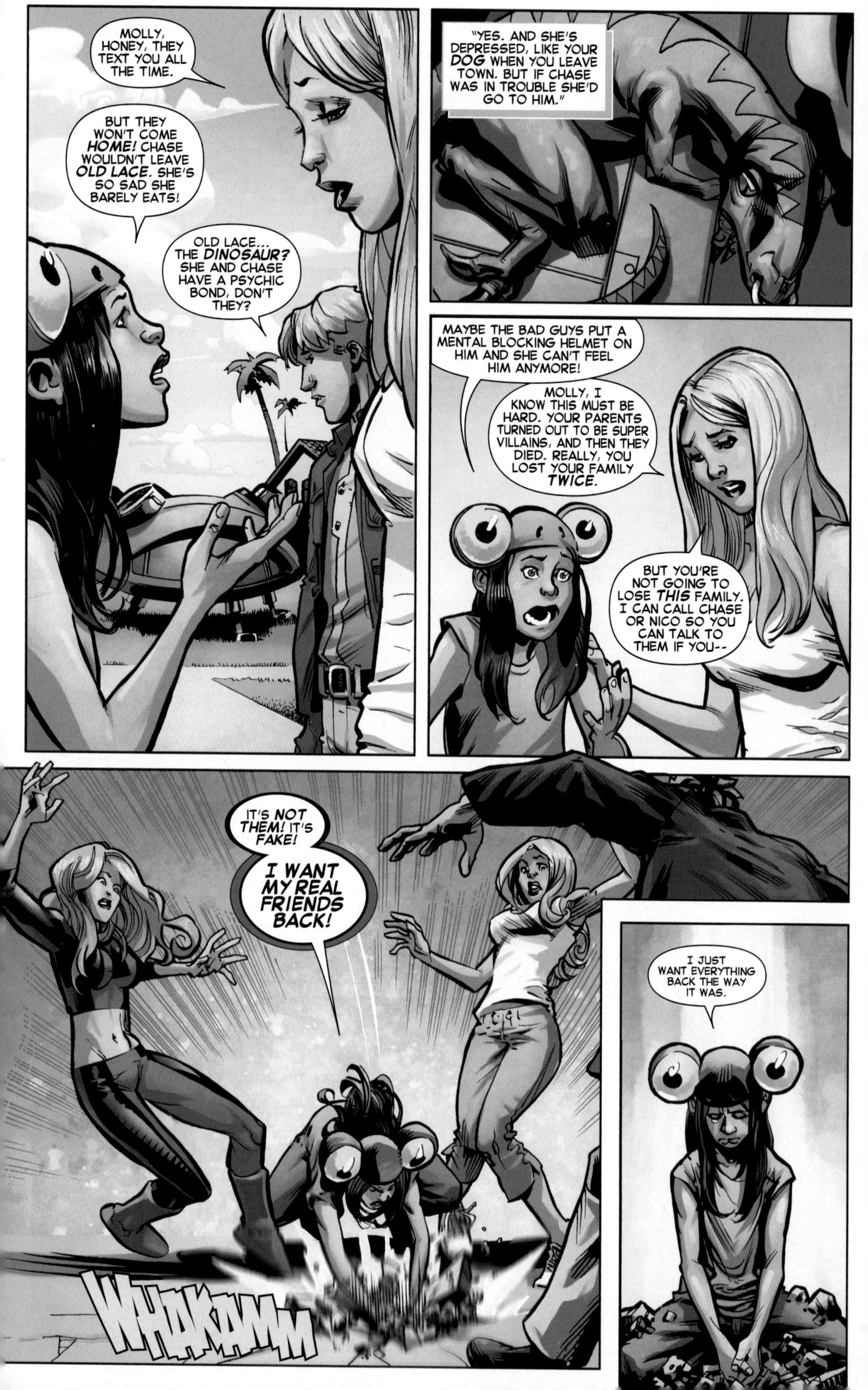

MOLLY, HONEY, THEY TEXT YOU ALL THE TIME.
BUT THEY WON'T COME HOME! CHASE WOULDN'T LEAVE OLD LACE. SHE'S SO SAD SHE BARELY EATS!
OLD LACE... THE DINOSAUR? SHE AND CHASE HAVE A PSYCHIC BOND, DON'T THEY?
"YES. AND SHE'S DEPRESSED, LIKE YOUR DOG WHEN YOU LEAVE TOWN. BUT IF CHASE WAS IN TROUBLE SHE'D GO TO HIM."
MAYBE THE BAD GUYS PUT A MENTAL BLOCKING HELMET ON HIM AND SHE CAN'T FEEL HIM ANYMORE!
MOLLY, I KNOW THIS MUST BE HARD. YOUR PARENTS TURNED OUT TO BE SUPER VILLAINS, AND THEN THEY DIED. REALLY, YOU LOST YOUR FAMILY TWICE.
BUT YOU'RE NOT GOING TO LOSE THIS FAMILY. I CAN CALL CHASE OR NICO SO YOU CAN TALK TO THEM IF YOU--
IT'S NOT THEM! IT'S FAKE!
I WANT MY REAL FRIENDS BACK!
WHAKAMM
I JUST WANT EVERYTHING BACK THE WAY IT WAS.

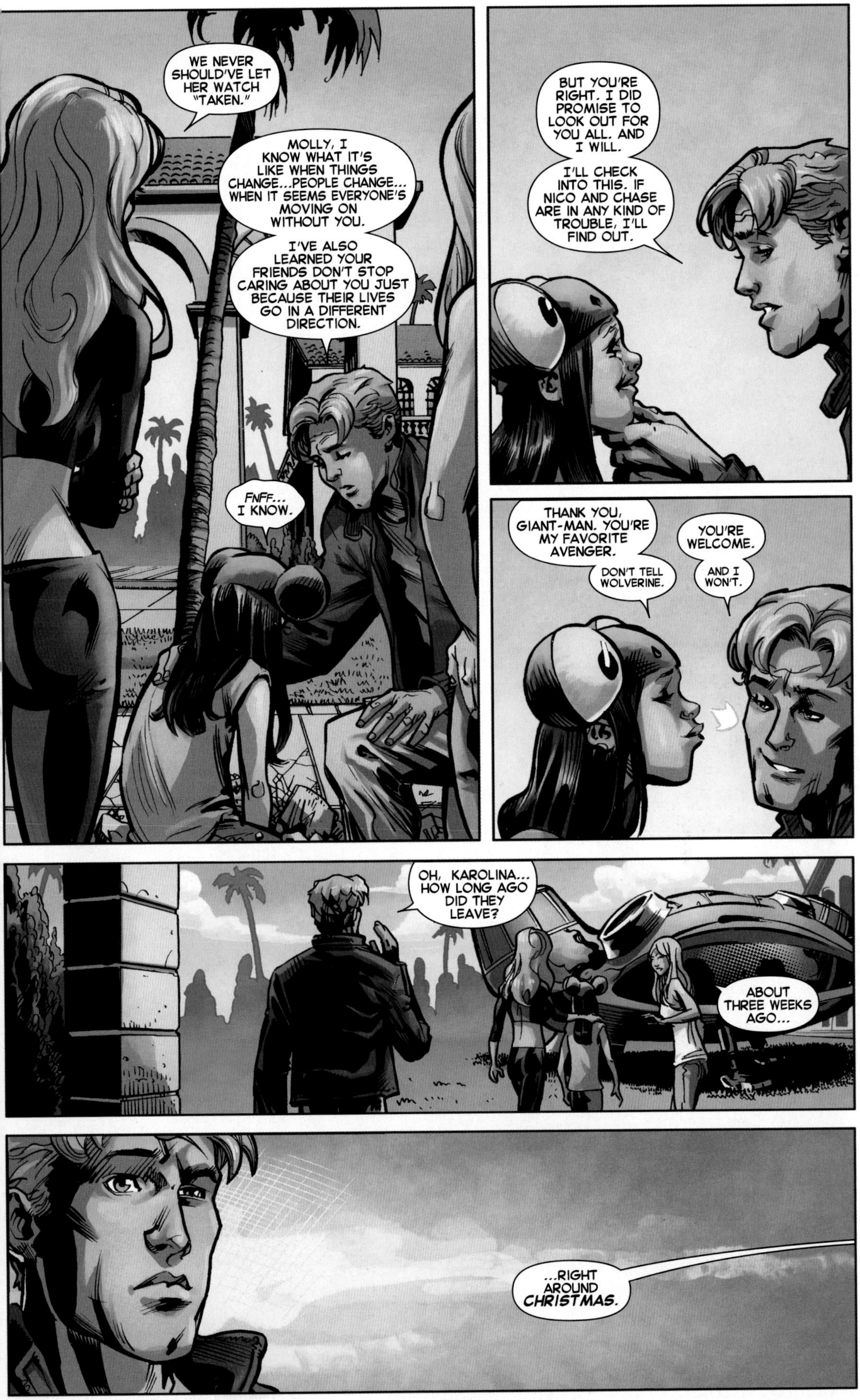
WE NEVER SHOULD'VE LET HER WATCH "TAKEN."
MOLLY, I KNOW WHAT IT'S LIKE WHEN THINGS CHANGE...PEOPLE CHANGE... WHEN IT SEEMS EVERYONE'S MOVING ON WITHOUT YOU.
I'VE ALSO LEARNED YOUR FRIENDS DON'T STOP CARING ABOUT YOU JUST BECAUSE THEIR LIVES GO IN A DIFFERENT DIRECTION.
FNFF... I KNOW.
BUT YOU'RE RIGHT. I DID PROMISE TO LOOK OUT FOR YOU ALL. AND I WILL.
I'LL CHECK INTO THIS. IF NICO AND CHASE ARE IN ANY KIND OF TROUBLE, I'LL FIND OUT.
THANK YOU, GIANT-MAN. YOU'RE MY FAVORITE AVENGER.
DON'T TELL WOLVERINE.
YOU'RE WELCOME.
AND I WON'T.
OH, KAROLINA... HOW LONG AGO DID THEY LEAVE?
ABOUT THREE WEEKS AGO...
...RIGHT AROUND CHRISTMAS.

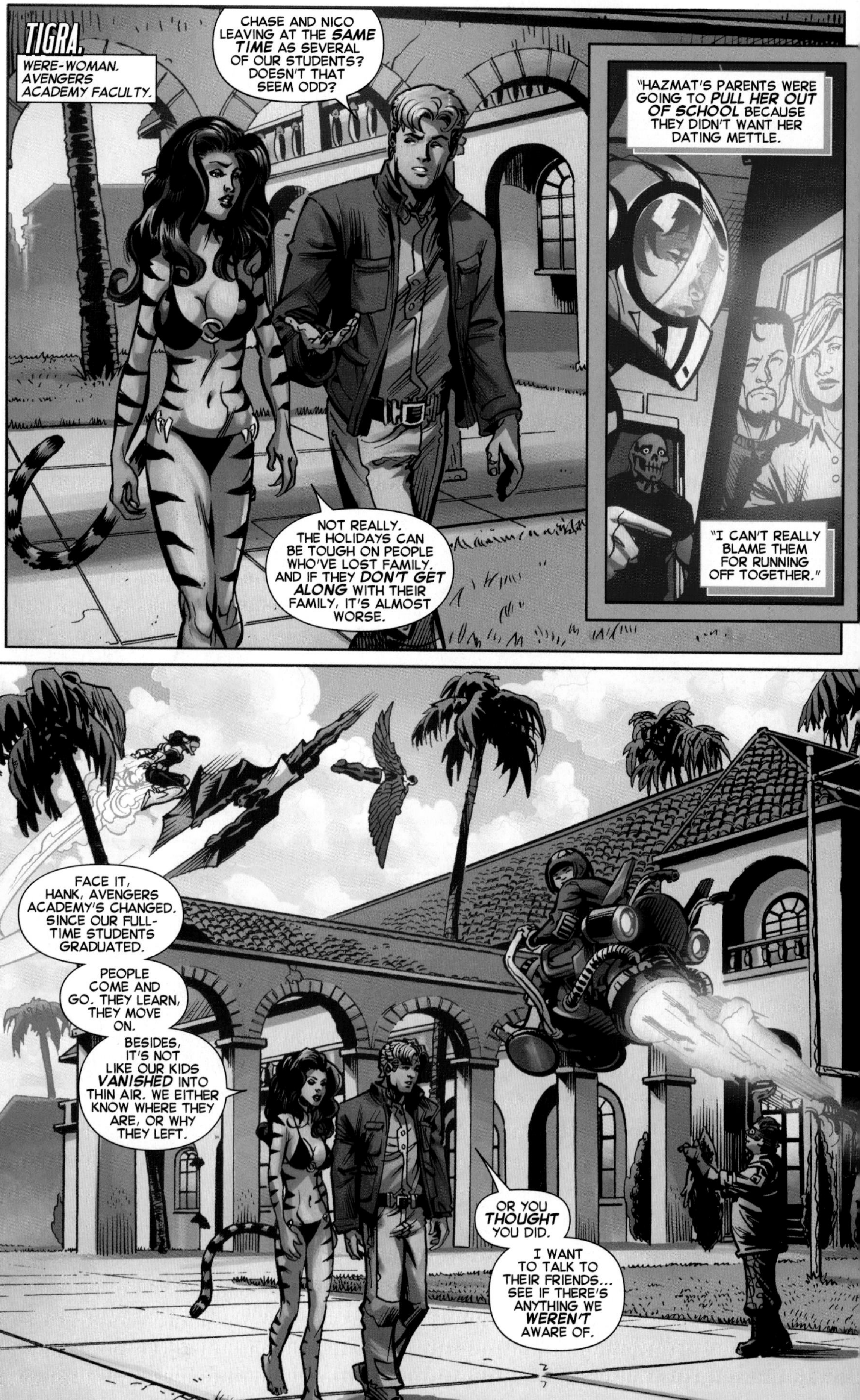
TIGRA.
WERE-WOMAN. AVENGERS ACADEMY FACULTY.
CHASE AND NICO LEAVING AT THE SAME TIME AS SEVERAL OF OUR STUDENTS? DOESN'T THAT SEEM ODD?
"HAZMAT'S PARENTS WERE GOING TO PULL HER OUT OF SCHOOL BECAUSE THEY DIDN'T WANT HER DATING METTLE.
NOT REALLY. THE HOLIDAYS CAN BE TOUGH ON PEOPLE WHO'VE LOST FAMILY. AND IF THEY DON'T GET ALONG WITH THEIR FAMILY, IT'S ALMOST WORSE.
"I CAN'T REALLY BLAME THEM FOR RUNNING OFF TOGETHER."
FACE IT, HANK, AVENGERS ACADEMY'S CHANGED. SINCE OUR FULL-TIME STUDENTS GRADUATED.
PEOPLE COME AND GO. THEY LEARN, THEY MOVE ON.
BESIDES, IT'S NOT LIKE OUR KIDS VANISHED INTO THIN AIR. WE EITHER KNOW WHERE THEY ARE, OR WHY THEY LEFT.
OR YOU THOUGHT YOU DID.
I WANT TO TALK TO THEIR FRIENDS... SEE IF THERE'S ANYTHING WE WEREN'T AWARE OF.

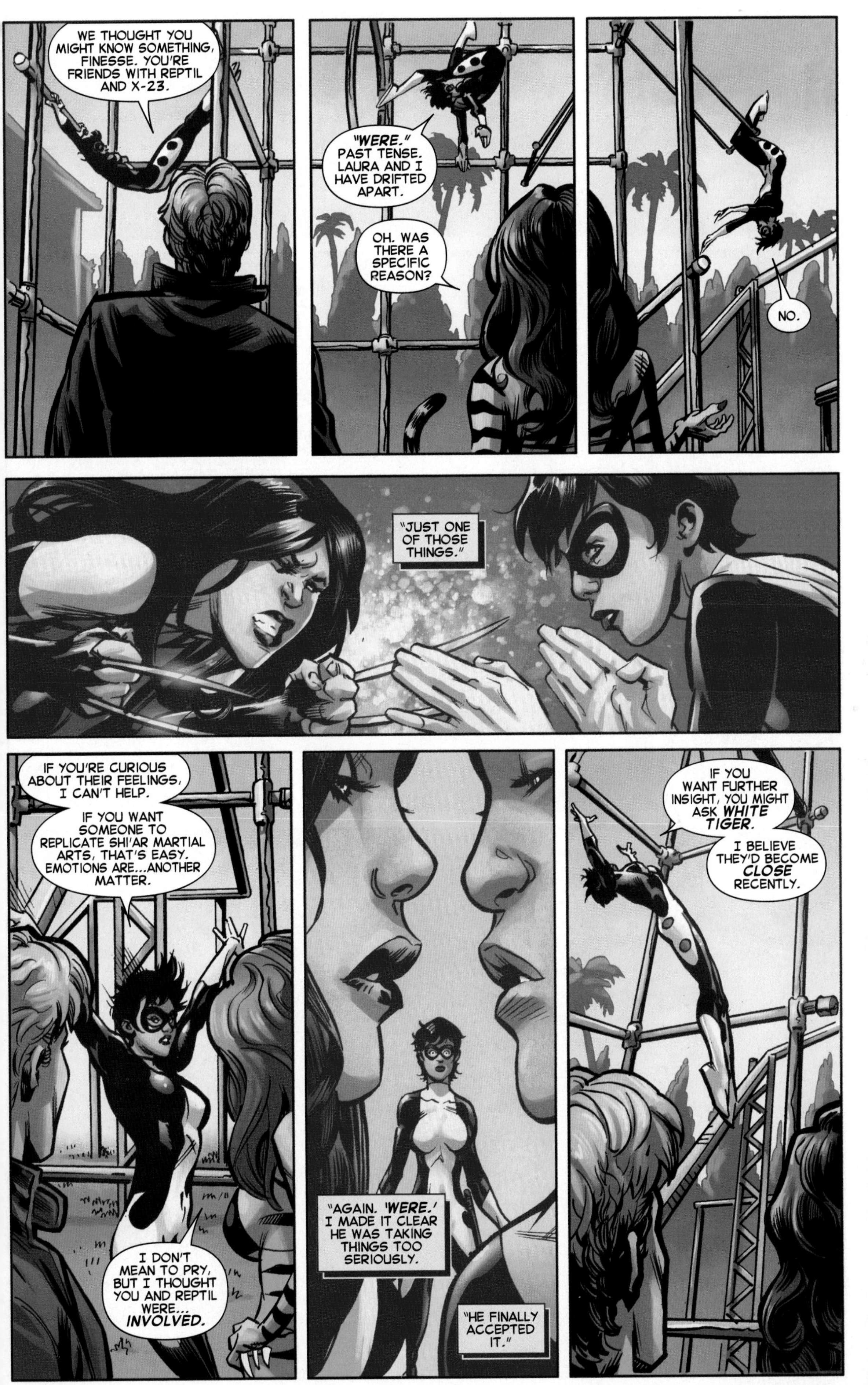
WE THOUGHT YOU MIGHT KNOW SOMETHING, FINESSE. YOU'RE FRIENDS WITH REPTIL AND X-23.
"WERE." PAST TENSE. LAURA AND I HAVE DRIFTED APART.
OH. WAS THERE A SPECIFIC REASON?
NO.
"JUST ONE OF THOSE THINGS."
IF YOU'RE CURIOUS ABOUT THEIR FEELINGS, I CAN'T HELP.
IF YOU WANT SOMEONE TO REPLICATE SHI'AR MARTIAL ARTS, THAT'S EASY. EMOTIONS ARE...ANOTHER MATTER.
I DON'T MEAN TO PRY, BUT I THOUGHT YOU AND REPTIL WERE... INVOLVED.
"AGAIN. 'WERE.' I MADE IT CLEAR HE WAS TAKING THINGS TOO SERIOUSLY.
"HE FINALLY ACCEPTED IT."
IF YOU WANT FURTHER INSIGHT, YOU MIGHT ASK WHITE TIGER.
I BELIEVE THEY'D BECOME CLOSE RECENTLY.

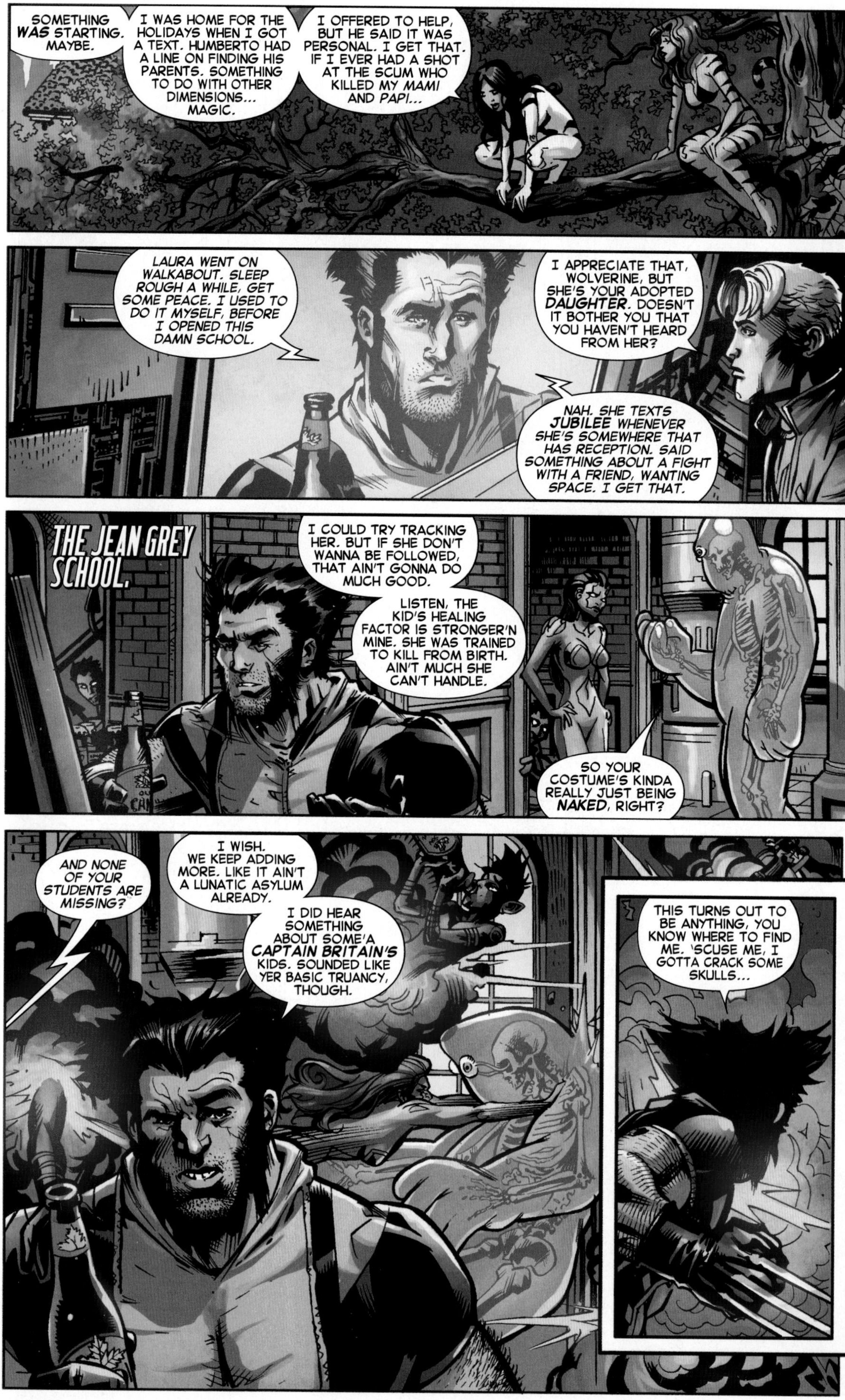
SOMETHING WAS STARTING. MAYBE.
I WAS HOME FOR THE HOLIDAYS WHEN I GOT A TEXT. HUMBERTO HAD A LINE ON FINDING HIS PARENTS. SOMETHING TO DO WITH OTHER DIMENSIONS... MAGIC.
I OFFERED TO HELP, BUT HE SAID IT WAS PERSONAL. I GET THAT. IF I EVER HAD A SHOT AT THE SCUM WHO KILLED MY MAMI AND PAPI...
LAURA WENT ON WALKABOUT. SLEEP ROUGH A WHILE, GET SOME PEACE. I USED TO DO IT MYSELF, BEFORE I OPENED THIS DAMN SCHOOL.
I APPRECIATE THAT, WOLVERINE, BUT SHE'S YOUR ADOPTED DAUGHTER. DOESN'T IT BOTHER YOU THAT YOU HAVEN'T HEARD FROM HER?
NAH. SHE TEXTS JUBILEE WHENEVER SHE'S SOMEWHERE THAT HAS RECEPTION. SAID SOMETHING ABOUT A FIGHT WITH A FRIEND, WANTING SPACE. I GET THAT.
THE JEAN GREY SCHOOL.
I COULD TRY TRACKING HER. BUT IF SHE DON'T WANNA BE FOLLOWED, THAT AIN'T GONNA DO MUCH GOOD.
LISTEN, THE KID'S HEALING FACTOR IS STRONGER'N MINE. SHE WAS TRAINED TO KILL FROM BIRTH. AIN'T MUCH SHE CAN'T HANDLE.
SO YOUR COSTUME'S KINDA REALLY JUST BEING NAKED, RIGHT?
AND NONE OF YOUR STUDENTS ARE MISSING?
I WISH. WE KEEP ADDING MORE. LIKE IT AIN'T A LUNATIC ASYLUM ALREADY.
I DID HEAR SOMETHING ABOUT SOME'A CAPTAIN BRITAIN'S KIDS. SOUNDED LIKE YER BASIC TRUANCY, THOUGH.
THIS TURNS OUT TO BE ANYTHING, YOU KNOW WHERE TO FIND ME. 'SCUSE ME, I GOTTA CRACK SOME SKULLS...

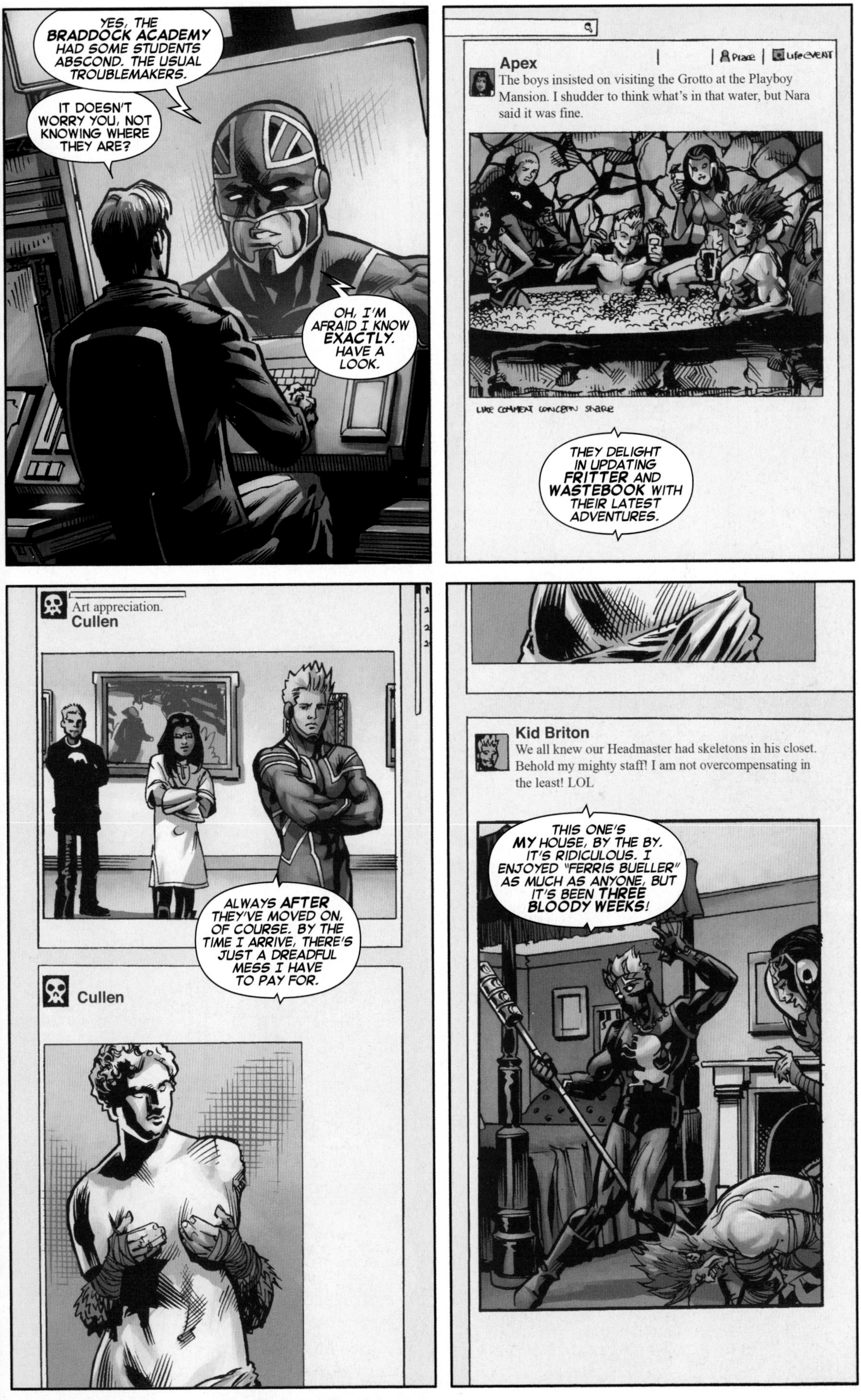

YES, THE BRADDOCK ACADEMY HAD SOME STUDENTS ABSCOND. THE USUAL TROUBLEMAKERS.
IT DOESN'T WORRY YOU, NOT KNOWING WHERE THEY ARE?
OH, I'M AFRAID I KNOW EXACTLY. HAVE A LOOK.
Apex
Place
Life Event
The boys insisted on visiting the Grotto at the Playboy Mansion. I shudder to think what's in that water, but Nara said it was fine.
LIKE COMMENT CONCERN SHARE
THEY DELIGHT IN UPDATING FRITTER AND WASTEBOOK WITH THEIR LATEST ADVENTURES.
Art appreciation.
Cullen
ALWAYS AFTER THEY'VE MOVED ON, OF COURSE. BY THE TIME I ARRIVE, THERE'S JUST A DREADFUL MESS I HAVE TO PAY FOR.
Cullen
Kid Briton
We all knew our Headmaster had skeletons in his closet. Behold my mighty staff! I am not overcompensating in the least! LOL
THIS ONE'S MY HOUSE, BY THE BY. IT'S RIDICULOUS. I ENJOYED "FERRIS BUELLER" AS MUCH AS ANYONE, BUT IT'S BEEN THREE BLOODY WEEKS!

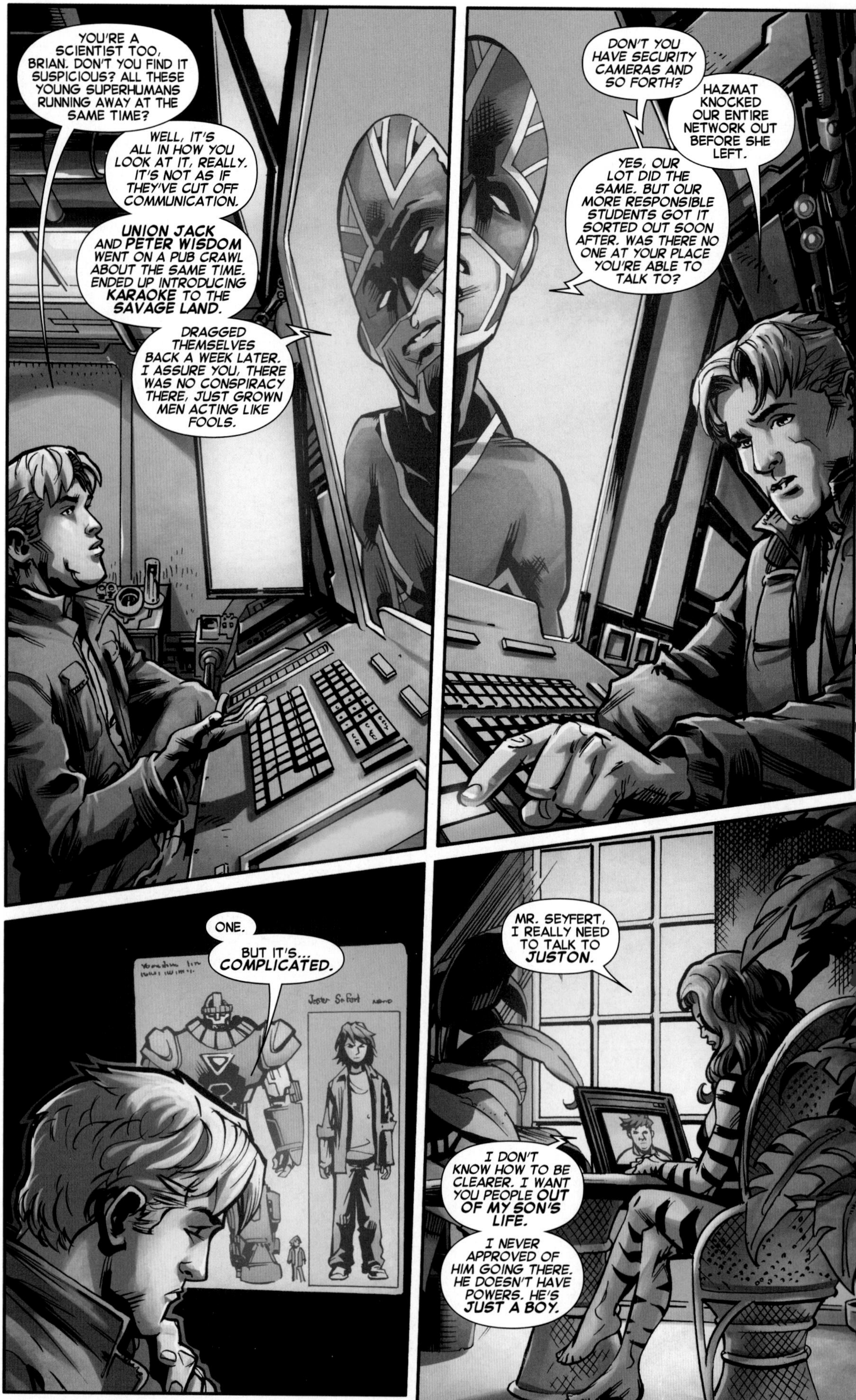
YOU'RE A SCIENTIST TOO, BRIAN. DON'T YOU FIND IT SUSPICIOUS? ALL THESE YOUNG SUPERHUMANS RUNNING AWAY AT THE SAME TIME?
WELL, IT'S ALL IN HOW YOU LOOK AT IT, REALLY. IT'S NOT AS IF THEY'VE CUT OFF COMMUNICATION.
UNION JACK AND PETER WISDOM WENT ON A PUB CRAWL ABOUT THE SAME TIME. ENDED UP INTRODUCING KARAOKE TO THE SAVAGE LAND.
DRAGGED THEMSELVES BACK A WEEK LATER. I ASSURE YOU, THERE WAS NO CONSPIRACY THERE, JUST GROWN MEN ACTING LIKE FOOLS.
DON'T YOU HAVE SECURITY CAMERAS AND SO FORTH?
HAZMAT KNOCKED OUR ENTIRE NETWORK OUT BEFORE SHE LEFT.
YES, OUR LOT DID THE SAME. BUT OUR MORE RESPONSIBLE STUDENTS GOT IT SORTED OUT SOON AFTER. WAS THERE NO ONE AT YOUR PLACE YOU'RE ABLE TO TALK TO?
ONE.
BUT IT'S... COMPLICATED.
MR. SEYFERT, I REALLY NEED TO TALK TO JUSTON.
I DON'T KNOW HOW TO BE CLEARER. I WANT YOU PEOPLE OUT OF MY SON'S LIFE.
I NEVER APPROVED OF HIM GOING THERE. HE DOESN'T HAVE POWERS. HE'S JUST A BOY.

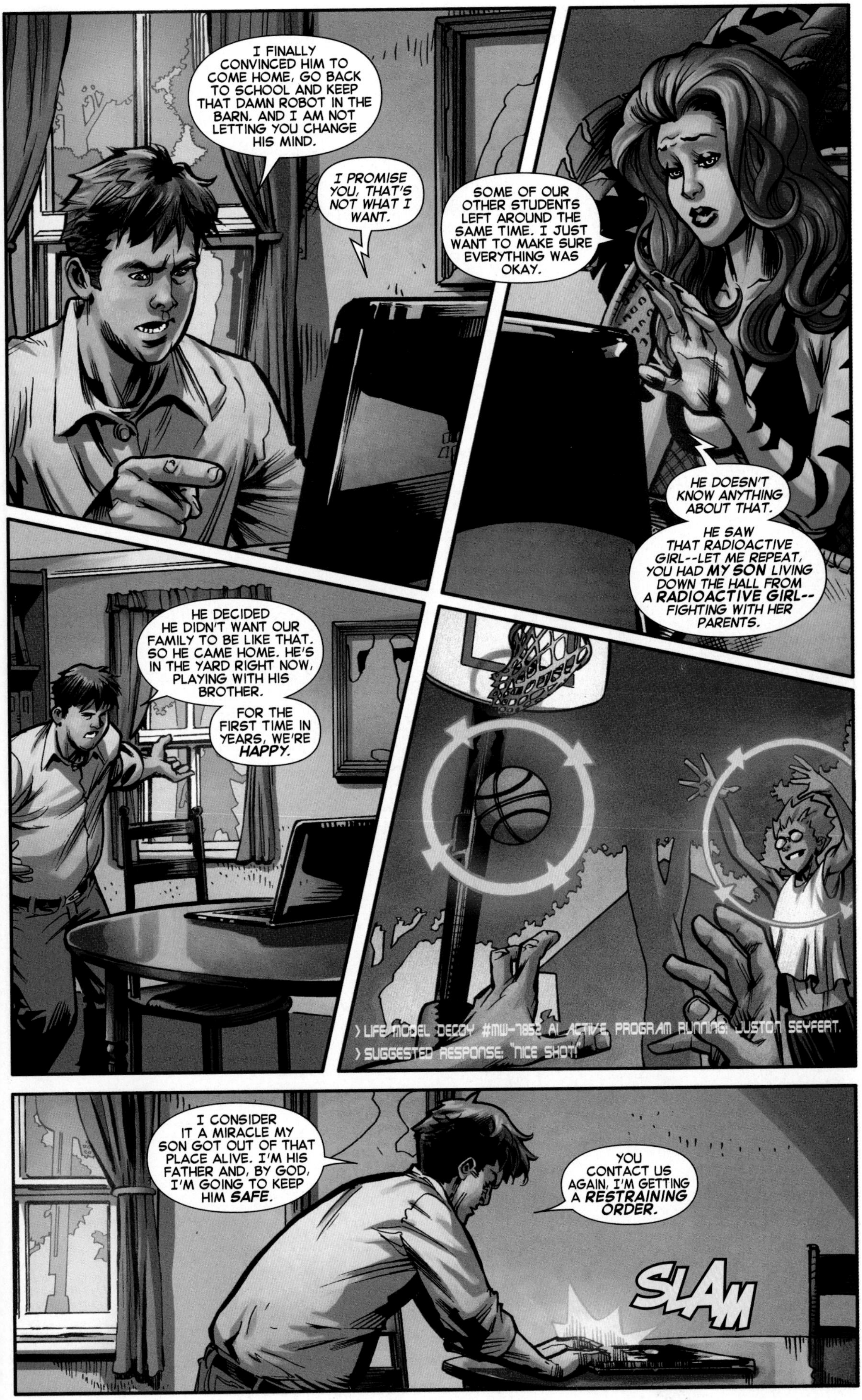

I FINALLY CONVINCED HIM TO COME HOME, GO BACK TO SCHOOL AND KEEP THAT DAMN ROBOT IN THE BARN. AND I AM NOT LETTING YOU CHANGE HIS MIND.
I PROMISE YOU, THAT'S NOT WHAT I WANT.
SOME OF OUR OTHER STUDENTS LEFT AROUND THE SAME TIME. I JUST WANT TO MAKE SURE EVERYTHING WAS OKAY.
HE DOESN'T KNOW ANYTHING ABOUT THAT.
HE SAW THAT RADIOACTIVE GIRL--LET ME REPEAT, YOU HAD MY SON LIVING DOWN THE HALL FROM A RADIOACTIVE GIRL--FIGHTING WITH HER PARENTS.
HE DECIDED HE DIDN'T WANT OUR FAMILY TO BE LIKE THAT. SO HE CAME HOME. HE'S IN THE YARD RIGHT NOW, PLAYING WITH HIS BROTHER.
FOR THE FIRST TIME IN YEARS, WE'RE HAPPY.
> LIFE MODEL DECOY #MW-7852 AI ACTIVE, PROGRAM RUNNING: JUSTON SEYFERT.
> SUGGESTED RESPONSE: "NICE SHOT!"
I CONSIDER IT A MIRACLE MY SON GOT OUT OF THAT PLACE ALIVE. I'M HIS FATHER AND, BY GOD, I'M GOING TO KEEP HIM SAFE.
YOU CONTACT US AGAIN, I'M GETTING A RESTRAINING ORDER.
SLAM

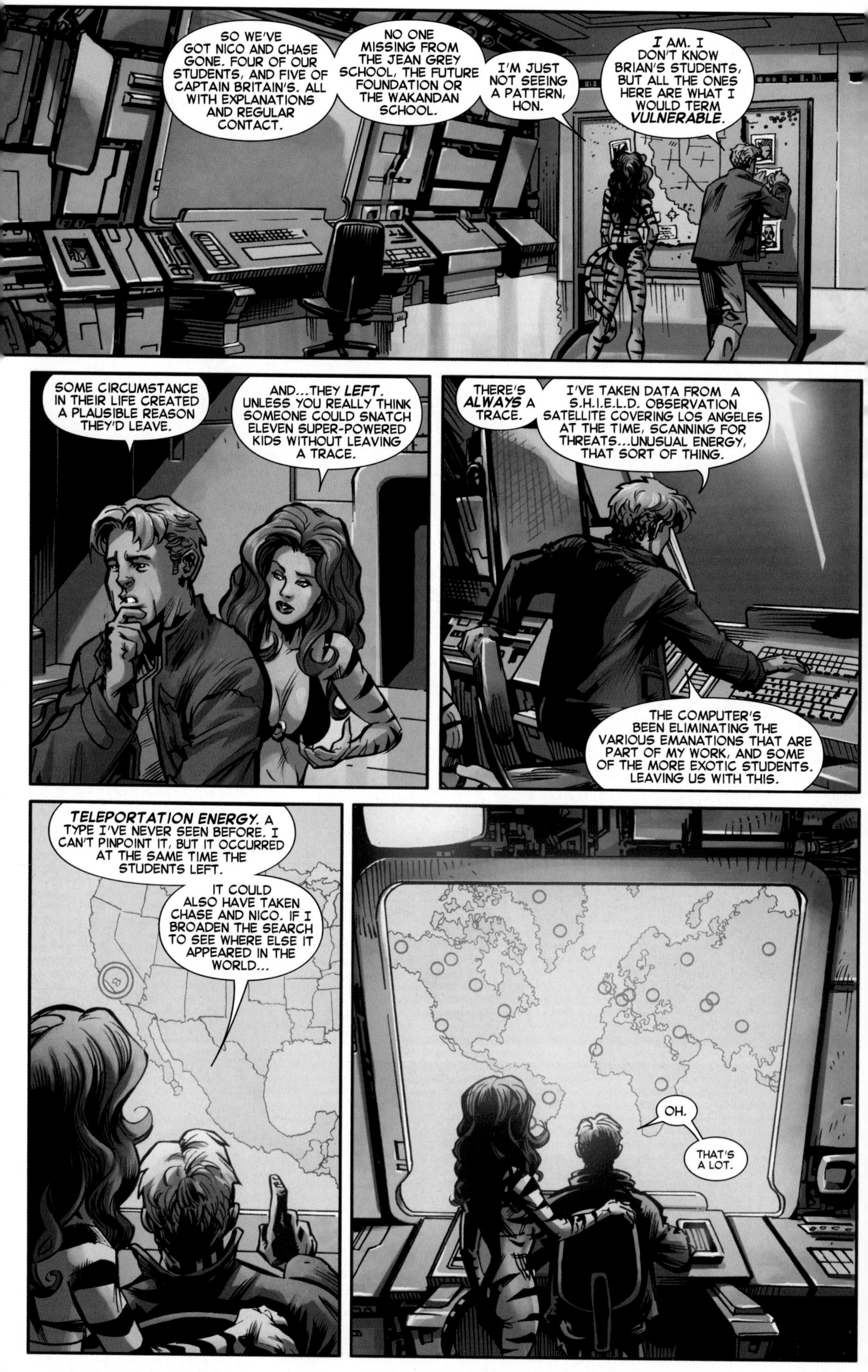
SO WE'VE GOT NICO AND CHASE GONE. FOUR OF OUR STUDENTS, AND FIVE OF CAPTAIN BRITAIN'S. ALL WITH EXPLANATIONS AND REGULAR CONTACT.
NO ONE MISSING FROM THE JEAN GREY SCHOOL, THE FUTURE FOUNDATION OR THE WAKANDAN SCHOOL.
I'M JUST NOT SEEING A PATTERN, HON.
I AM. I DON'T KNOW BRIAN'S STUDENTS, BUT ALL THE ONES HERE ARE WHAT I WOULD TERM VULNERABLE.
SOME CIRCUMSTANCE IN THEIR LIFE CREATED A PLAUSIBLE REASON THEY'D LEAVE.
AND...THEY LEFT. UNLESS YOU REALLY THINK SOMEONE COULD SNATCH ELEVEN SUPER-POWERED KIDS WITHOUT LEAVING A TRACE.
THERE'S ALWAYS A TRACE.
I'VE TAKEN DATA FROM A S.H.I.E.L.D. OBSERVATION SATELLITE COVERING LOS ANGELES AT THE TIME, SCANNING FOR THREATS...UNUSUAL ENERGY, THAT SORT OF THING.
THE COMPUTER'S BEEN ELIMINATING THE VARIOUS EMANATIONS THAT ARE PART OF MY WORK, AND SOME OF THE MORE EXOTIC STUDENTS. LEAVING US WITH THIS.
TELEPORTATION ENERGY. A TYPE I'VE NEVER SEEN BEFORE. I CAN'T PINPOINT IT, BUT IT OCCURRED AT THE SAME TIME THE STUDENTS LEFT.
IT COULD ALSO HAVE TAKEN CHASE AND NICO. IF I BROADEN THE SEARCH TO SEE WHERE ELSE IT APPEARED IN THE WORLD...
OH.
THAT'S A LOT.

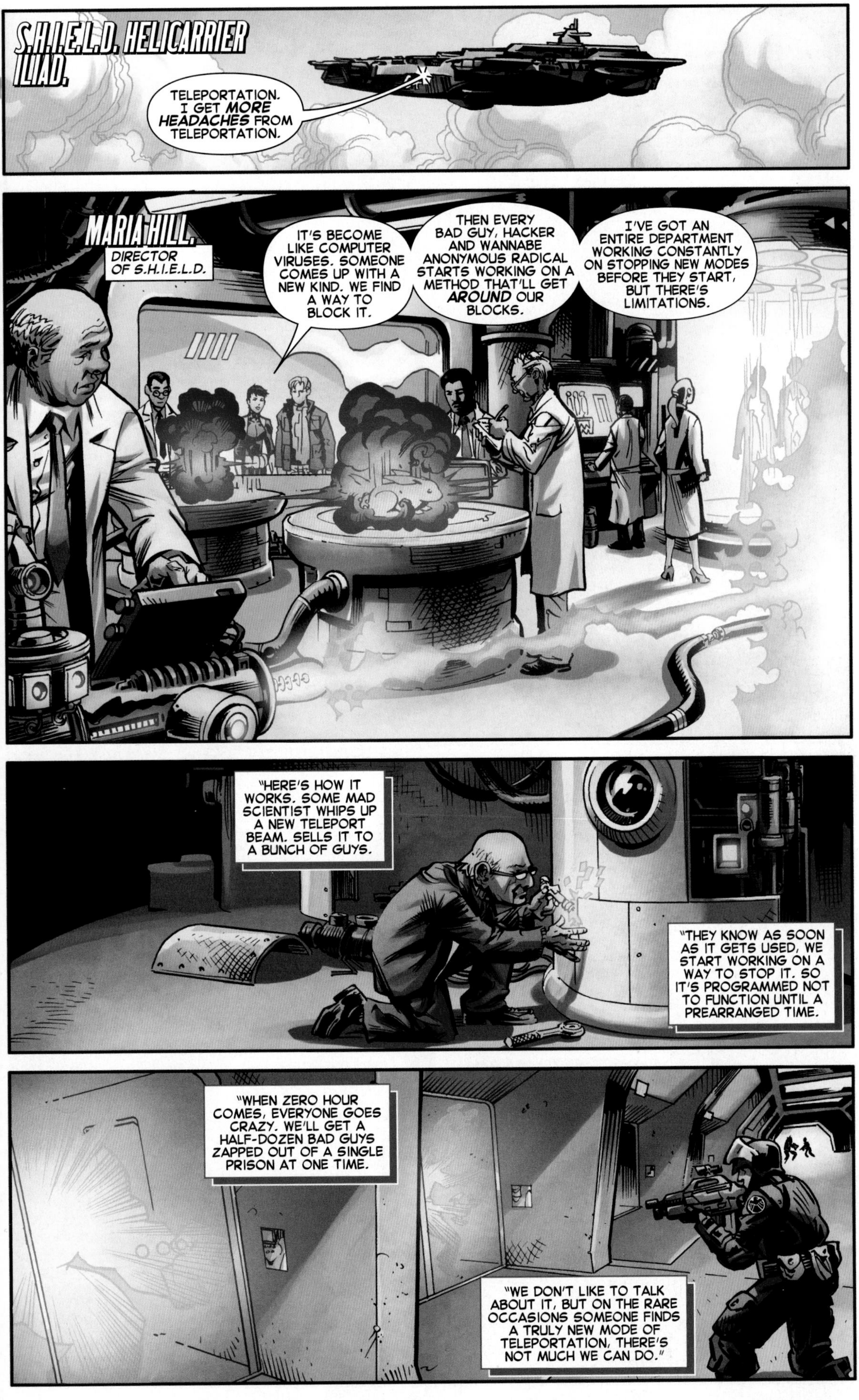
S.H.I.E.L.D. HELICARRIER ILIAD.
TELEPORTATION. I GET MORE HEADACHES FROM TELEPORTATION.
MARIA HILL, DIRECTOR OF S.H.I.E.L.D.
IT'S BECOME LIKE COMPUTER VIRUSES. SOMEONE COMES UP WITH A NEW KIND. WE FIND A WAY TO BLOCK IT.
THEN EVERY BAD GUY, HACKER AND WANNABE ANONYMOUS RADICAL STARTS WORKING ON A METHOD THAT'LL GET AROUND OUR BLOCKS.
I'VE GOT AN ENTIRE DEPARTMENT WORKING CONSTANTLY ON STOPPING NEW MODES BEFORE THEY START, BUT THERE'S LIMITATIONS.
"HERE'S HOW IT WORKS. SOME MAD SCIENTIST WHIPS UP A NEW TELEPORT BEAM. SELLS IT TO A BUNCH OF GUYS.
"THEY KNOW AS SOON AS IT GETS USED, WE START WORKING ON A WAY TO STOP IT. SO IT'S PROGRAMMED NOT TO FUNCTION UNTIL A PREARRANGED TIME.
"WHEN ZERO HOUR COMES, EVERYONE GOES CRAZY. WE'LL GET A HALF-DOZEN BAD GUYS ZAPPED OUT OF A SINGLE PRISON AT ONE TIME.
"WE DON'T LIKE TO TALK ABOUT IT, BUT ON THE RARE OCCASIONS SOMEONE FINDS A TRULY NEW MODE OF TELEPORTATION, THERE'S NOT MUCH WE CAN DO."

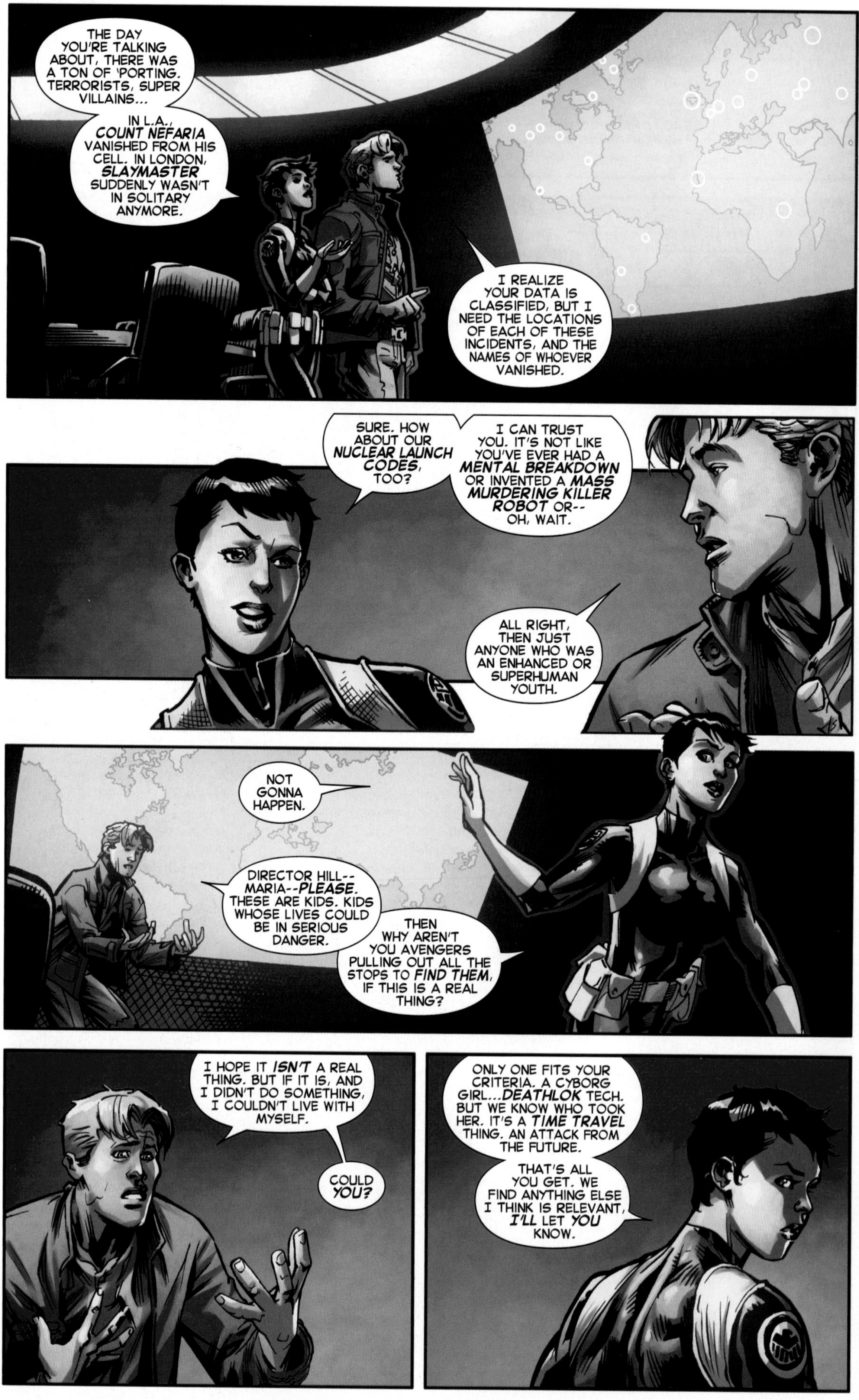

THE DAY YOU'RE TALKING ABOUT, THERE WAS A TON OF 'PORTING. TERRORISTS, SUPER VILLAINS...
IN L.A., COUNT NEFARIA VANISHED FROM HIS CELL. IN LONDON, SLAYMASTER SUDDENLY WASN'T IN SOLITARY ANYMORE.
I REALIZE YOUR DATA IS CLASSIFIED, BUT I NEED THE LOCATIONS OF EACH OF THESE INCIDENTS, AND THE NAMES OF WHOEVER VANISHED.
SURE. HOW ABOUT OUR NUCLEAR LAUNCH CODES, TOO?
I CAN TRUST YOU. IT'S NOT LIKE YOU'VE EVER HAD A MENTAL BREAKDOWN OR INVENTED A MASS MURDERING KILLER ROBOT OR-- OH, WAIT.
ALL RIGHT, THEN JUST ANYONE WHO WAS AN ENHANCED OR SUPERHUMAN YOUTH.
NOT GONNA HAPPEN.
DIRECTOR HILL-- MARIA--PLEASE. THESE ARE KIDS. KIDS WHOSE LIVES COULD BE IN SERIOUS DANGER.
THEN WHY AREN'T YOU AVENGERS PULLING OUT ALL THE STOPS TO FIND THEM, IF THIS IS A REAL THING?
I HOPE IT ISN'T A REAL THING. BUT IF IT IS, AND I DIDN'T DO SOMETHING, I COULDN'T LIVE WITH MYSELF.
COULD YOU?
ONLY ONE FITS YOUR CRITERIA. A CYBORG GIRL...DEATHLOK TECH. BUT WE KNOW WHO TOOK HER. IT'S A TIME TRAVEL THING. AN ATTACK FROM THE FUTURE.
THAT'S ALL YOU GET. WE FIND ANYTHING ELSE I THINK IS RELEVANT, I'LL LET YOU KNOW.

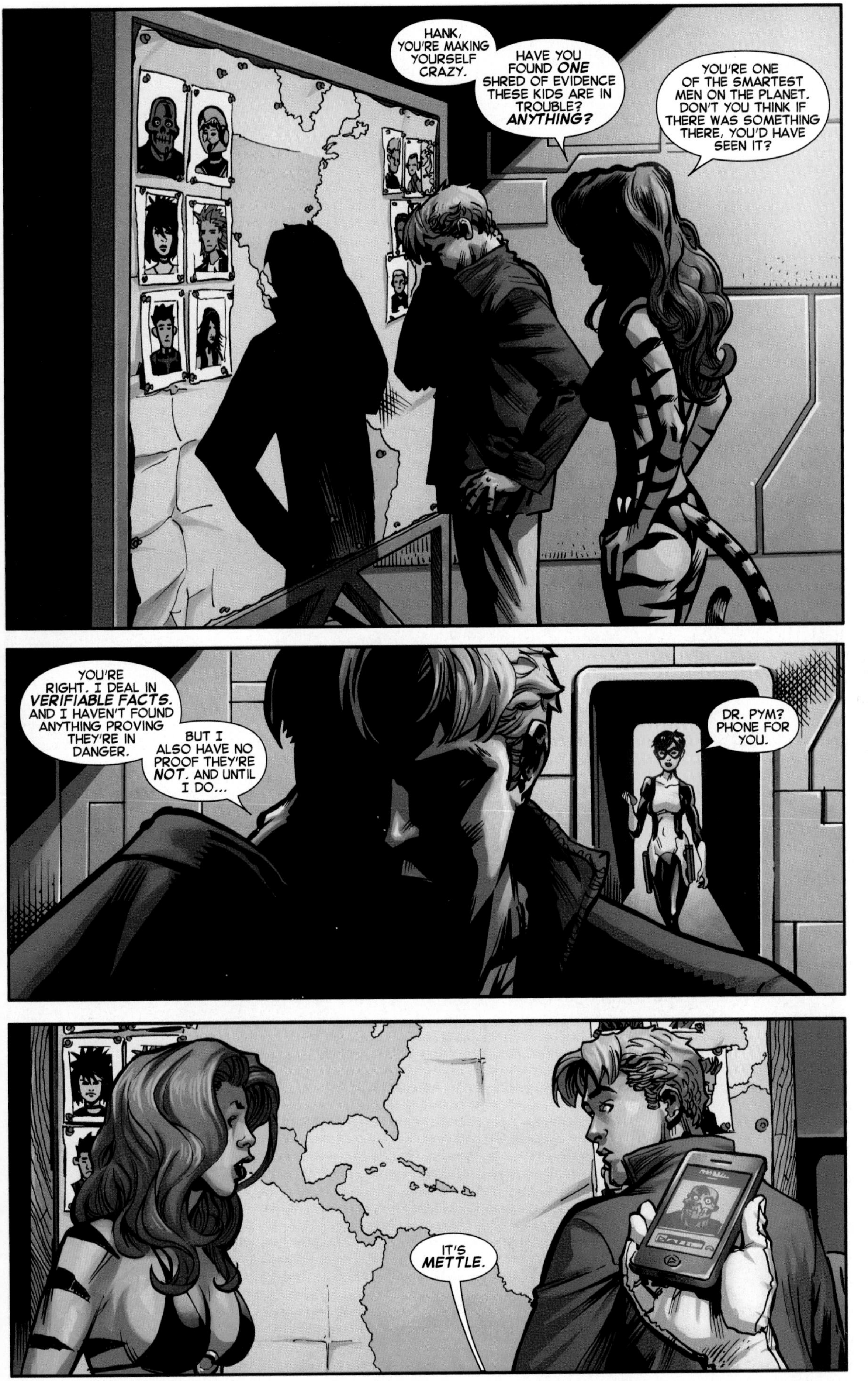
HANK, YOU'RE MAKING YOURSELF CRAZY.
HAVE YOU FOUND ONE SHRED OF EVIDENCE THESE KIDS ARE IN TROUBLE? ANYTHING?
YOU'RE ONE OF THE SMARTEST MEN ON THE PLANET. DON'T YOU THINK IF THERE WAS SOMETHING THERE, YOU'D HAVE SEEN IT?
YOU'RE RIGHT. I DEAL IN VERIFIABLE FACTS. AND I HAVEN'T FOUND ANYTHING PROVING THEY'RE IN DANGER.
BUT I ALSO HAVE NO PROOF THEY'RE NOT. AND UNTIL I DO...
DR. PYM? PHONE FOR YOU.
IT'S METTLE.

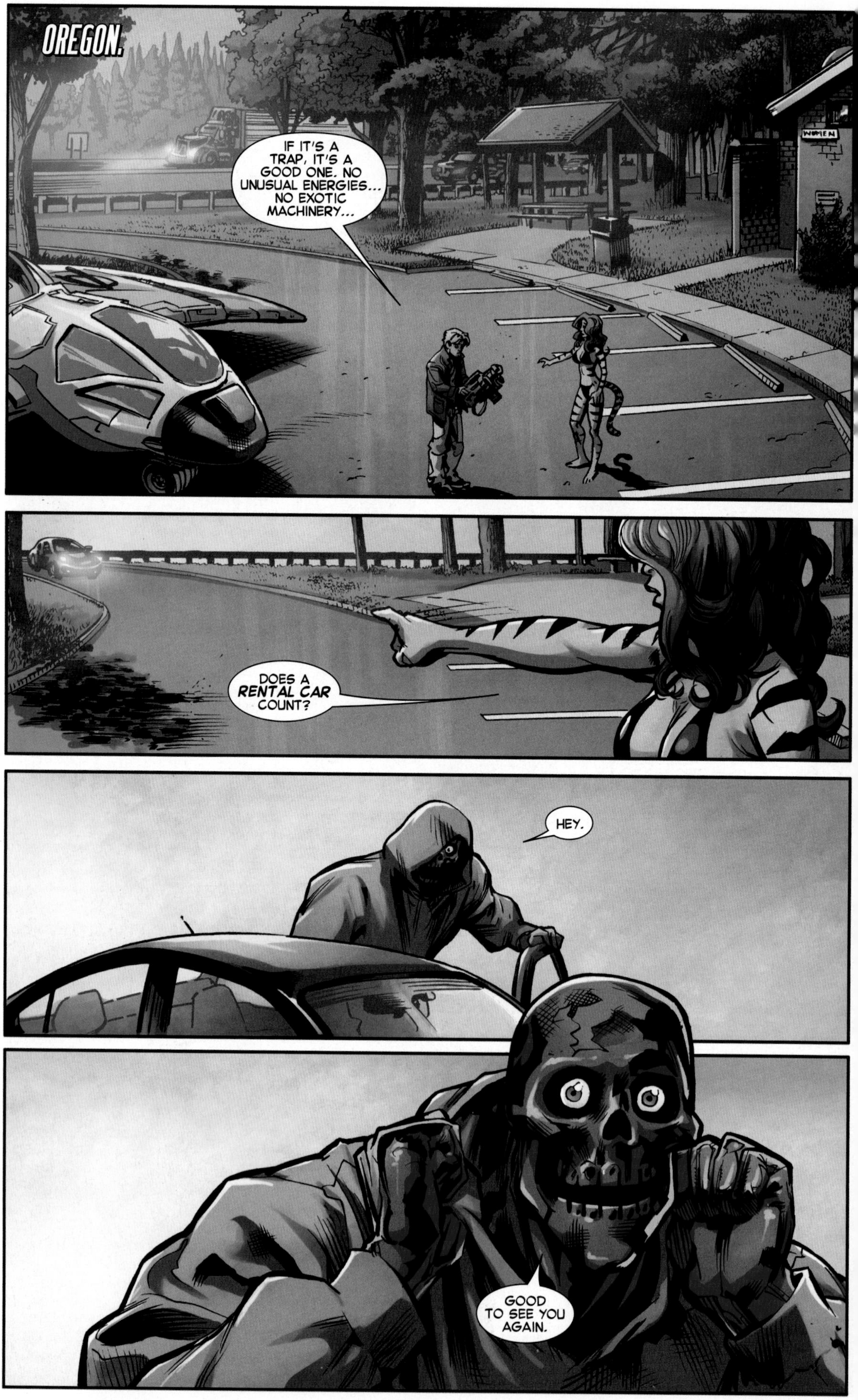
OREGON.
IF IT'S A TRAP, IT'S A GOOD ONE. NO UNUSUAL ENERGIES... NO EXOTIC MACHINERY...
WOMEN
DOES A RENTAL CAR COUNT?
HEY.
GOOD TO SEE YOU AGAIN.

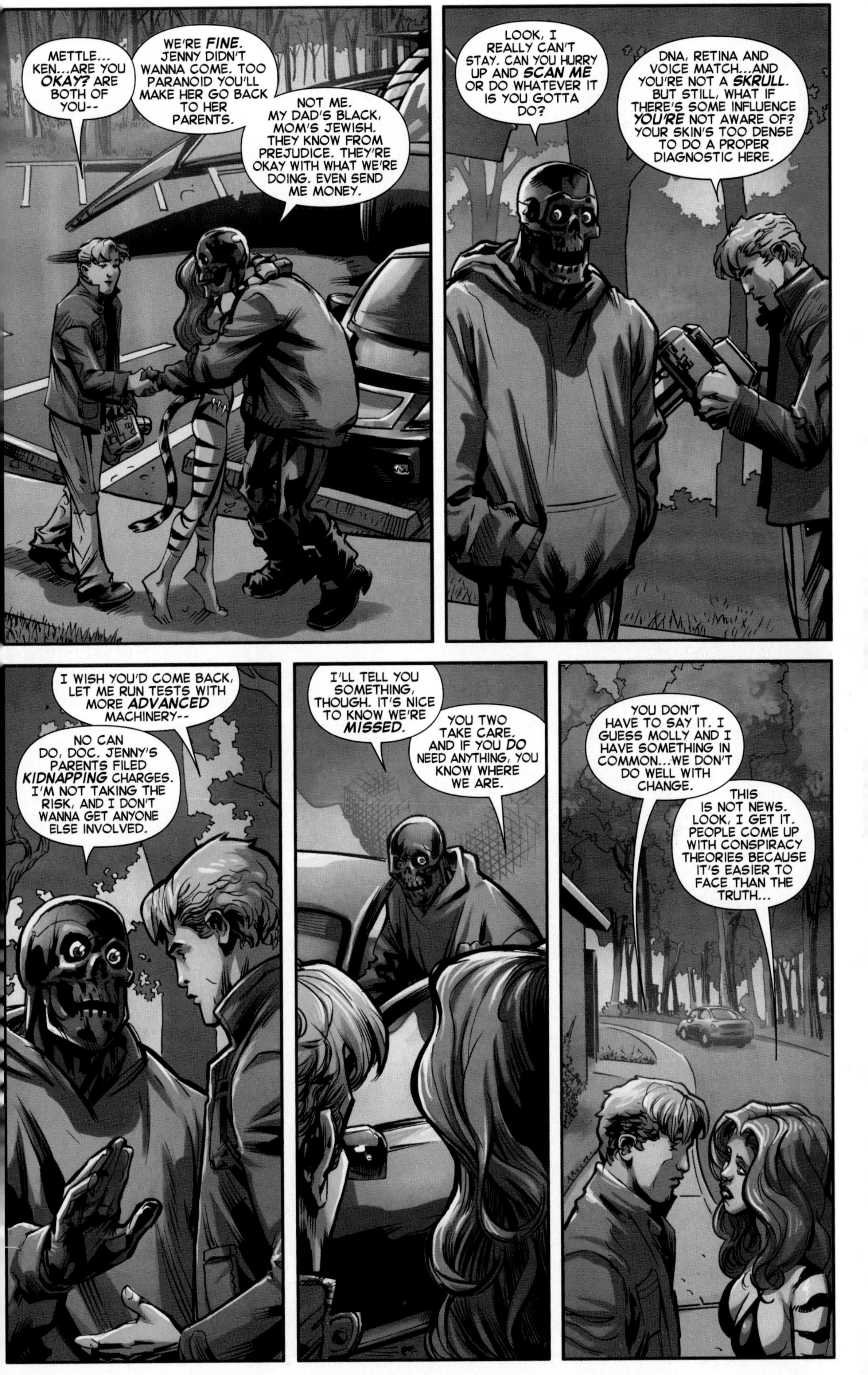
METTLE... KEN...ARE YOU OKAY? ARE BOTH OF YOU--
WE'RE FINE. JENNY DIDN'T WANNA COME. TOO PARANOID YOU'LL MAKE HER GO BACK TO HER PARENTS.
NOT ME. MY DAD'S BLACK, MOM'S JEWISH. THEY KNOW FROM PREJUDICE. THEY'RE OKAY WITH WHAT WE'RE DOING. EVEN SEND ME MONEY.
LOOK, I REALLY CAN'T STAY. CAN YOU HURRY UP AND SCAN ME OR DO WHATEVER IT IS YOU GOTTA DO?
DNA, RETINA AND VOICE MATCH...AND YOU'RE NOT A SKRULL. BUT STILL, WHAT IF THERE'S SOME INFLUENCE YOU'RE NOT AWARE OF? YOUR SKIN'S TOO DENSE TO DO A PROPER DIAGNOSTIC HERE.
I WISH YOU'D COME BACK, LET ME RUN TESTS WITH MORE ADVANCED MACHINERY--
NO CAN DO, DOC. JENNY'S PARENTS FILED KIDNAPPING CHARGES. I'M NOT TAKING THE RISK, AND I DON'T WANNA GET ANYONE ELSE INVOLVED.
I'LL TELL YOU SOMETHING, THOUGH. IT'S NICE TO KNOW WE'RE MISSED.
YOU TWO TAKE CARE. AND IF YOU DO NEED ANYTHING, YOU KNOW WHERE WE ARE.
YOU DON'T HAVE TO SAY IT. I GUESS MOLLY AND I HAVE SOMETHING IN COMMON...WE DON'T DO WELL WITH CHANGE.
THIS IS NOT NEWS. LOOK, I GET IT. PEOPLE COME UP WITH CONSPIRACY THEORIES BECAUSE IT'S EASIER TO FACE THAN THE TRUTH...

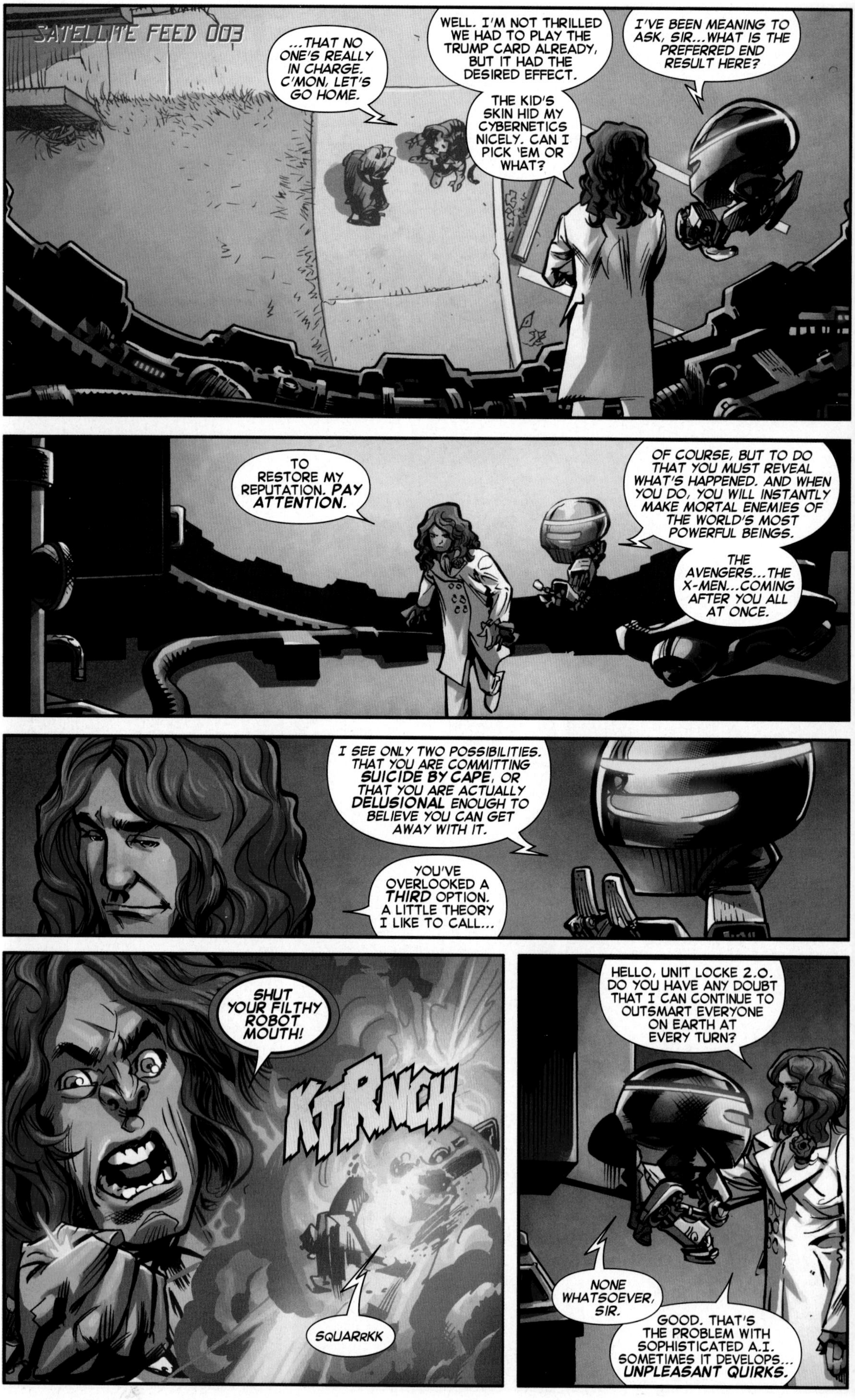
SATELLITE FEED 003
...THAT NO ONE'S REALLY IN CHARGE. C'MON, LET'S GO HOME.
WELL. I'M NOT THRILLED WE HAD TO PLAY THE TRUMP CARD ALREADY, BUT IT HAD THE DESIRED EFFECT.
THE KID'S SKIN HID MY CYBERNETICS NICELY. CAN I PICK 'EM OR WHAT?
I'VE BEEN MEANING TO ASK, SIR...WHAT IS THE PREFERRED END RESULT HERE?
TO RESTORE MY REPUTATION. PAY ATTENTION.
OF COURSE, BUT TO DO THAT YOU MUST REVEAL WHAT'S HAPPENED. AND WHEN YOU DO, YOU WILL INSTANTLY MAKE MORTAL ENEMIES OF THE WORLD'S MOST POWERFUL BEINGS.
THE AVENGERS...THE X-MEN...COMING AFTER YOU ALL AT ONCE.
I SEE ONLY TWO POSSIBILITIES. THAT YOU ARE COMMITTING SUICIDE BY CAPE, OR THAT YOU ARE ACTUALLY DELUSIONAL ENOUGH TO BELIEVE YOU CAN GET AWAY WITH IT.
YOU'VE OVERLOOKED A THIRD OPTION. A LITTLE THEORY I LIKE TO CALL...
SHUT YOUR FILTHY ROBOT MOUTH!
KTRNCH
SQUARRKK
HELLO, UNIT LOCKE 2.0. DO YOU HAVE ANY DOUBT THAT I CAN CONTINUE TO OUTSMART EVERYONE ON EARTH AT EVERY TURN?
NONE WHATSOEVER, SIR.
GOOD. THAT'S THE PROBLEM WITH SOPHISTICATED A.I. SOMETIMES IT DEVELOPS... UNPLEASANT QUIRKS.

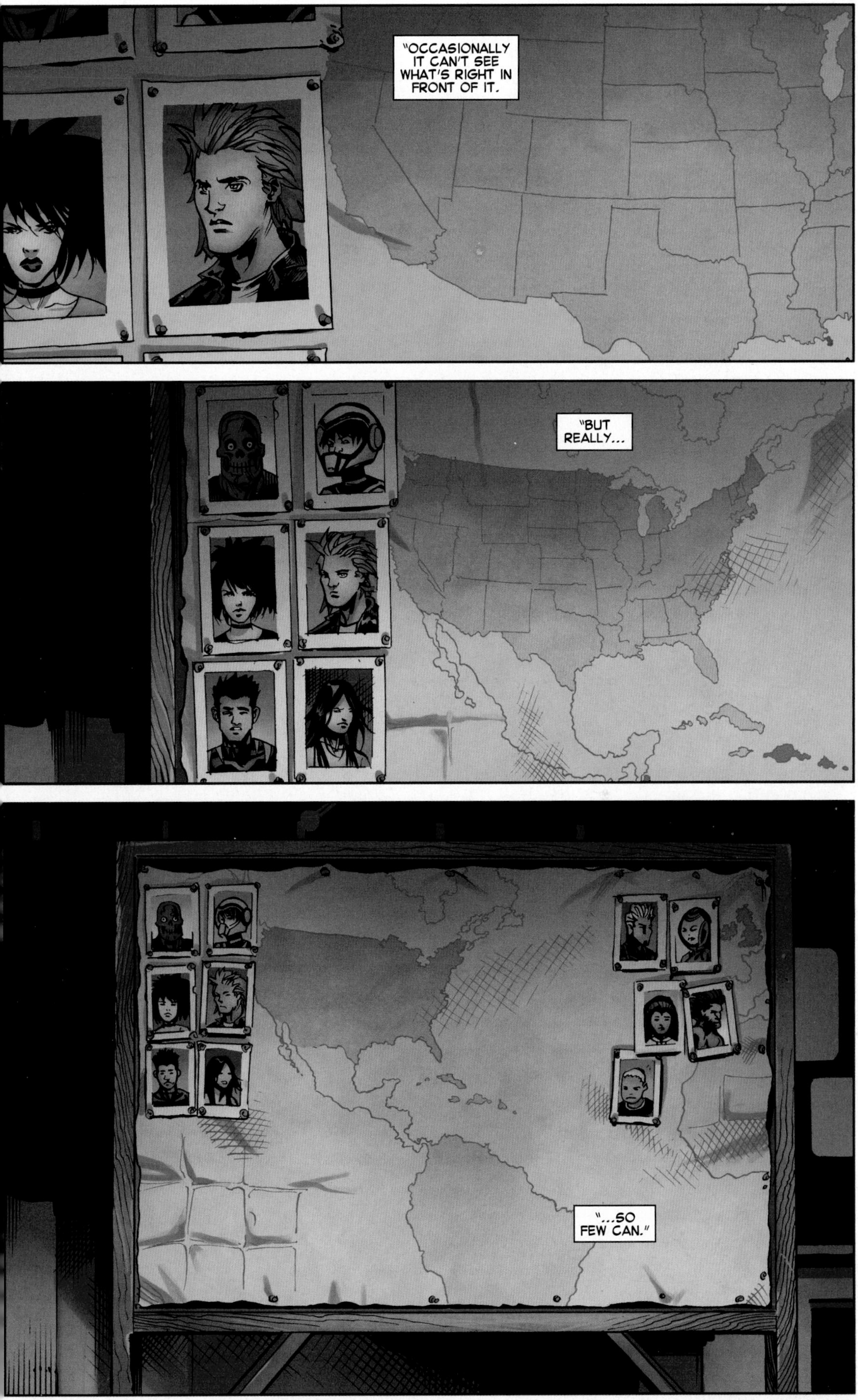
"OCCASIONALLY IT CAN'T SEE WHAT'S RIGHT IN FRONT OF IT.
"BUT REALLY...
"...SO FEW CAN."

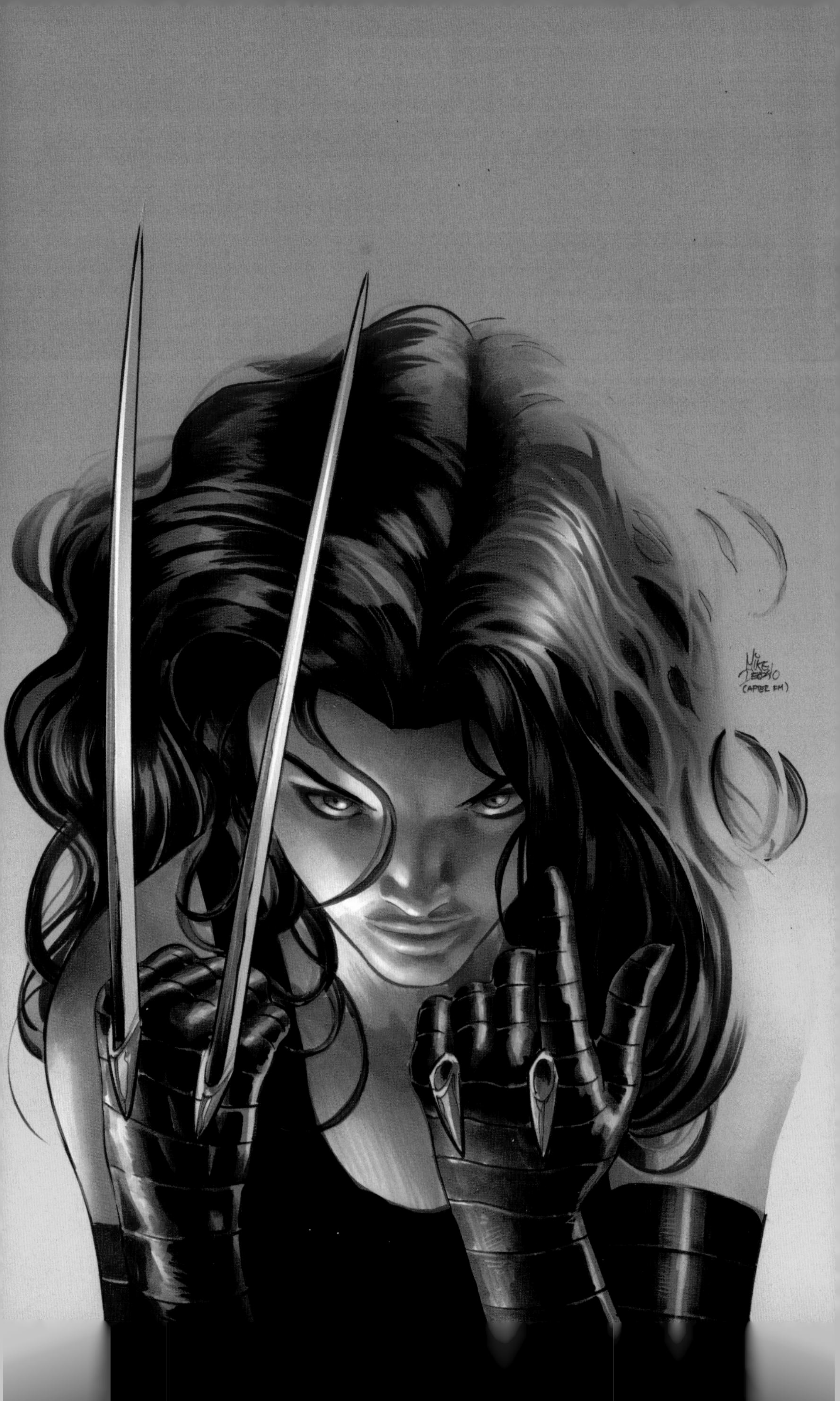
(AFTER FM)

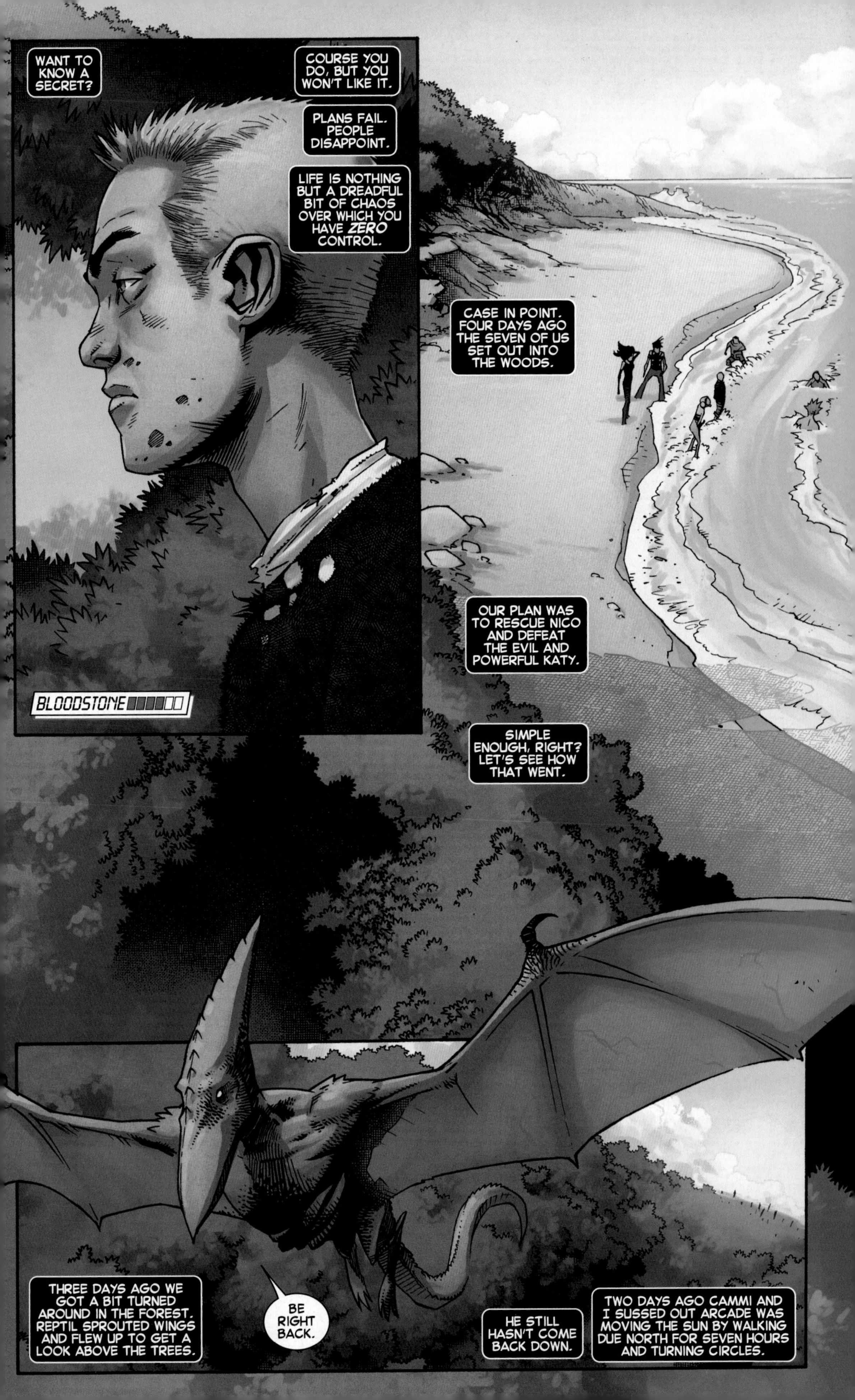
WANT TO KNOW A SECRET?
COURSE YOU DO, BUT YOU WON'T LIKE IT.
PLANS FAIL. PEOPLE DISAPPOINT.
LIFE IS NOTHING BUT A DREADFUL BIT OF CHAOS OVER WHICH YOU HAVE ZERO CONTROL.
BLOODSTONE
CASE IN POINT. FOUR DAYS AGO THE SEVEN OF US SET OUT INTO THE WOODS.
OUR PLAN WAS TO RESCUE NICO AND DEFEAT THE EVIL AND POWERFUL KATY.
SIMPLE ENOUGH, RIGHT? LET'S SEE HOW THAT WENT.
THREE DAYS AGO WE GOT A BIT TURNED AROUND IN THE FOREST. REPTIL SPROUTED WINGS AND FLEW UP TO GET A LOOK ABOVE THE TREES.
BE RIGHT BACK.
HE STILL HASN'T COME BACK DOWN.
TWO DAYS AGO CAMMI AND I SUSSED OUT ARCADE WAS MOVING THE SUN BY WALKING DUE NORTH FOR SEVEN HOURS AND TURNING CIRCLES.

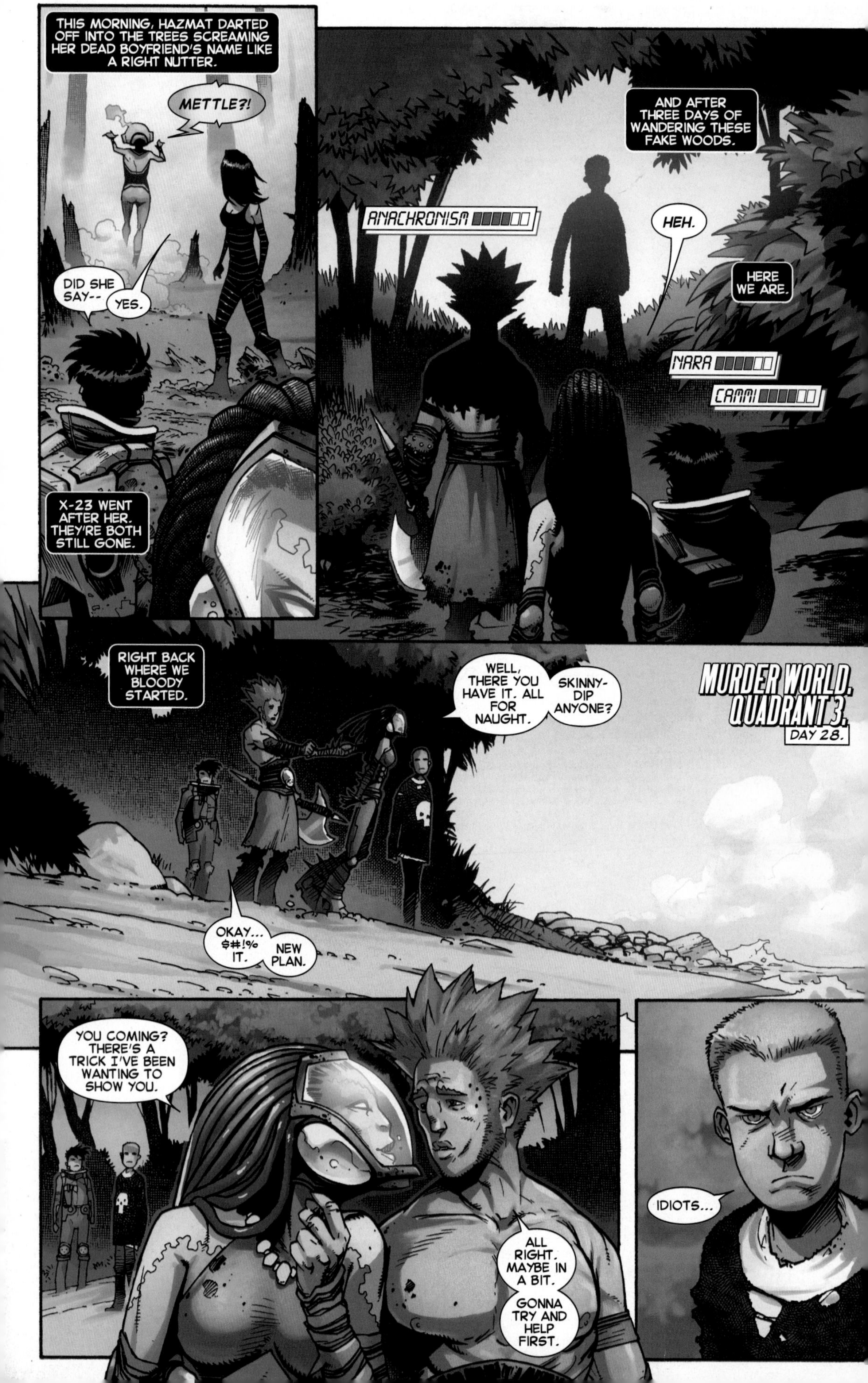
THIS MORNING, HAZMAT DARTED OFF INTO THE TREES SCREAMING HER DEAD BOYFRIEND'S NAME LIKE A RIGHT NUTTER.
METTLE?!
DID SHE SAY--
YES.
X-23 WENT AFTER HER. THEY'RE BOTH STILL GONE.
AND AFTER THREE DAYS OF WANDERING THESE FAKE WOODS.
ANACHRONISM
HEH.
HERE WE ARE.
NARA
CAMMI
RIGHT BACK WHERE WE BLOODY STARTED.
WELL, THERE YOU HAVE IT. ALL FOR NAUGHT.
SKINNY-DIP ANYONE?
MURDER WORLD. QUADRANT 3.
DAY 28.
OKAY... $#!% IT.
NEW PLAN.
YOU COMING? THERE'S A TRICK I'VE BEEN WANTING TO SHOW YOU.
ALL RIGHT. MAYBE IN A BIT.
GONNA TRY AND HELP FIRST.
IDIOTS...

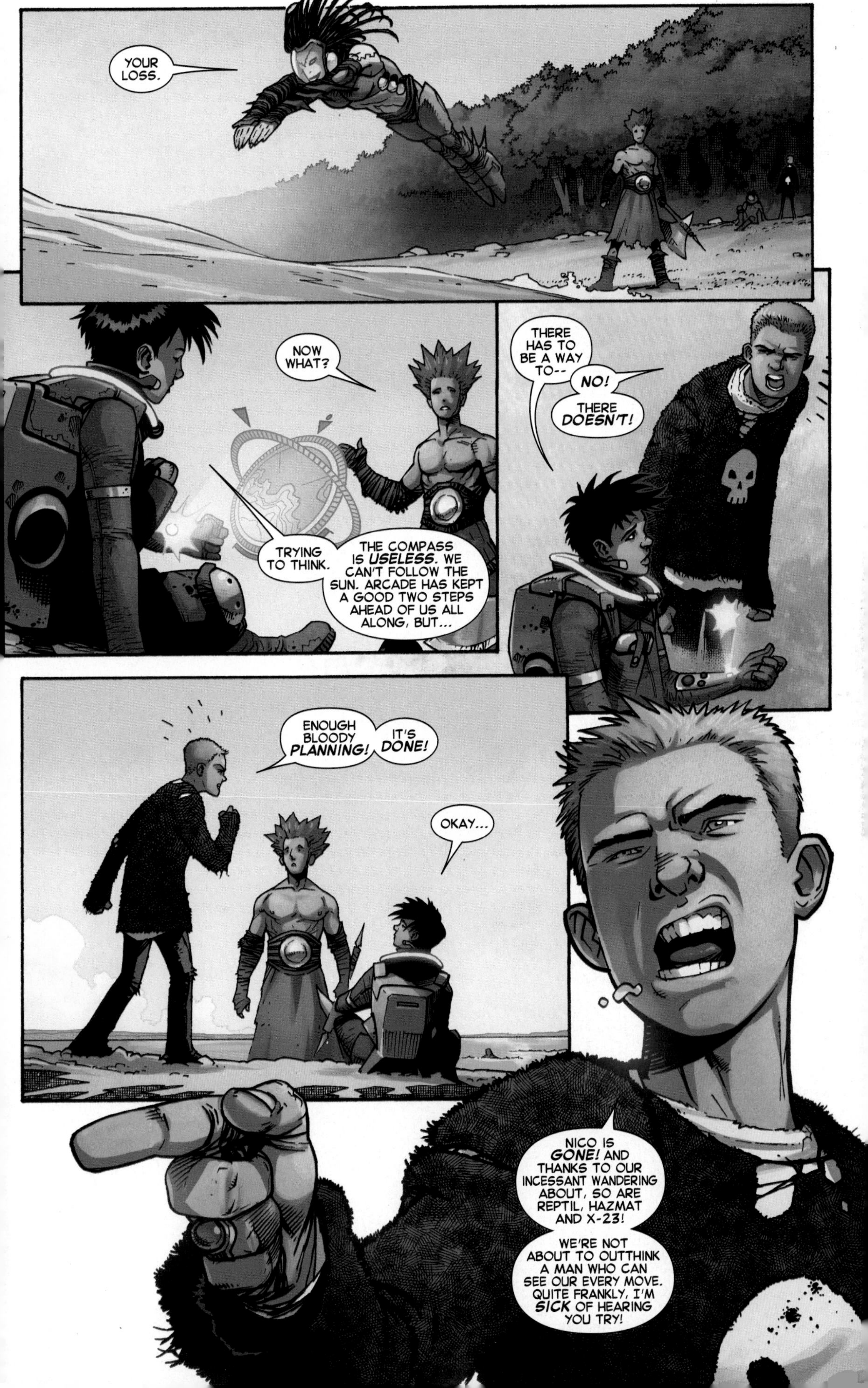
YOUR LOSS.
NOW WHAT?
TRYING TO THINK.
THE COMPASS IS USELESS. WE CAN'T FOLLOW THE SUN. ARCADE HAS KEPT A GOOD TWO STEPS AHEAD OF US ALL ALONG, BUT...
THERE HAS TO BE A WAY TO--
NO!
THERE DOESN'T!
ENOUGH BLOODY PLANNING!
IT'S DONE!
OKAY...
NICO IS GONE! AND THANKS TO OUR INCESSANT WANDERING ABOUT, SO ARE REPTIL, HAZMAT AND X-23!
WE'RE NOT ABOUT TO OUTTHINK A MAN WHO CAN SEE OUR EVERY MOVE. QUITE FRANKLY, I'M SICK OF HEARING YOU TRY!

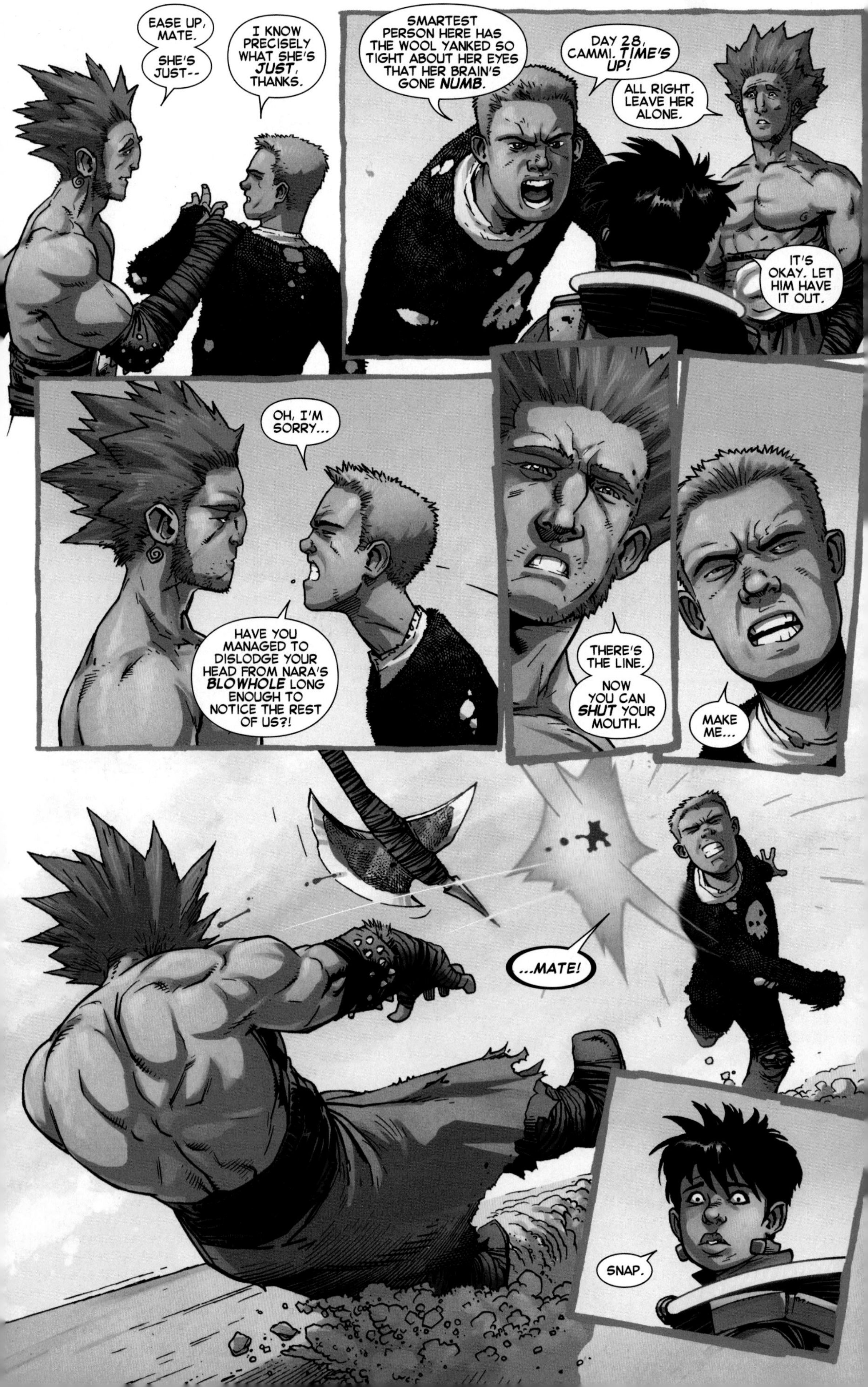
EASE UP, MATE.
SHE'S JUST--
I KNOW PRECISELY WHAT SHE'S JUST, THANKS.
SMARTEST PERSON HERE HAS THE WOOL YANKED SO TIGHT ABOUT HER EYES THAT HER BRAIN'S GONE NUMB.
DAY 28, CAMMI. TIME'S UP!
ALL RIGHT. LEAVE HER ALONE.
IT'S OKAY. LET HIM HAVE IT OUT.
OH, I'M SORRY...
HAVE YOU MANAGED TO DISLODGE YOUR HEAD FROM NARA'S BLOWHOLE LONG ENOUGH TO NOTICE THE REST OF US?!
THERE'S THE LINE.
NOW YOU CAN SHUT YOUR MOUTH.
MAKE ME...
...MATE!
SNAP.

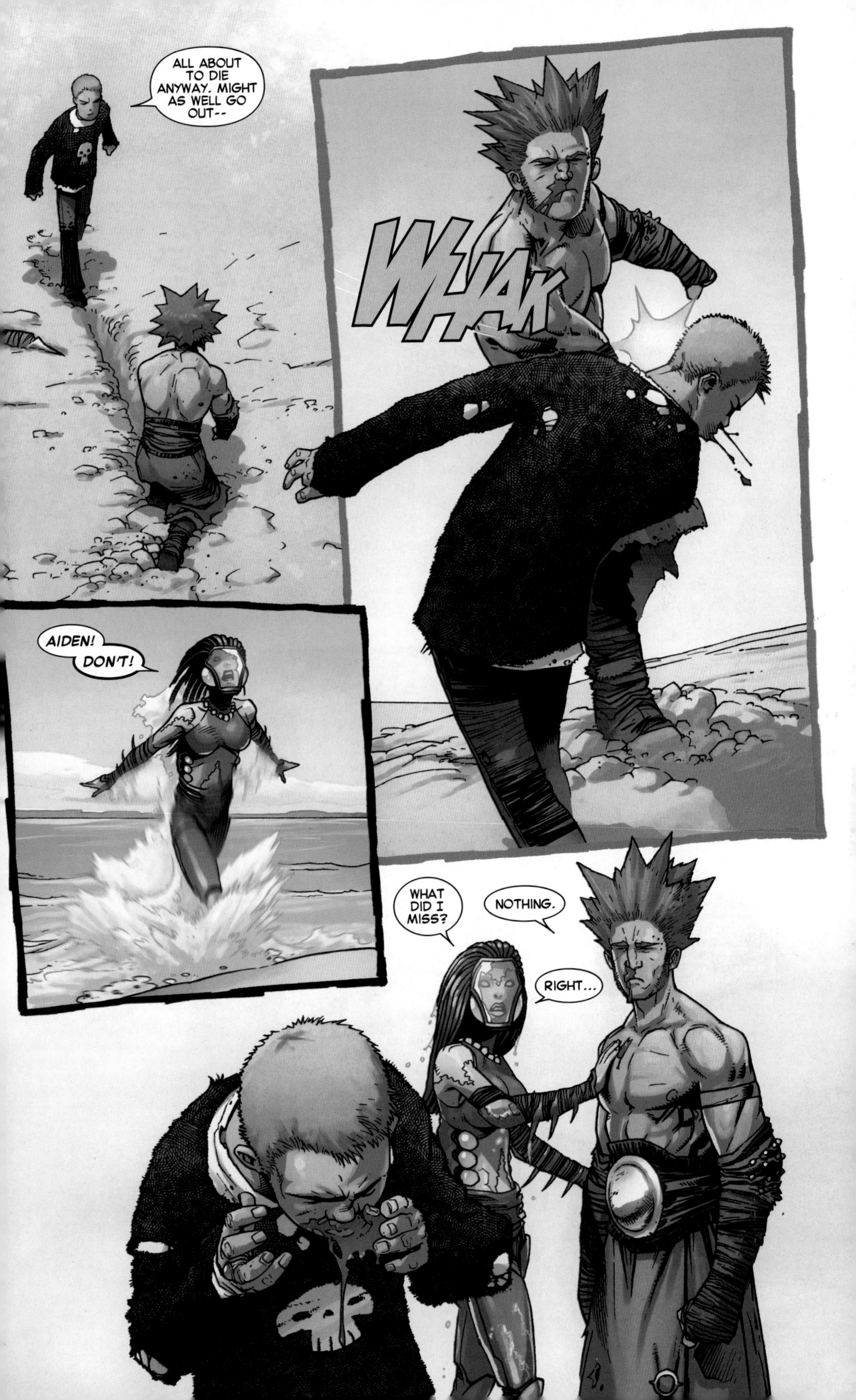

ALL ABOUT TO DIE ANYWAY. MIGHT AS WELL GO OUT--
WHAK
AIDEN!
DON'T!
WHAT DID I MISS?
NOTHING.
RIGHT...

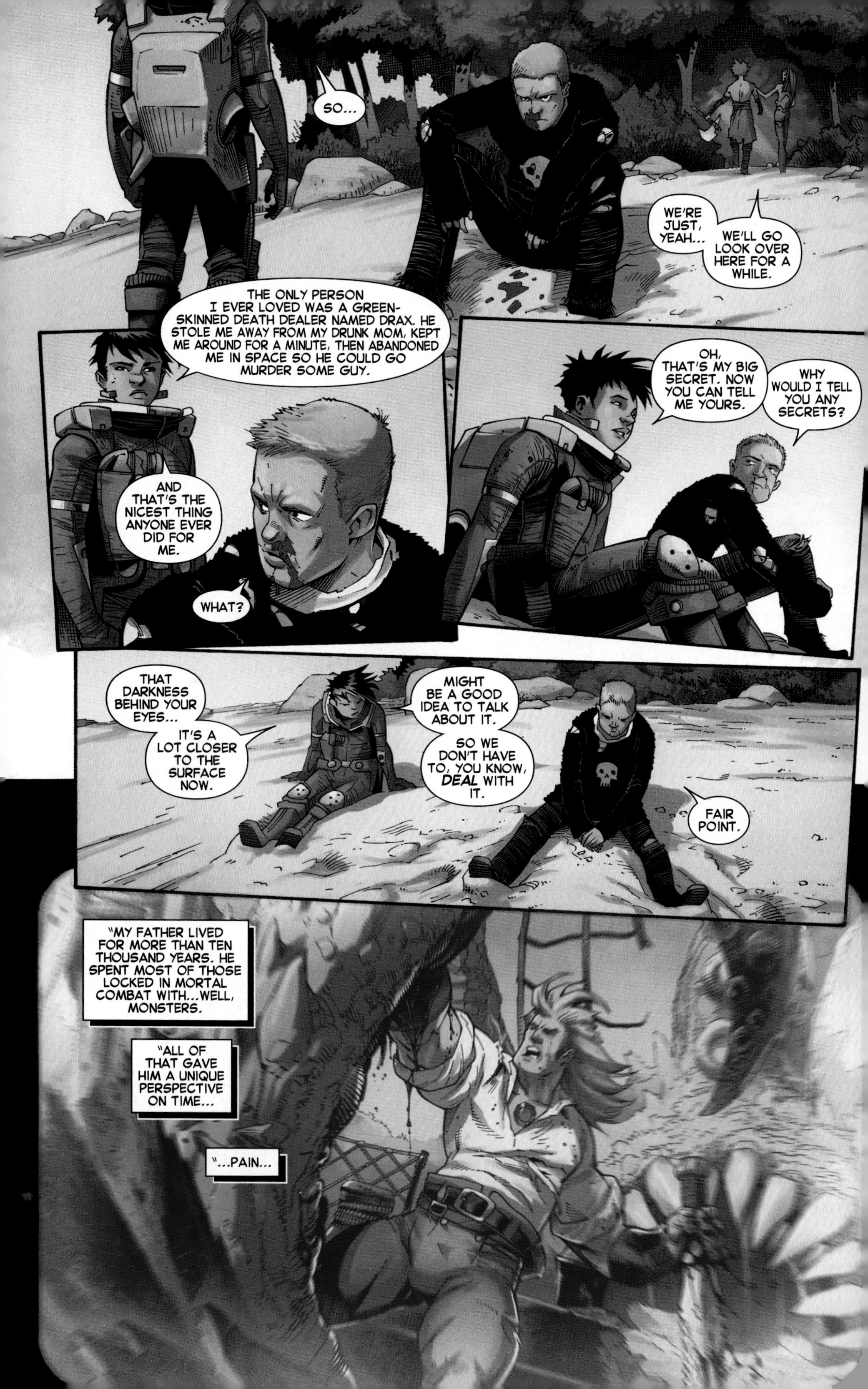
SO...
WE'RE JUST, YEAH...
WE'LL GO LOOK OVER HERE FOR A WHILE.
THE ONLY PERSON I EVER LOVED WAS A GREEN-SKINNED DEATH DEALER NAMED DRAX. HE STOLE ME AWAY FROM MY DRUNK MOM, KEPT ME AROUND FOR A MINUTE, THEN ABANDONED ME IN SPACE SO HE COULD GO MURDER SOME GUY.
AND THAT'S THE NICEST THING ANYONE EVER DID FOR ME.
WHAT?
OH, THAT'S MY BIG SECRET. NOW YOU CAN TELL ME YOURS.
WHY WOULD I TELL YOU ANY SECRETS?
THAT DARKNESS BEHIND YOUR EYES...
IT'S A LOT CLOSER TO THE SURFACE NOW.
MIGHT BE A GOOD IDEA TO TALK ABOUT IT.
SO WE DON'T HAVE TO, YOU KNOW, DEAL WITH IT.
FAIR POINT.
"MY FATHER LIVED FOR MORE THAN TEN THOUSAND YEARS. HE SPENT MOST OF THOSE LOCKED IN MORTAL COMBAT WITH...WELL, MONSTERS.
"ALL OF THAT GAVE HIM A UNIQUE PERSPECTIVE ON TIME...
"...PAIN...

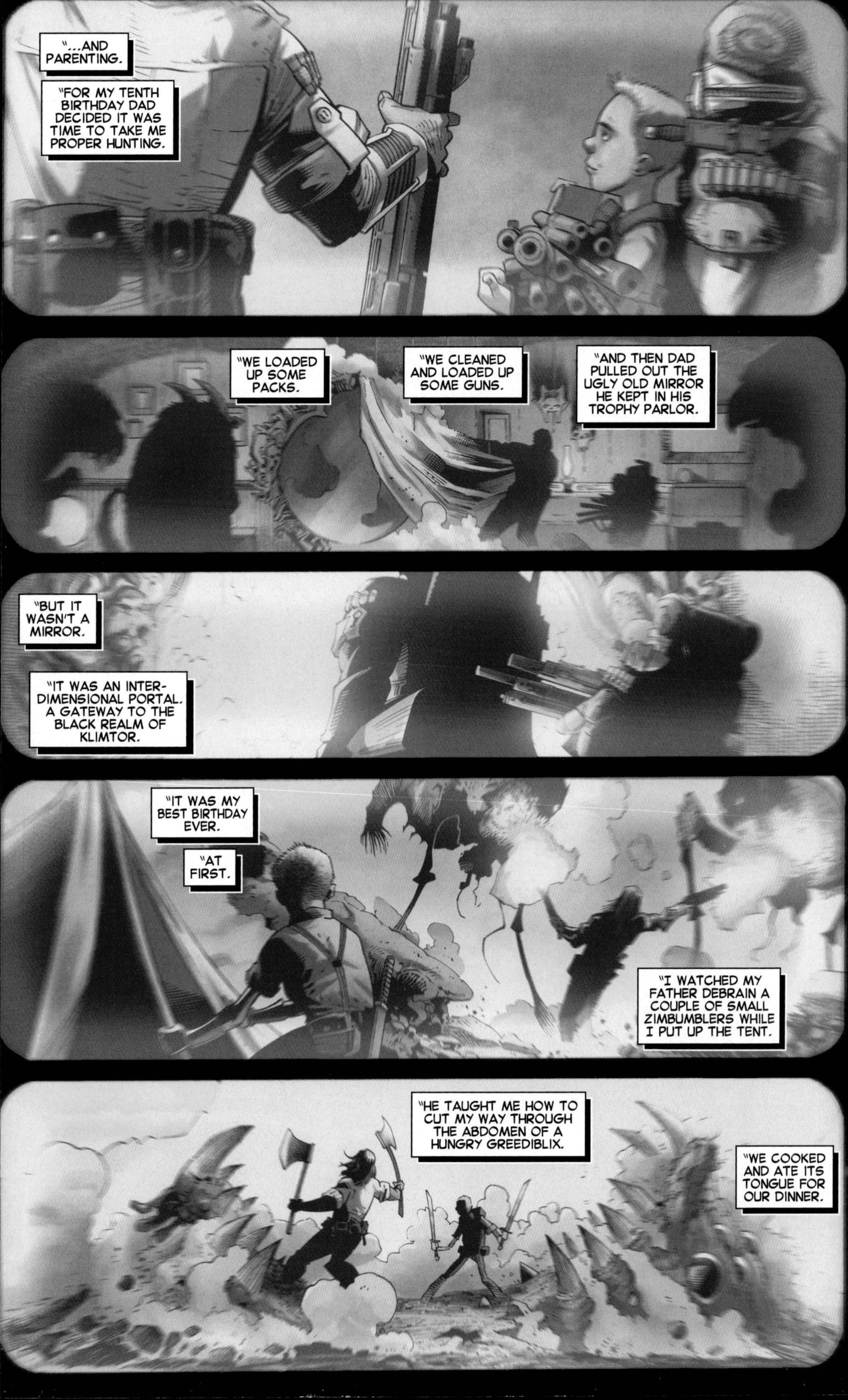
"...AND PARENTING.
"FOR MY TENTH BIRTHDAY DAD DECIDED IT WAS TIME TO TAKE ME PROPER HUNTING.
"WE LOADED UP SOME PACKS.
"WE CLEANED AND LOADED UP SOME GUNS.
"AND THEN DAD PULLED OUT THE UGLY OLD MIRROR HE KEPT IN HIS TROPHY PARLOR.
"BUT IT WASN'T A MIRROR.
"IT WAS AN INTER-DIMENSIONAL PORTAL. A GATEWAY TO THE BLACK REALM OF KLIMTOR.
"IT WAS MY BEST BIRTHDAY EVER.
"AT FIRST.
"I WATCHED MY FATHER DEBRAIN A COUPLE OF SMALL ZIMBUMBLERS WHILE I PUT UP THE TENT.
"HE TAUGHT ME HOW TO CUT MY WAY THROUGH THE ABDOMEN OF A HUNGRY GREEDIBLIX.
"WE COOKED AND ATE ITS TONGUE FOR OUR DINNER.

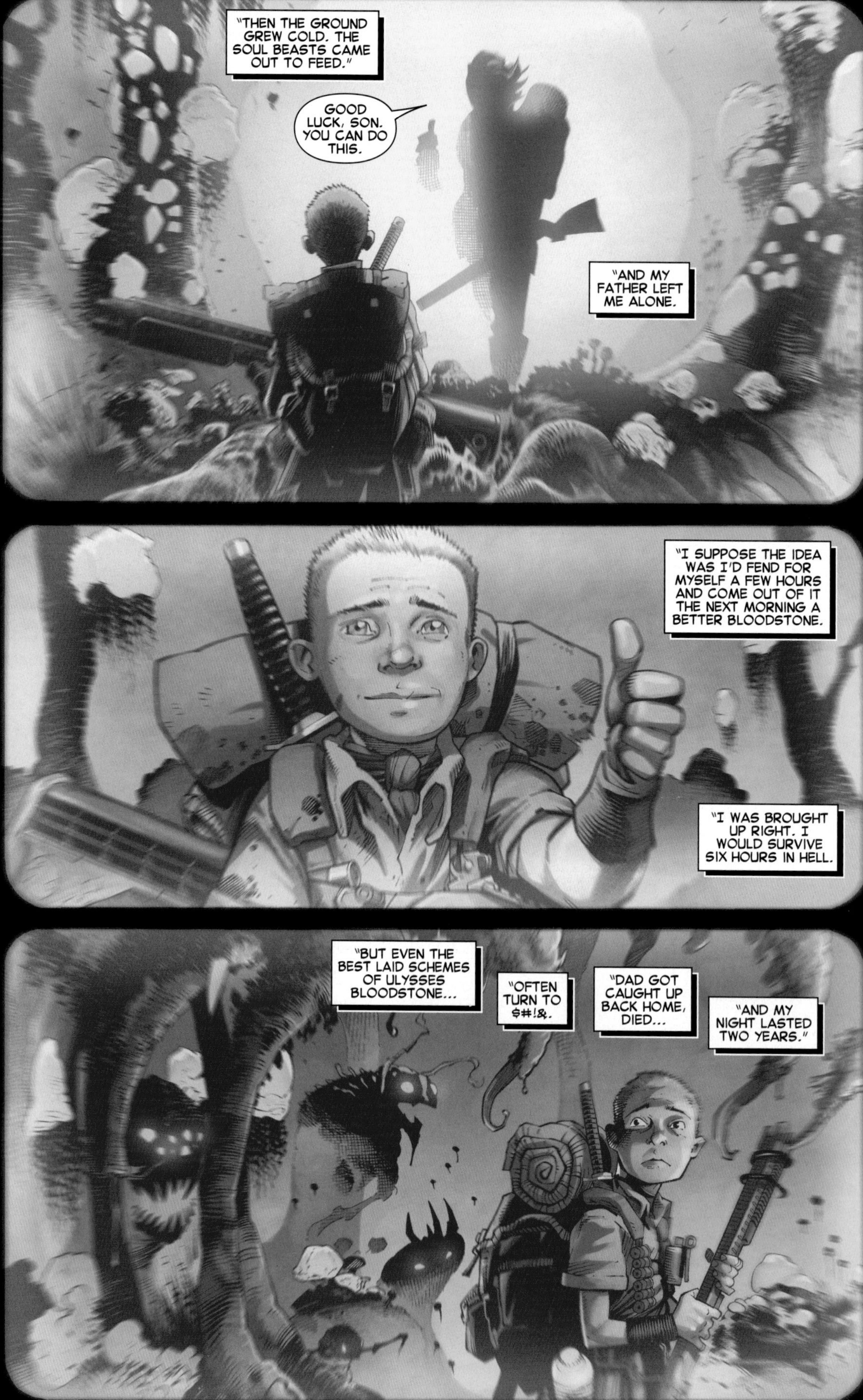
"THEN THE GROUND GREW COLD. THE SOUL BEASTS CAME OUT TO FEED."
GOOD LUCK, SON. YOU CAN DO THIS.
"AND MY FATHER LEFT ME ALONE.
"I SUPPOSE THE IDEA WAS I'D FEND FOR MYSELF A FEW HOURS AND COME OUT OF IT THE NEXT MORNING A BETTER BLOODSTONE.
"I WAS BROUGHT UP RIGHT. I WOULD SURVIVE SIX HOURS IN HELL.
"BUT EVEN THE BEST LAID SCHEMES OF ULYSSES BLOODSTONE...
"OFTEN TURN TO $#!&.
"DAD GOT CAUGHT UP BACK HOME, DIED...
"AND MY NIGHT LASTED TWO YEARS."

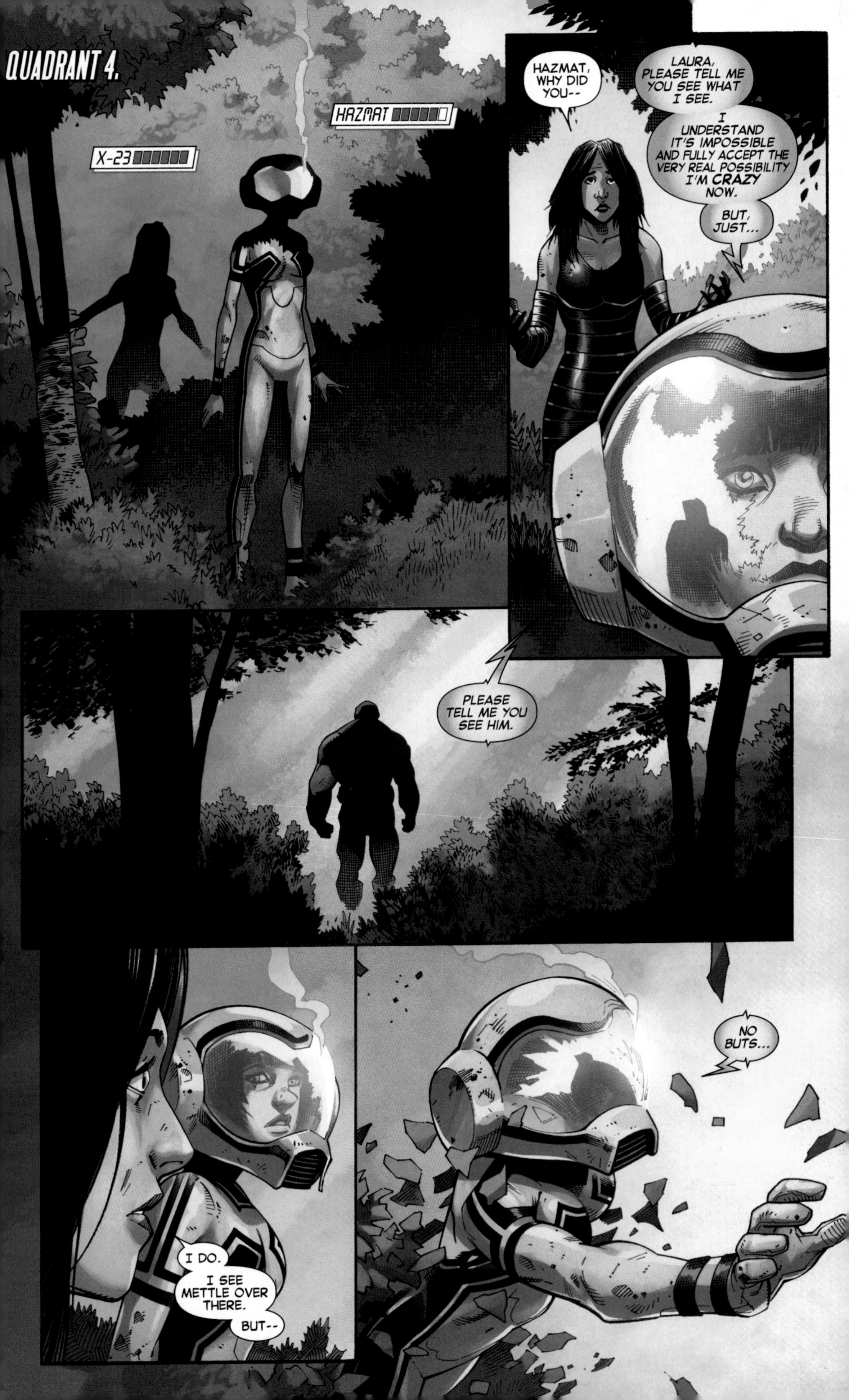
QUADRANT 4.
X-23
HAZMAT
HAZMAT, WHY DID YOU--
LAURA, PLEASE TELL ME YOU SEE WHAT I SEE.
I UNDERSTAND IT'S IMPOSSIBLE AND FULLY ACCEPT THE VERY REAL POSSIBILITY I'M CRAZY NOW.
BUT, JUST...
PLEASE TELL ME YOU SEE HIM.
I DO.
I SEE METTLE OVER THERE.
BUT--
NO BUTS...

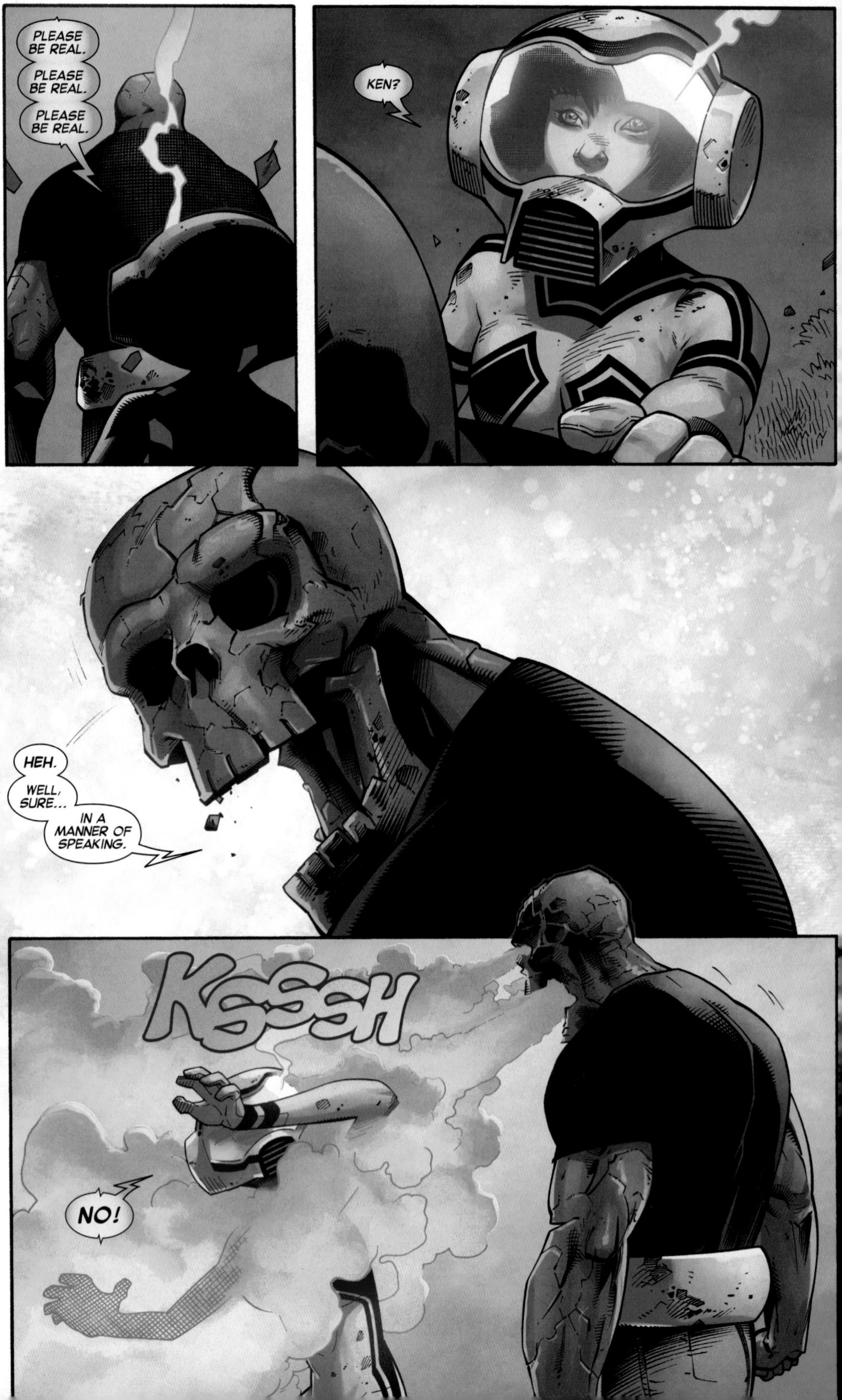
PLEASE BE REAL.
PLEASE BE REAL.
PLEASE BE REAL.
KEN?
HEH.
WELL, SURE...
IN A MANNER OF SPEAKING.
KSSSH
NO!

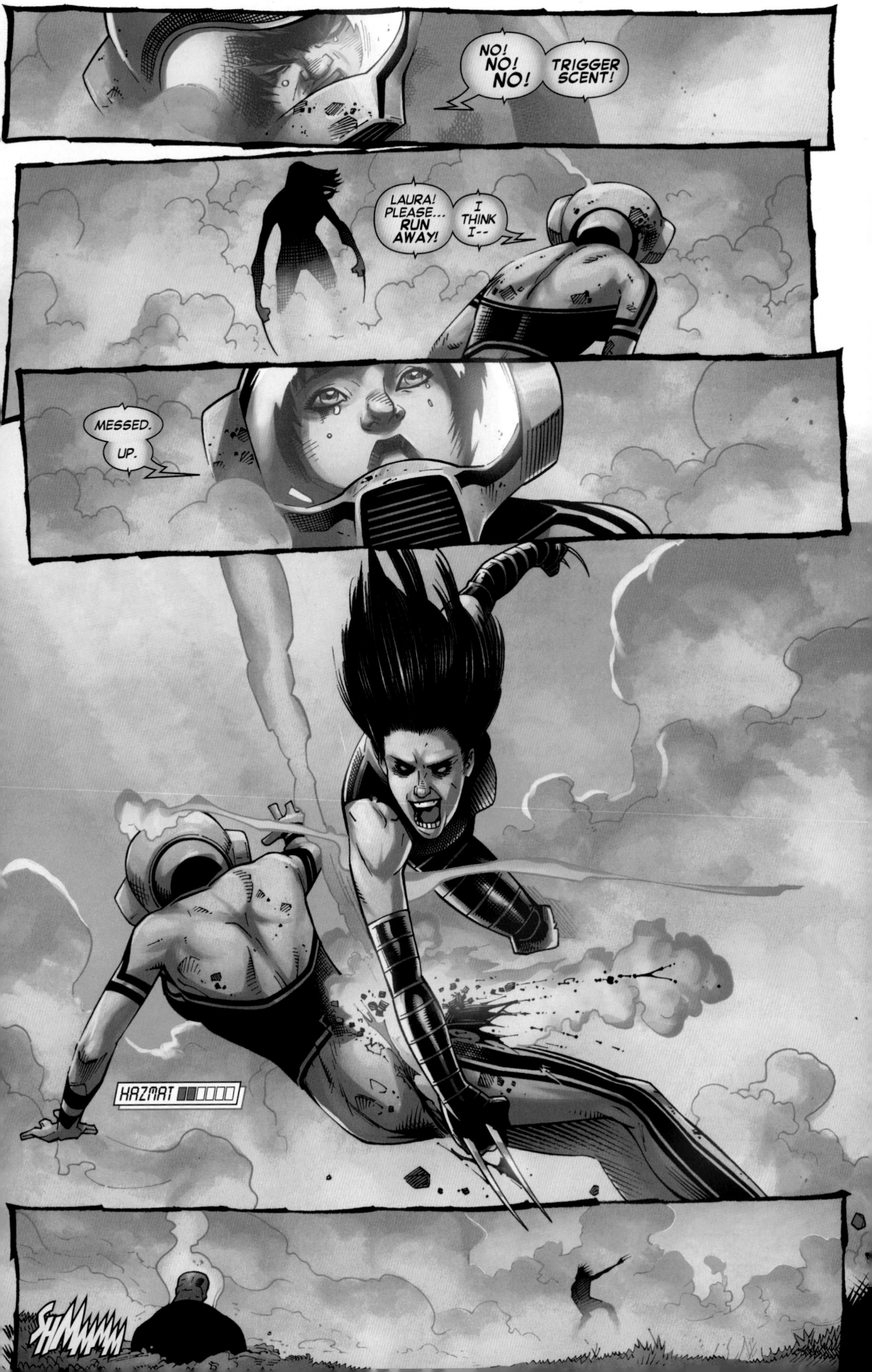

NO! NO! NO!
TRIGGER SCENT!
LAURA! PLEASE... RUN AWAY!
I THINK I--
MESSED. UP.
HAZMAT
SHMMMM

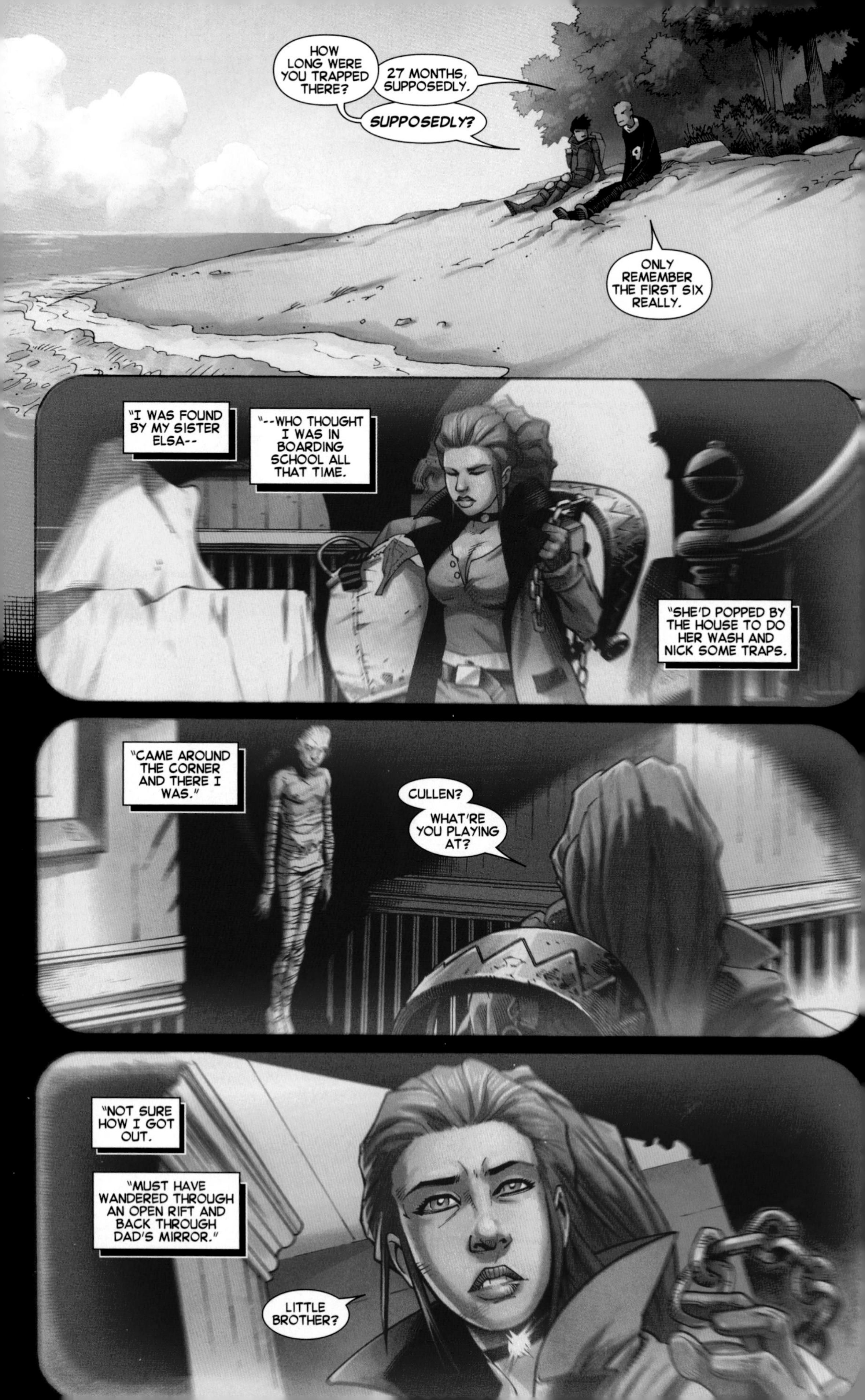
HOW LONG WERE YOU TRAPPED THERE?
27 MONTHS, SUPPOSEDLY.
SUPPOSEDLY?
ONLY REMEMBER THE FIRST SIX REALLY.
"I WAS FOUND BY MY SISTER ELSA--
"--WHO THOUGHT I WAS IN BOARDING SCHOOL ALL THAT TIME.
"SHE'D POPPED BY THE HOUSE TO DO HER WASH AND NICK SOME TRAPS.
"CAME AROUND THE CORNER AND THERE I WAS."
CULLEN?
WHAT'RE YOU PLAYING AT?
"NOT SURE HOW I GOT OUT.
"MUST HAVE WANDERED THROUGH AN OPEN RIFT AND BACK THROUGH DAD'S MIRROR."
LITTLE BROTHER?

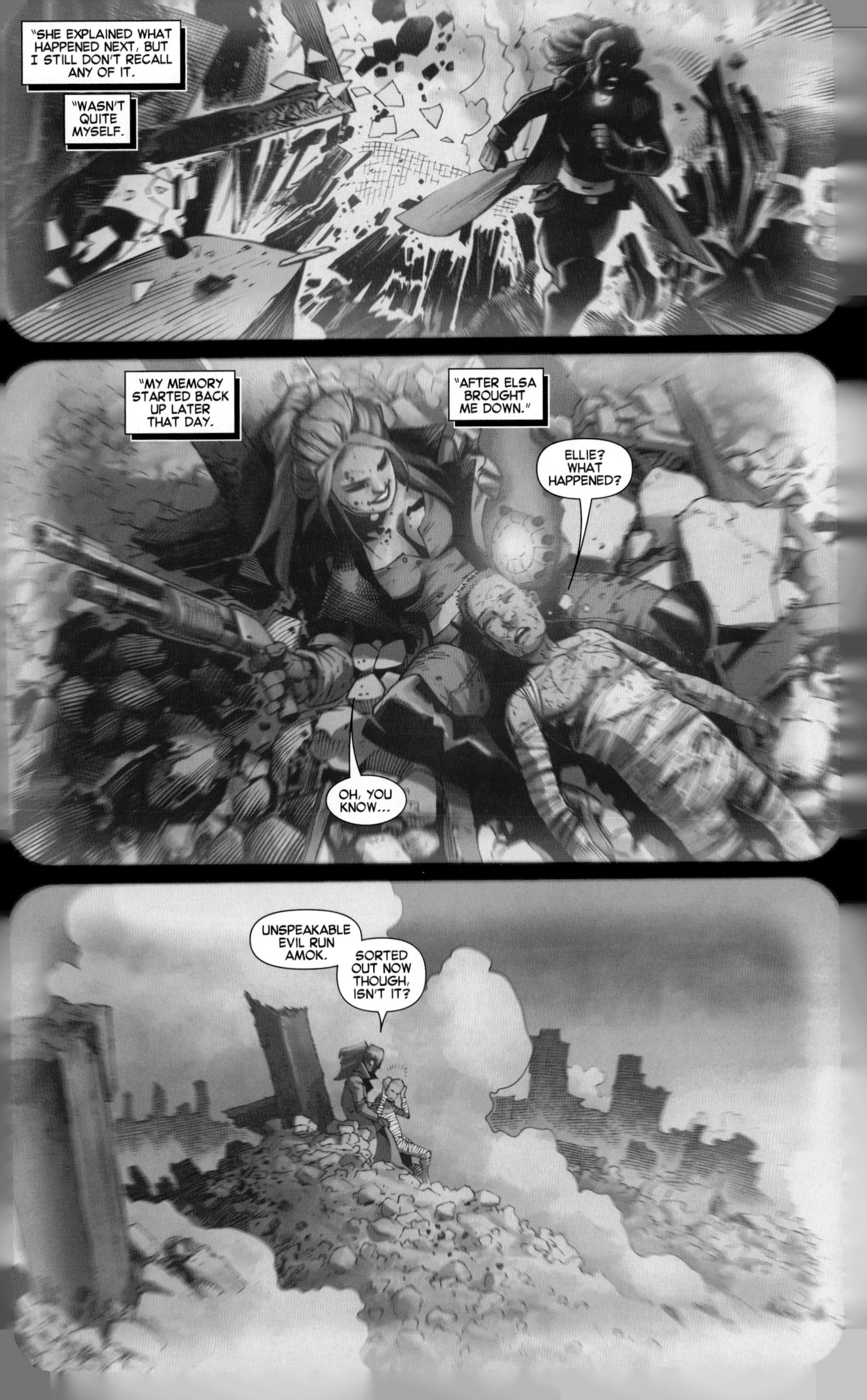
"SHE EXPLAINED WHAT HAPPENED NEXT, BUT I STILL DON'T RECALL ANY OF IT.
"WASN'T QUITE MYSELF.
"MY MEMORY STARTED BACK UP LATER THAT DAY.
"AFTER ELSA BROUGHT ME DOWN."
ELLIE? WHAT HAPPENED?
OH, YOU KNOW...
UNSPEAKABLE EVIL RUN AMOK.
SORTED OUT NOW THOUGH, ISN'T IT?

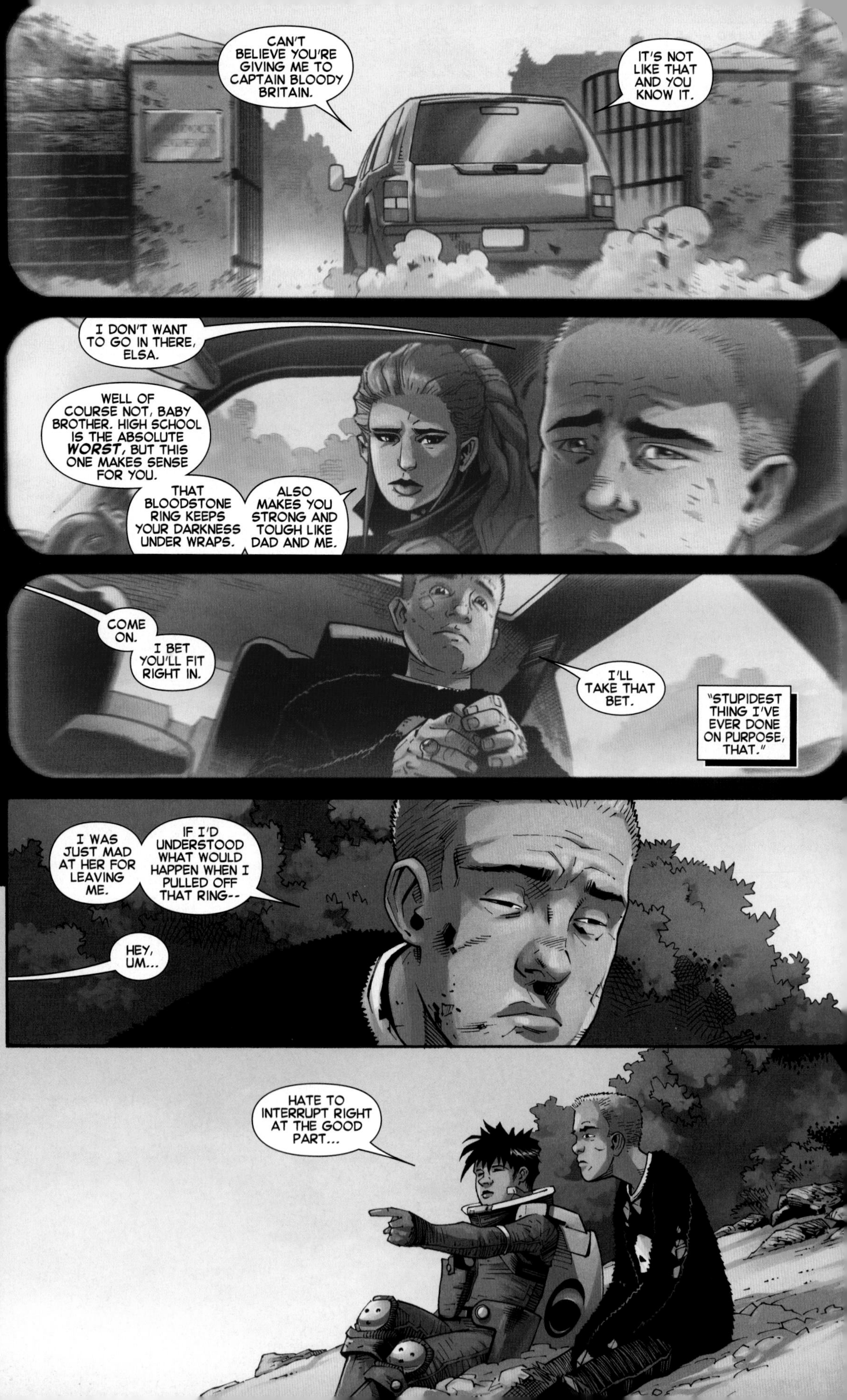
CAN'T BELIEVE YOU'RE GIVING ME TO CAPTAIN BLOODY BRITAIN.
IT'S NOT LIKE THAT AND YOU KNOW IT.
I DON'T WANT TO GO IN THERE, ELSA.
WELL OF COURSE NOT, BABY BROTHER. HIGH SCHOOL IS THE ABSOLUTE WORST, BUT THIS ONE MAKES SENSE FOR YOU.
THAT BLOODSTONE RING KEEPS YOUR DARKNESS UNDER WRAPS.
ALSO MAKES YOU STRONG AND TOUGH LIKE DAD AND ME.
COME ON.
I BET YOU'LL FIT RIGHT IN.
I'LL TAKE THAT BET.
"STUPIDEST THING I'VE EVER DONE ON PURPOSE, THAT."
I WAS JUST MAD AT HER FOR LEAVING ME.
IF I'D UNDERSTOOD WHAT WOULD HAPPEN WHEN I PULLED OFF THAT RING--
HEY, UM...
HATE TO INTERRUPT RIGHT AT THE GOOD PART...

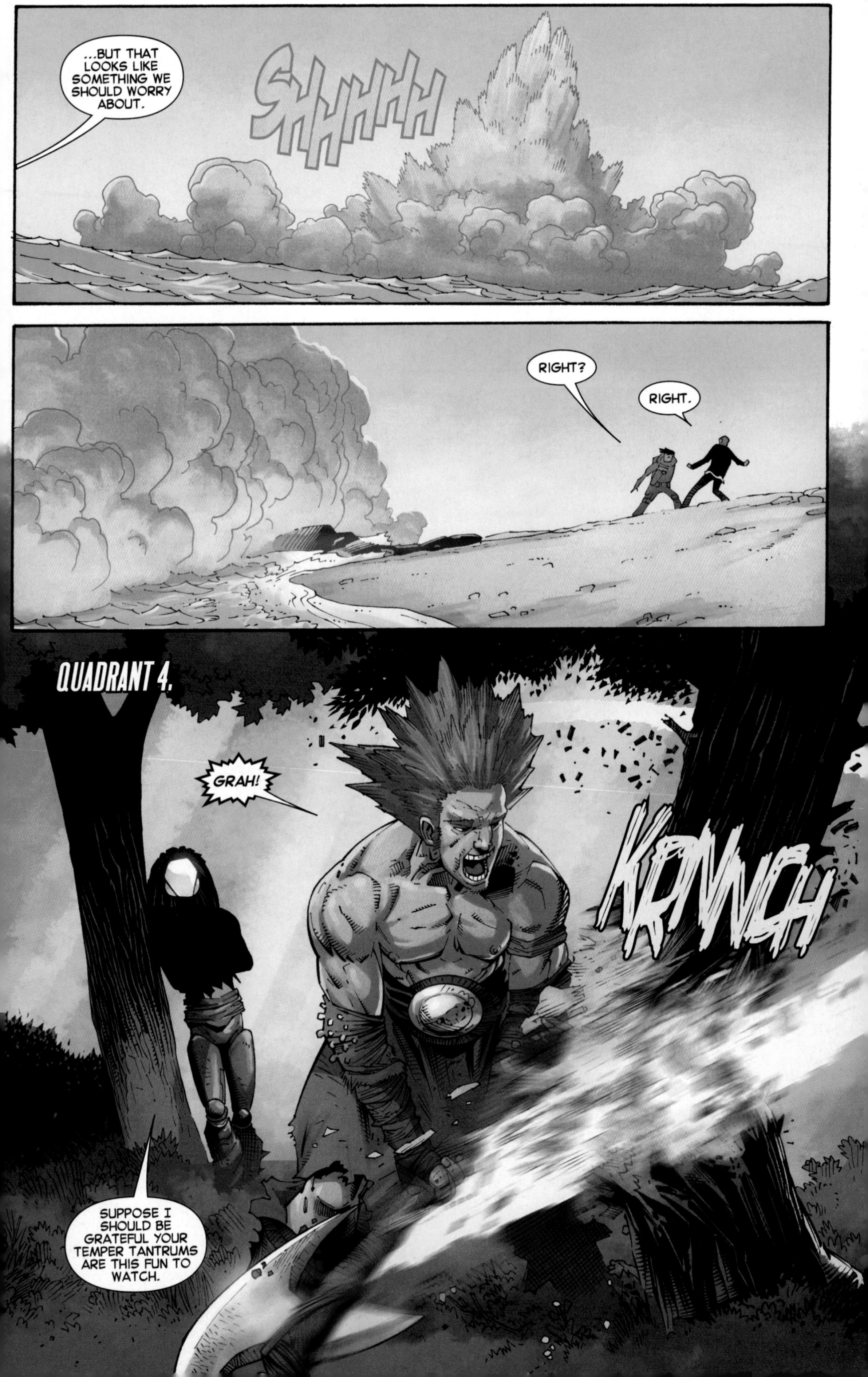
...BUT THAT LOOKS LIKE SOMETHING WE SHOULD WORRY ABOUT.
SHHHHH
RIGHT?
RIGHT.
QUADRANT 4.
GRAH!
KRNNCH
SUPPOSE I SHOULD BE GRATEFUL YOUR TEMPER TANTRUMS ARE THIS FUN TO WATCH.

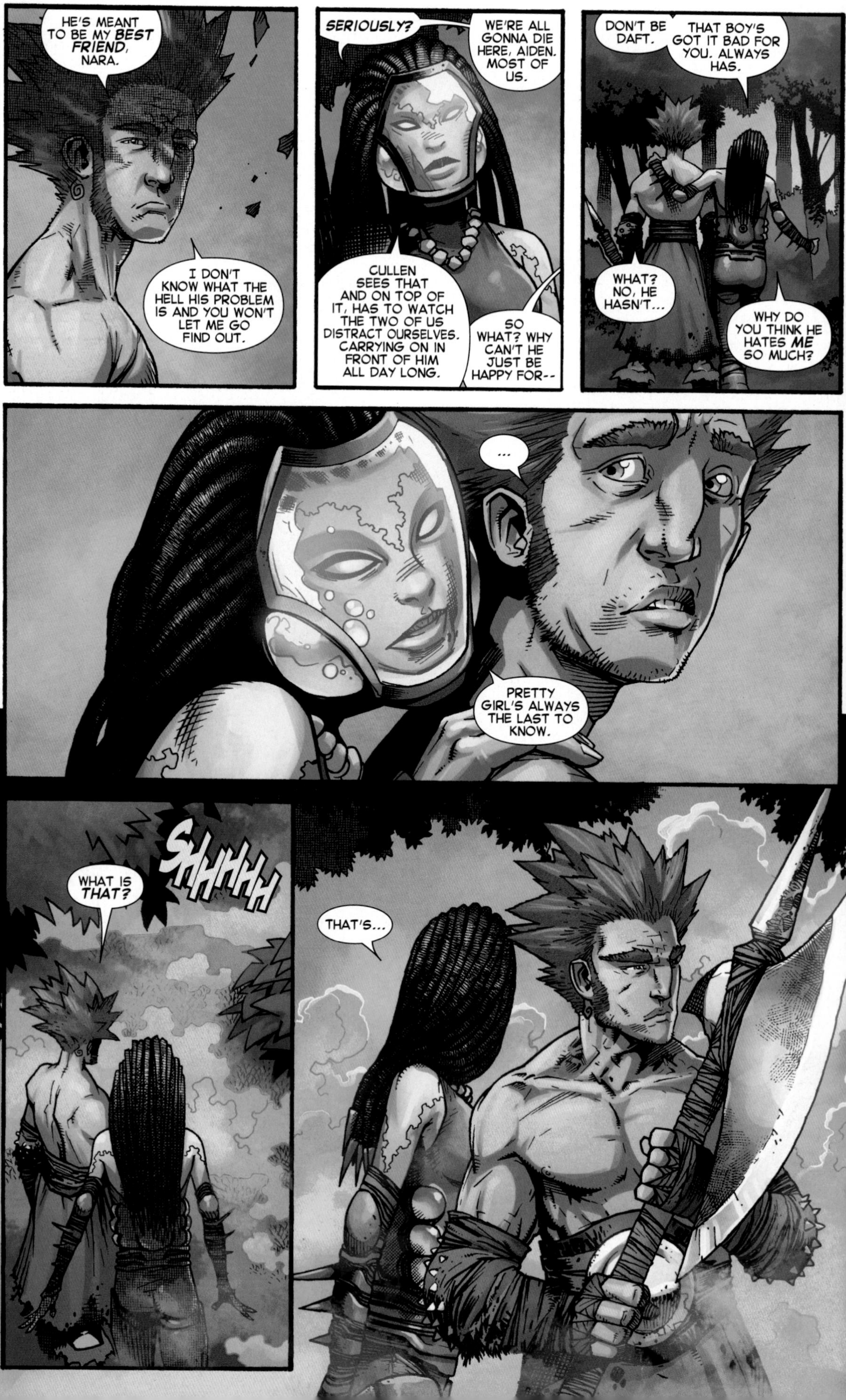
HE'S MEANT TO BE MY BEST FRIEND, NARA.
I DON'T KNOW WHAT THE HELL HIS PROBLEM IS AND YOU WON'T LET ME GO FIND OUT.
SERIOUSLY?
WE'RE ALL GONNA DIE HERE, AIDEN. MOST OF US.
CULLEN SEES THAT AND ON TOP OF IT, HAS TO WATCH THE TWO OF US DISTRACT OURSELVES. CARRYING ON IN FRONT OF HIM ALL DAY LONG.
SO WHAT? WHY CAN'T HE JUST BE HAPPY FOR--
DON'T BE DAFT.
THAT BOY'S GOT IT BAD FOR YOU. ALWAYS HAS.
WHAT? NO, HE HASN'T...
WHY DO YOU THINK HE HATES ME SO MUCH?
...
PRETTY GIRL'S ALWAYS THE LAST TO KNOW.
SHHHHH
WHAT IS THAT?
THAT'S...

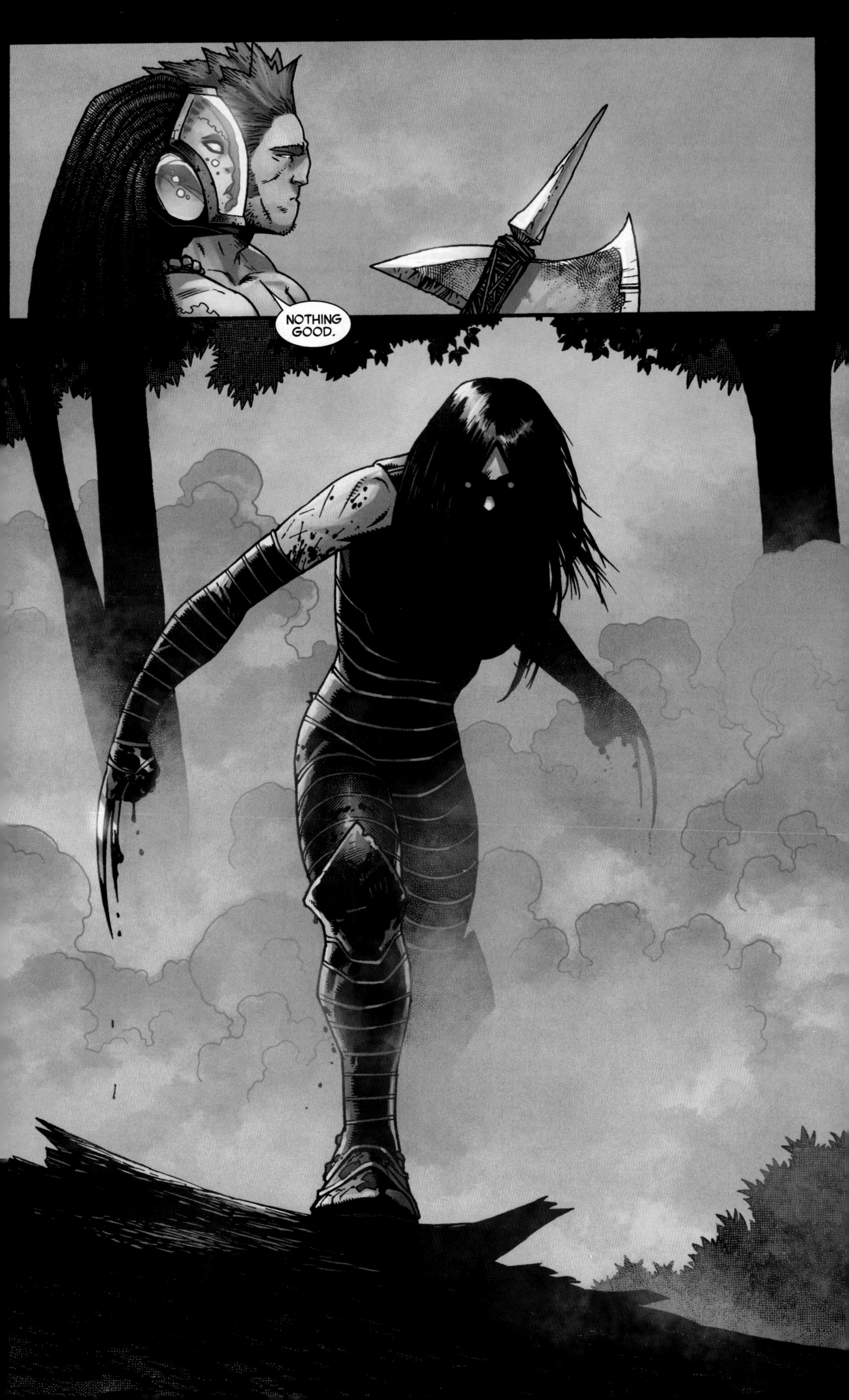
NOTHING GOOD.

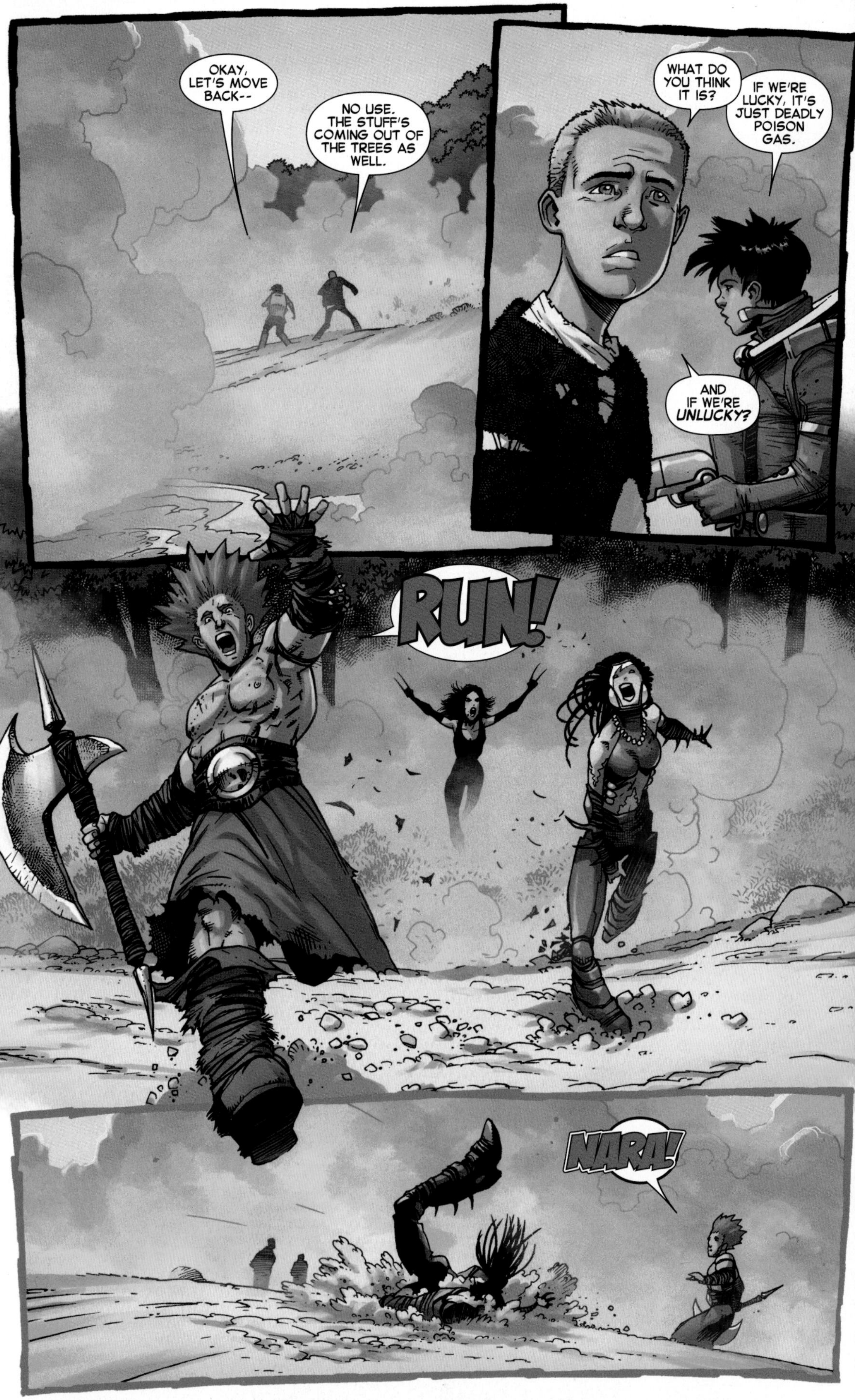
OKAY, LET'S MOVE BACK--
NO USE. THE STUFF'S COMING OUT OF THE TREES AS WELL.
WHAT DO YOU THINK IT IS?
IF WE'RE LUCKY, IT'S JUST DEADLY POISON GAS.
AND IF WE'RE UNLUCKY?
RUN!
NARA!

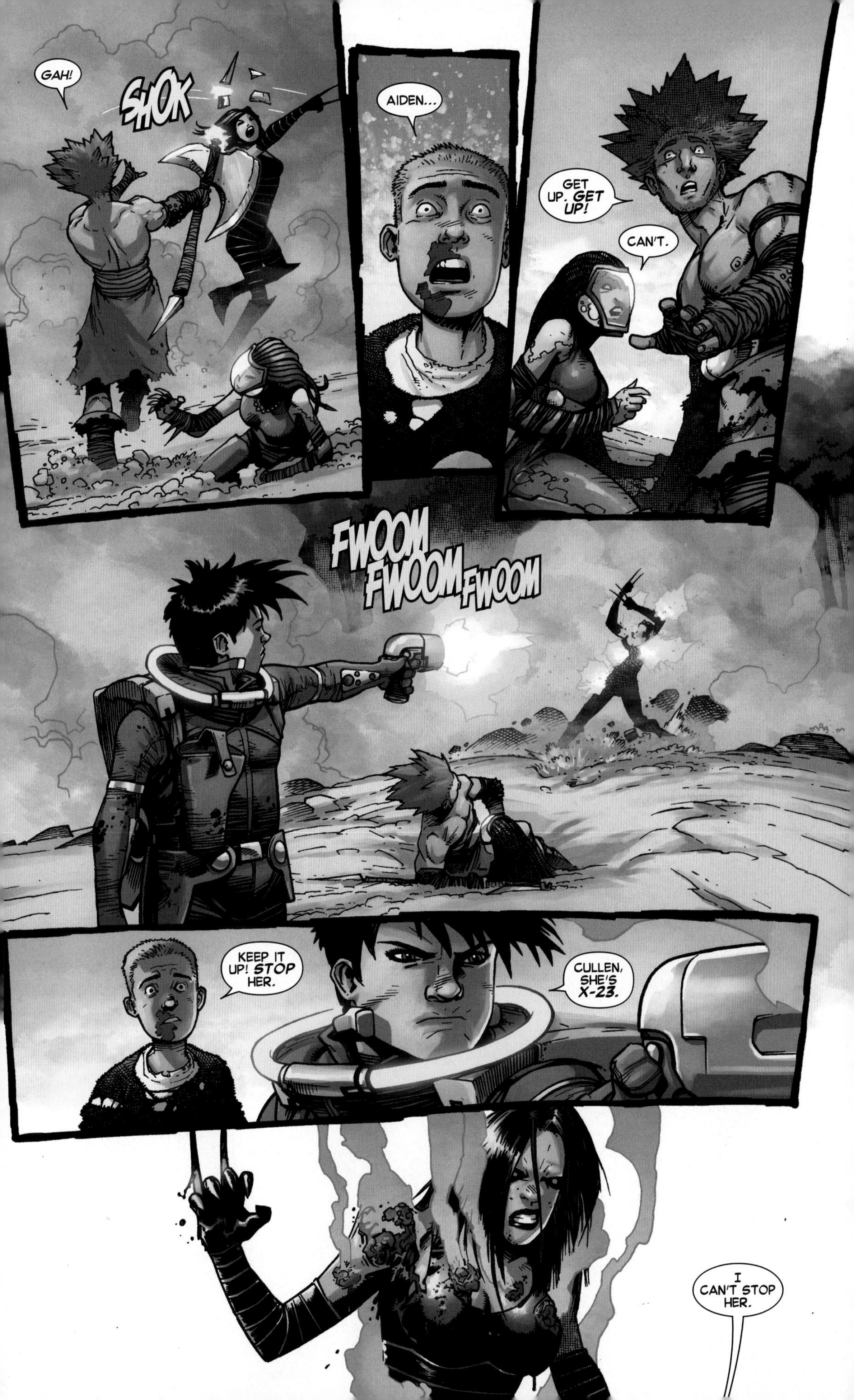
GAH!
SHOK
AIDEN...
GET UP. GET UP!
CAN'T.
FWOOM FWOOM FWOOM
KEEP IT UP! STOP HER.
CULLEN, SHE'S X-23.
I CAN'T STOP HER.

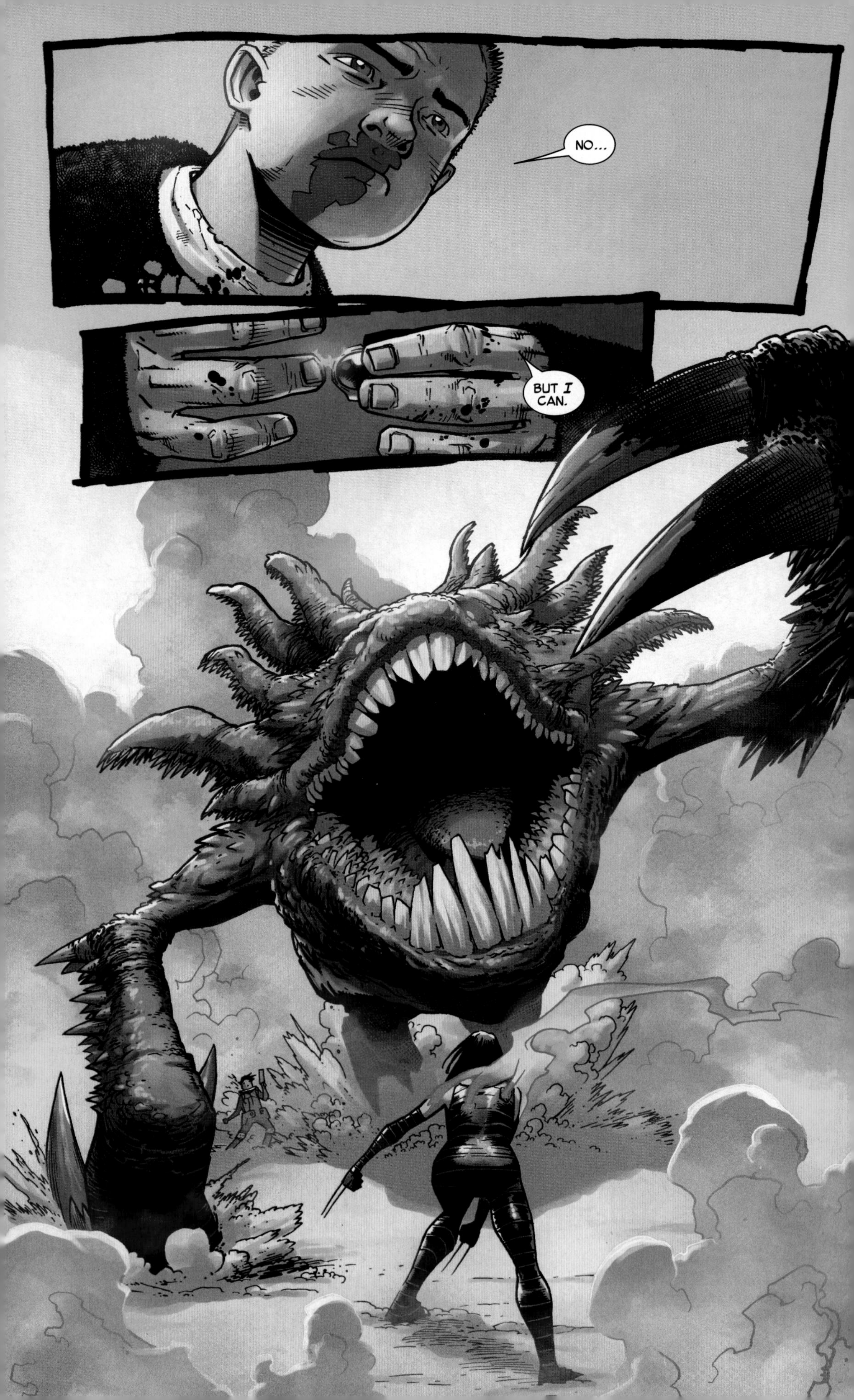
NO...
BUT I CAN.

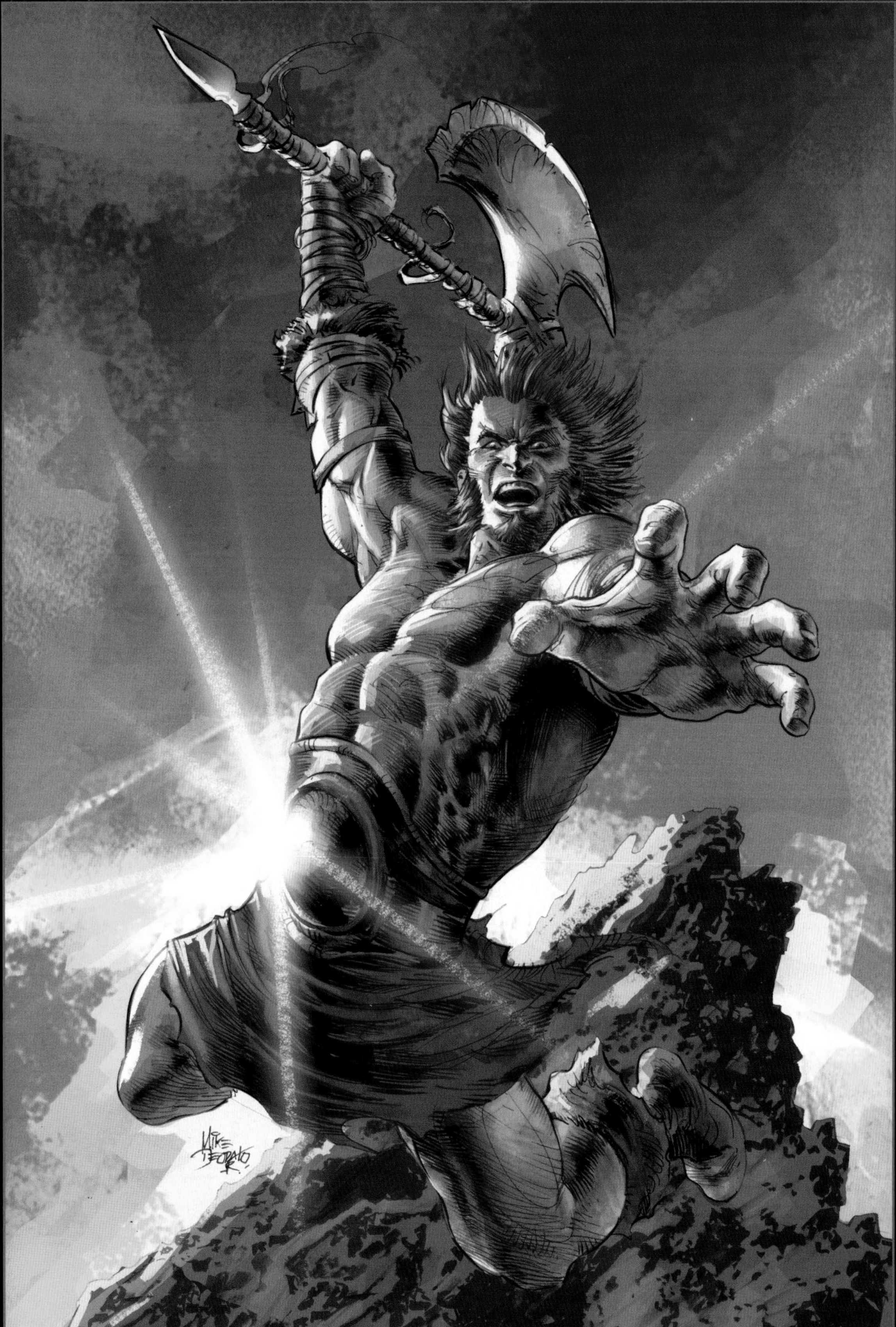

15: BOSS LEVEL PART 2

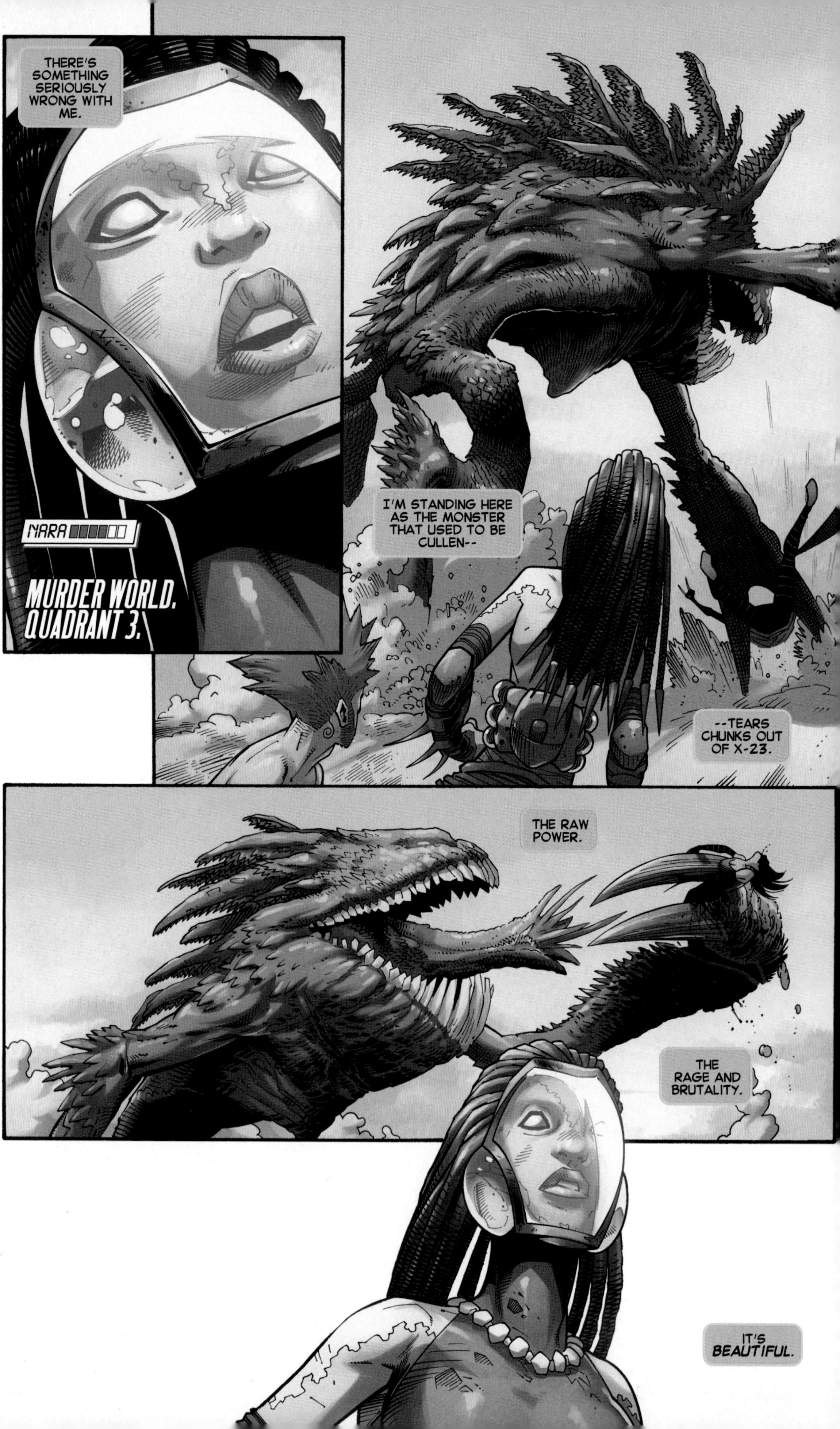
THERE'S SOMETHING SERIOUSLY WRONG WITH ME.
NARA
MURDER WORLD. QUADRANT 3.
I'M STANDING HERE AS THE MONSTER THAT USED TO BE CULLEN--
--TEARS CHUNKS OUT OF X-23.
THE RAW POWER.
THE RAGE AND BRUTALITY.
IT'S BEAUTIFUL.

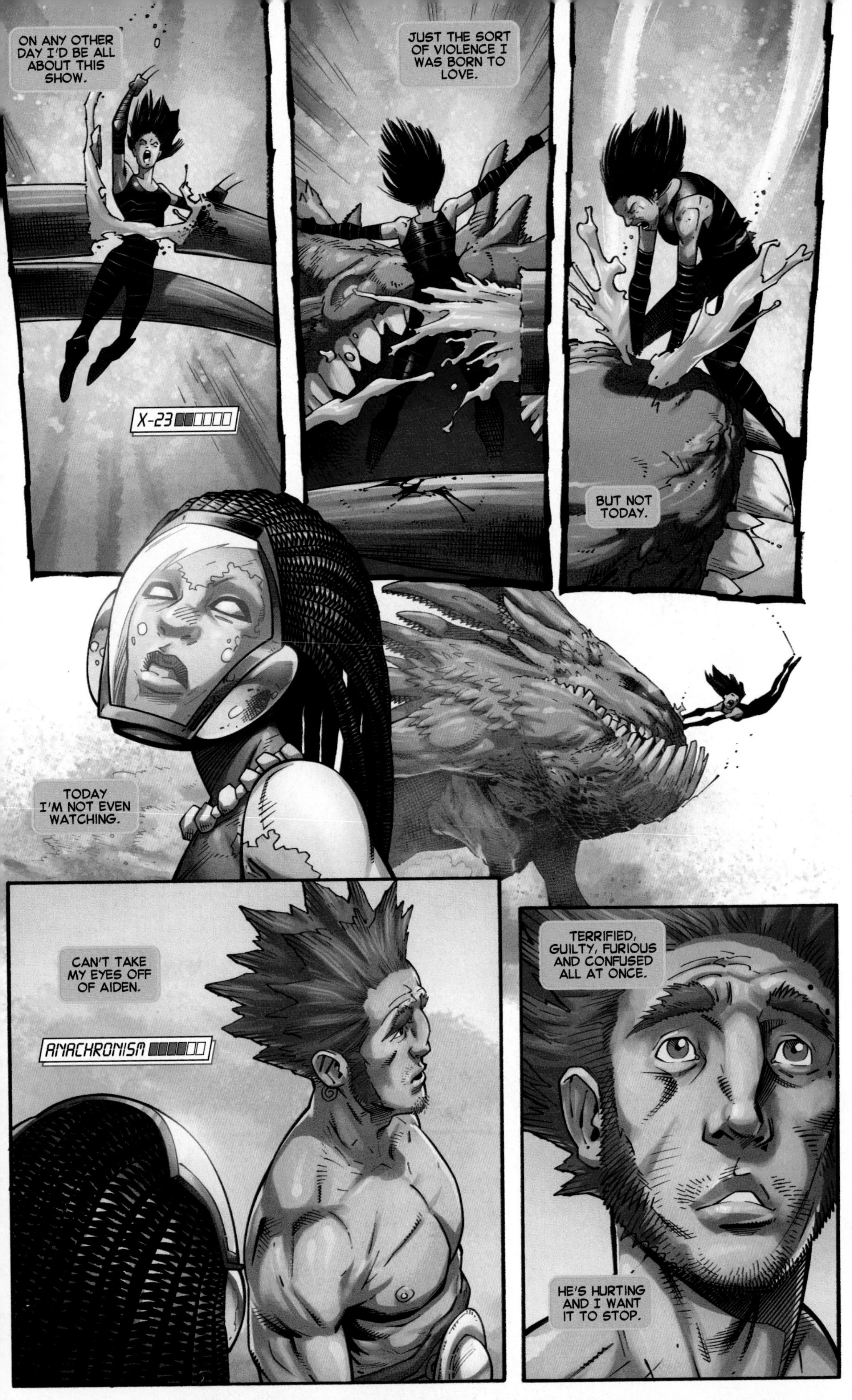
ON ANY OTHER DAY I'D BE ALL ABOUT THIS SHOW.
X-23
JUST THE SORT OF VIOLENCE I WAS BORN TO LOVE.
BUT NOT TODAY.
TODAY I'M NOT EVEN WATCHING.
CAN'T TAKE MY EYES OFF OF AIDEN.
ANACHRONISM
TERRIFIED, GUILTY, FURIOUS AND CONFUSED ALL AT ONCE.
HE'S HURTING AND I WANT IT TO STOP.

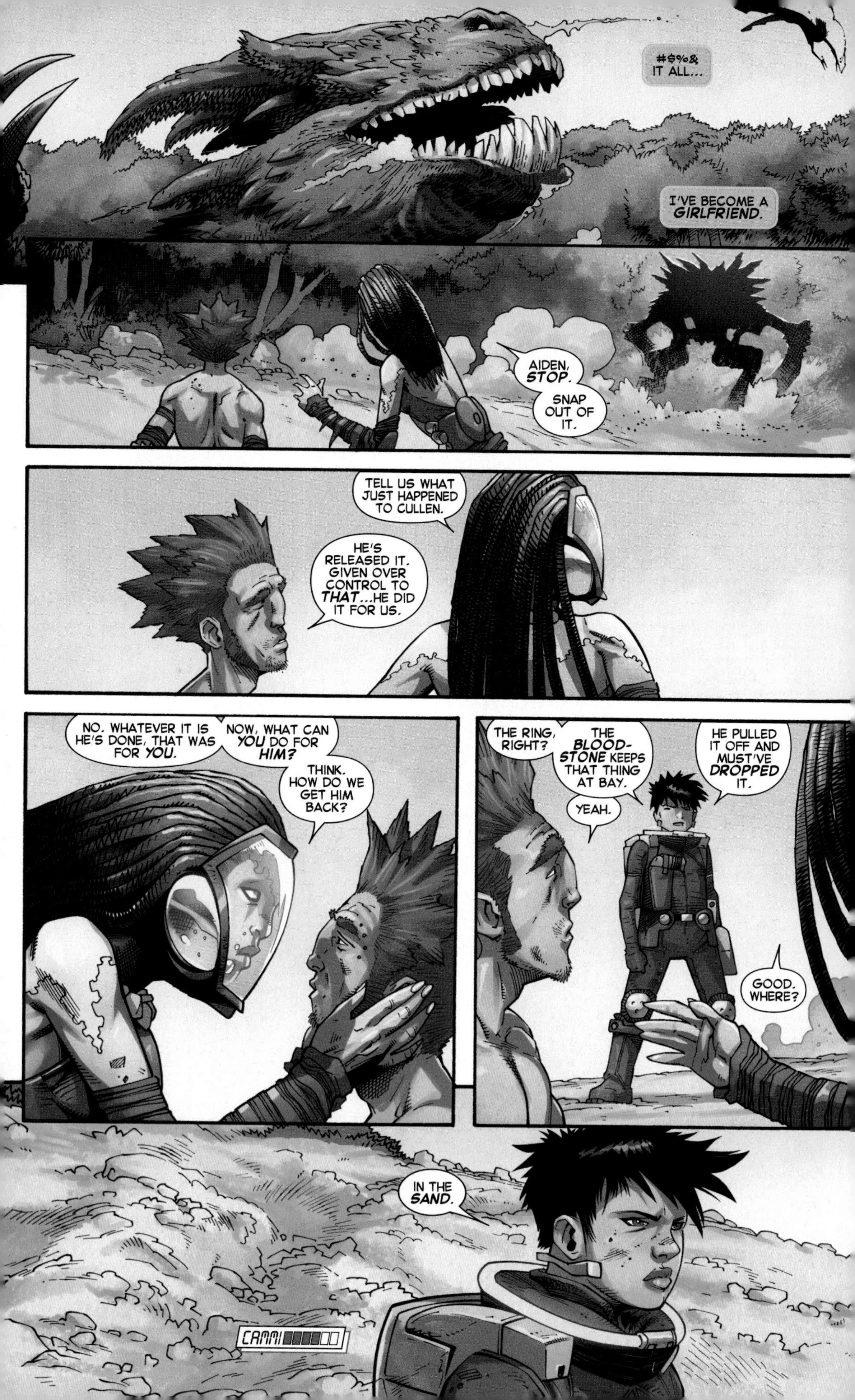

#$%&
IT ALL...
I'VE BECOME A GIRLFRIEND.
AIDEN, STOP.
SNAP OUT OF IT.
TELL US WHAT JUST HAPPENED TO CULLEN.
HE'S RELEASED IT. GIVEN OVER CONTROL TO THAT...HE DID IT FOR US.
NO. WHATEVER IT IS HE'S DONE, THAT WAS FOR YOU.
NOW, WHAT CAN YOU DO FOR HIM?
THINK. HOW DO WE GET HIM BACK?
THE RING, RIGHT?
THE BLOODSTONE KEEPS THAT THING AT BAY.
YEAH.
HE PULLED IT OFF AND MUST'VE DROPPED IT.
GOOD. WHERE?
IN THE SAND.
CAMMI

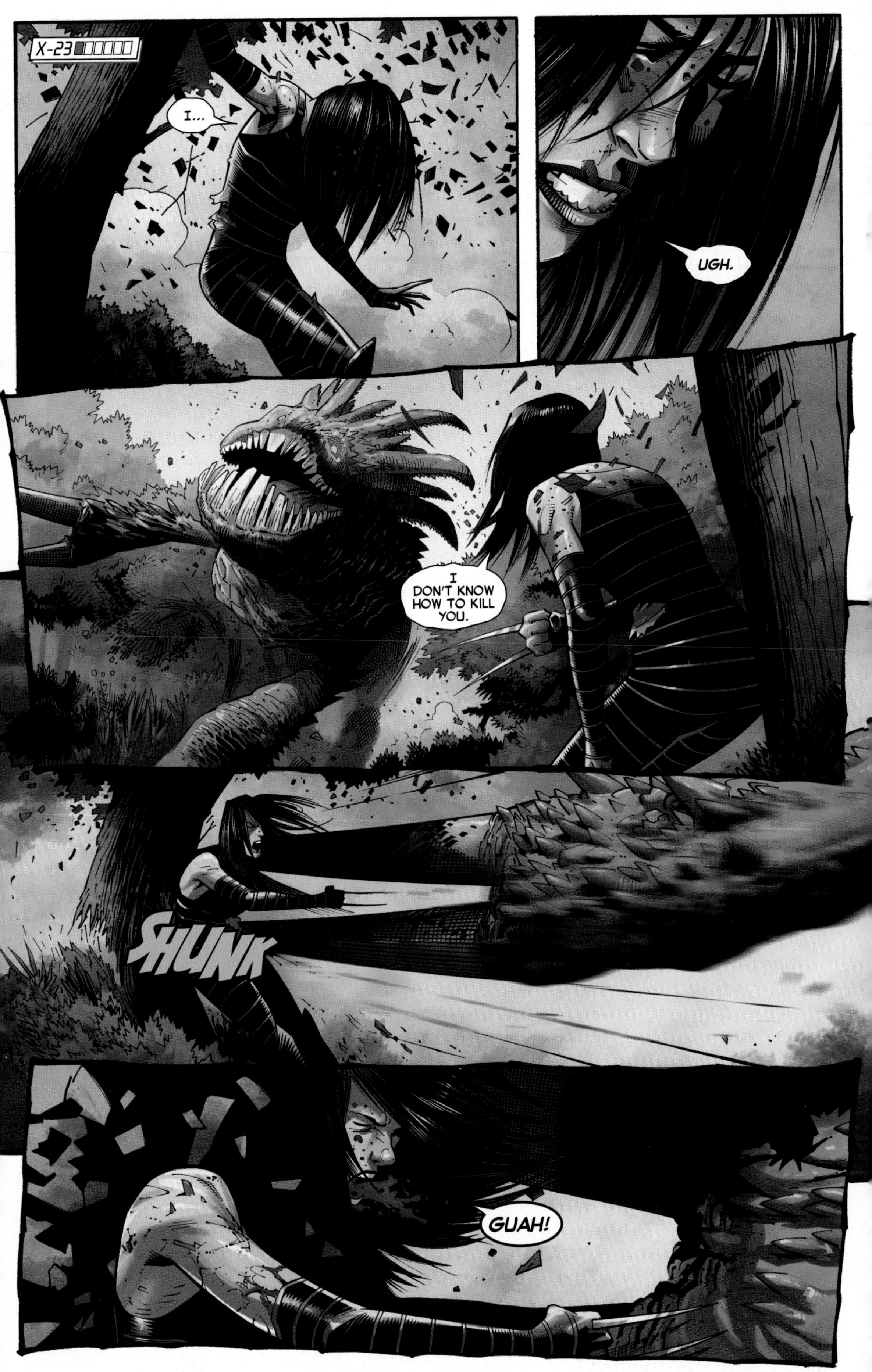
X-23
I...
UGH.
I DON'T KNOW HOW TO KILL YOU.
SHUNK
GUAH!

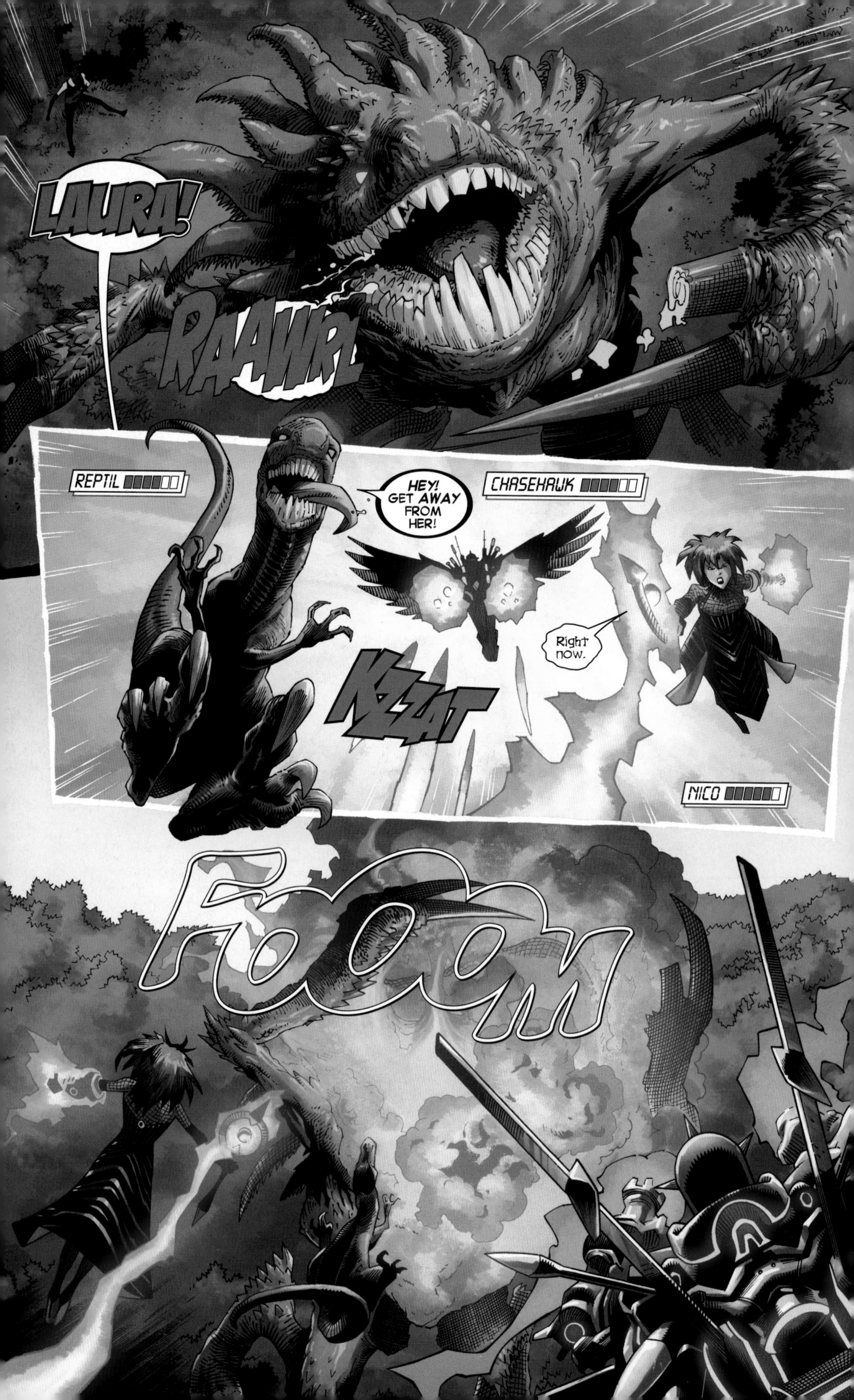
LAURA!
RAAWRL
REPTIL
HEY! GET AWAY FROM HER!
CHASEHAWK
Right now.
KZZAT
NICO
FOOOM

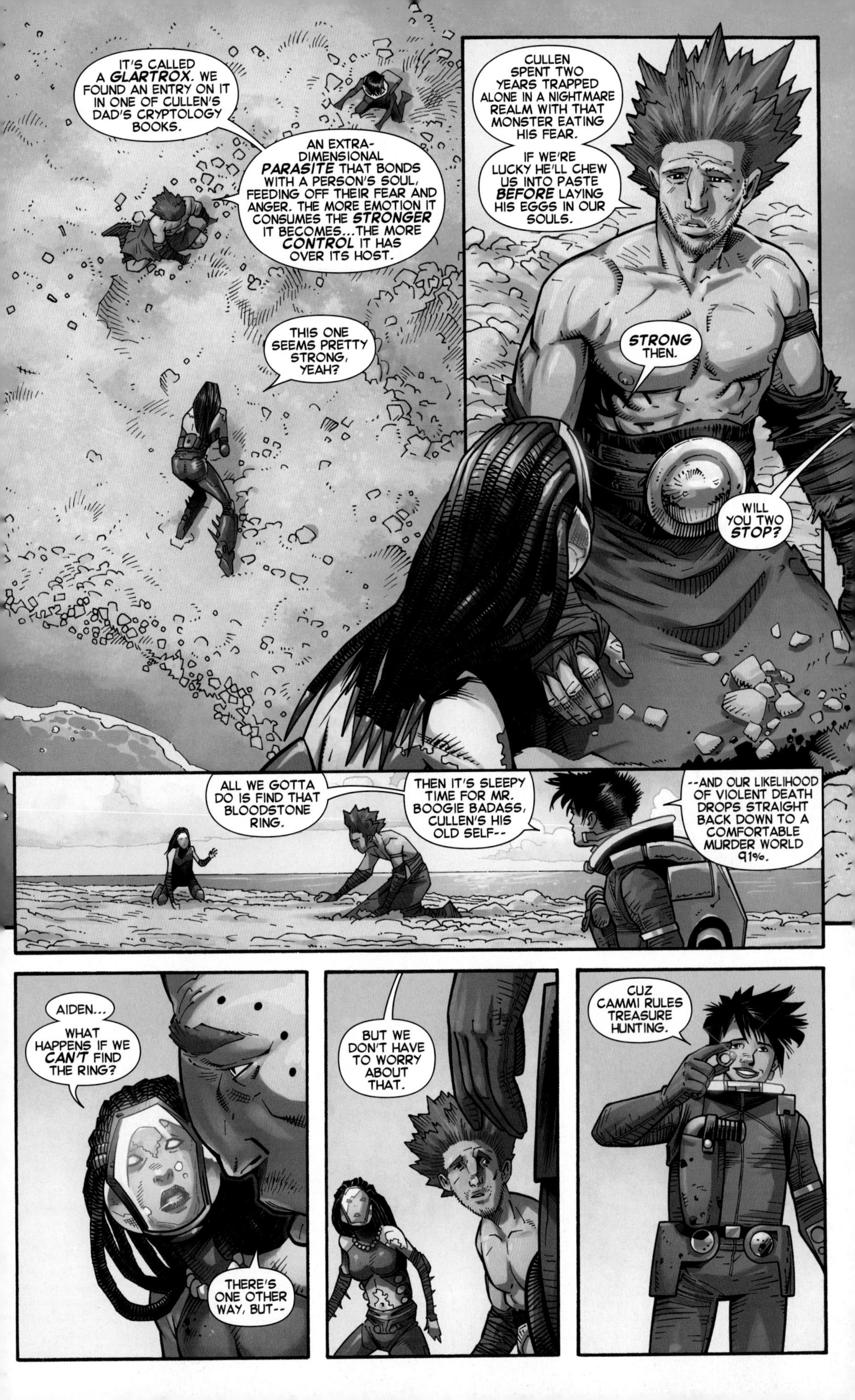
IT'S CALLED A GLARTROX. WE FOUND AN ENTRY ON IT IN ONE OF CULLEN'S DAD'S CRYPTOLOGY BOOKS.
AN EXTRA-DIMENSIONAL PARASITE THAT BONDS WITH A PERSON'S SOUL, FEEDING OFF THEIR FEAR AND ANGER. THE MORE EMOTION IT CONSUMES THE STRONGER IT BECOMES...THE MORE CONTROL IT HAS OVER ITS HOST.
THIS ONE SEEMS PRETTY STRONG, YEAH?
CULLEN SPENT TWO YEARS TRAPPED ALONE IN A NIGHTMARE REALM WITH THAT MONSTER EATING HIS FEAR.
IF WE'RE LUCKY HE'LL CHEW US INTO PASTE BEFORE LAYING HIS EGGS IN OUR SOULS.
STRONG THEN.
WILL YOU TWO STOP?
ALL WE GOTTA DO IS FIND THAT BLOODSTONE RING.
THEN IT'S SLEEPY TIME FOR MR. BOOGIE BADASS, CULLEN'S HIS OLD SELF--
--AND OUR LIKELIHOOD OF VIOLENT DEATH DROPS STRAIGHT BACK DOWN TO A COMFORTABLE MURDER WORLD 91%.
AIDEN...
WHAT HAPPENS IF WE CAN'T FIND THE RING?
THERE'S ONE OTHER WAY, BUT--
BUT WE DON'T HAVE TO WORRY ABOUT THAT.
CUZ CAMMI RULES TREASURE HUNTING.

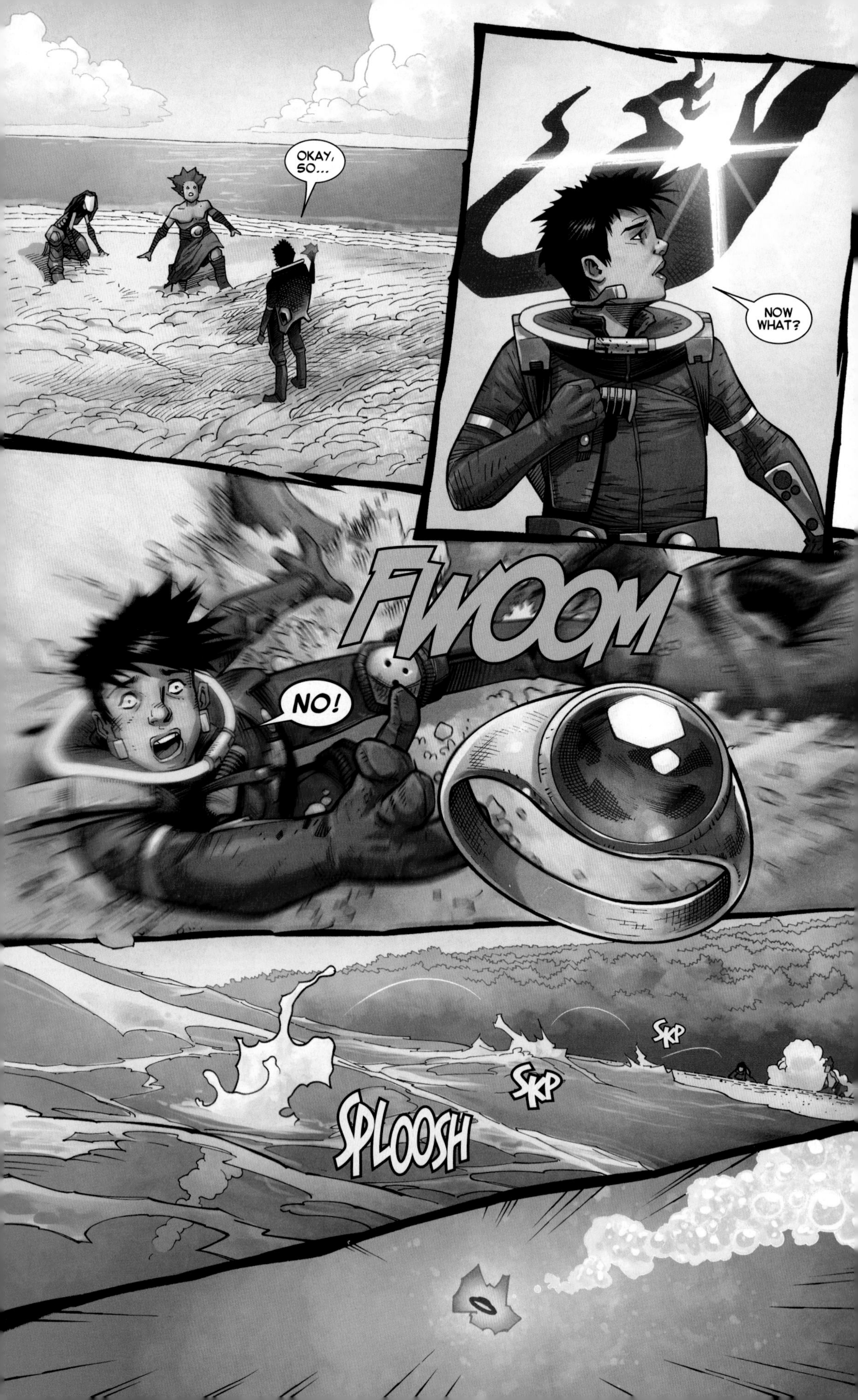
OKAY, SO...
NOW WHAT?
FWOOM
NO!
SKP
SKP
SPLOOSH

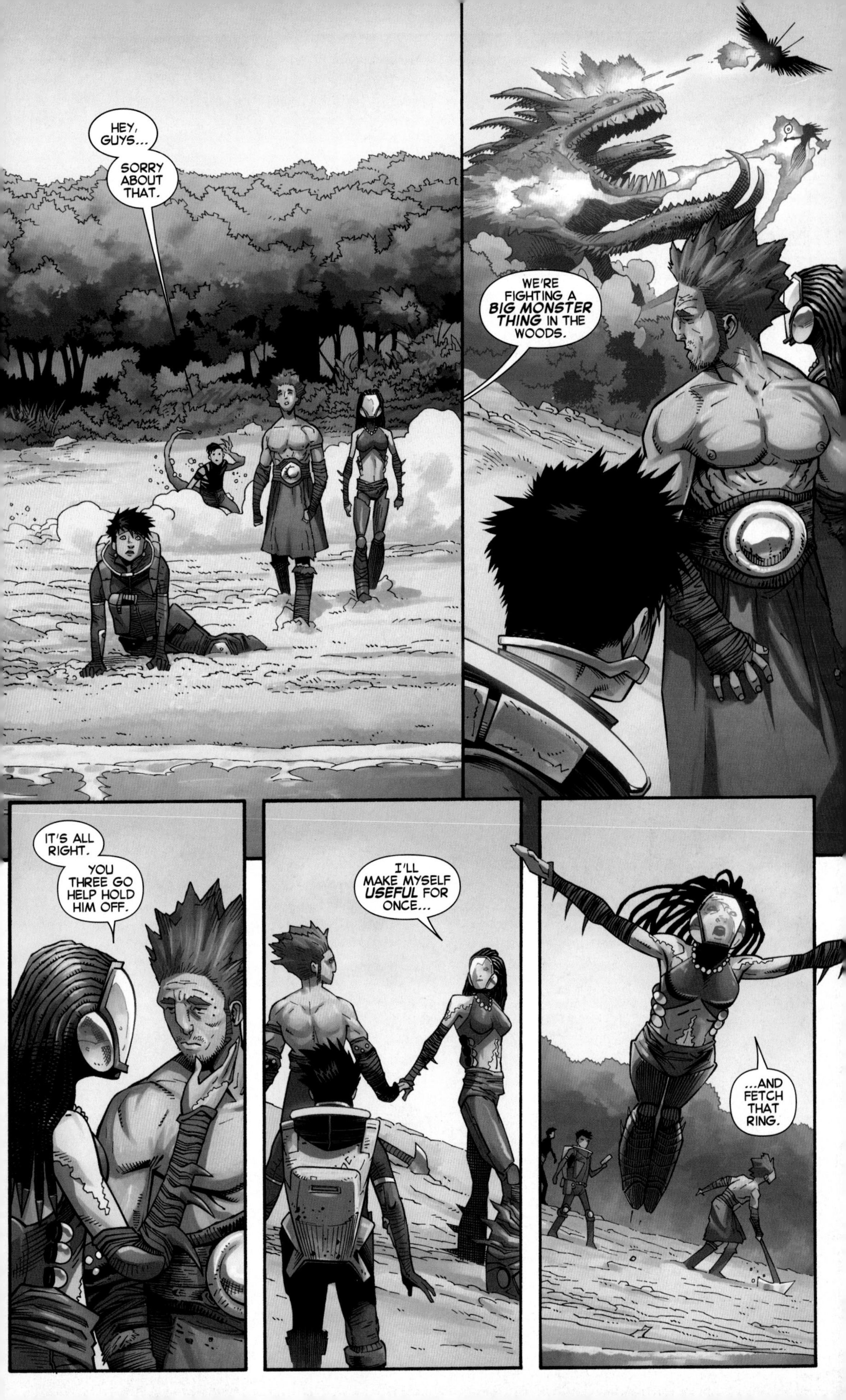
HEY, GUYS...
SORRY ABOUT THAT.
WE'RE FIGHTING A *BIG MONSTER THING* IN THE WOODS.
IT'S ALL RIGHT.
YOU THREE GO HELP HOLD HIM OFF.
I'LL MAKE MYSELF *USEFUL* FOR ONCE...
...AND FETCH THAT RING.

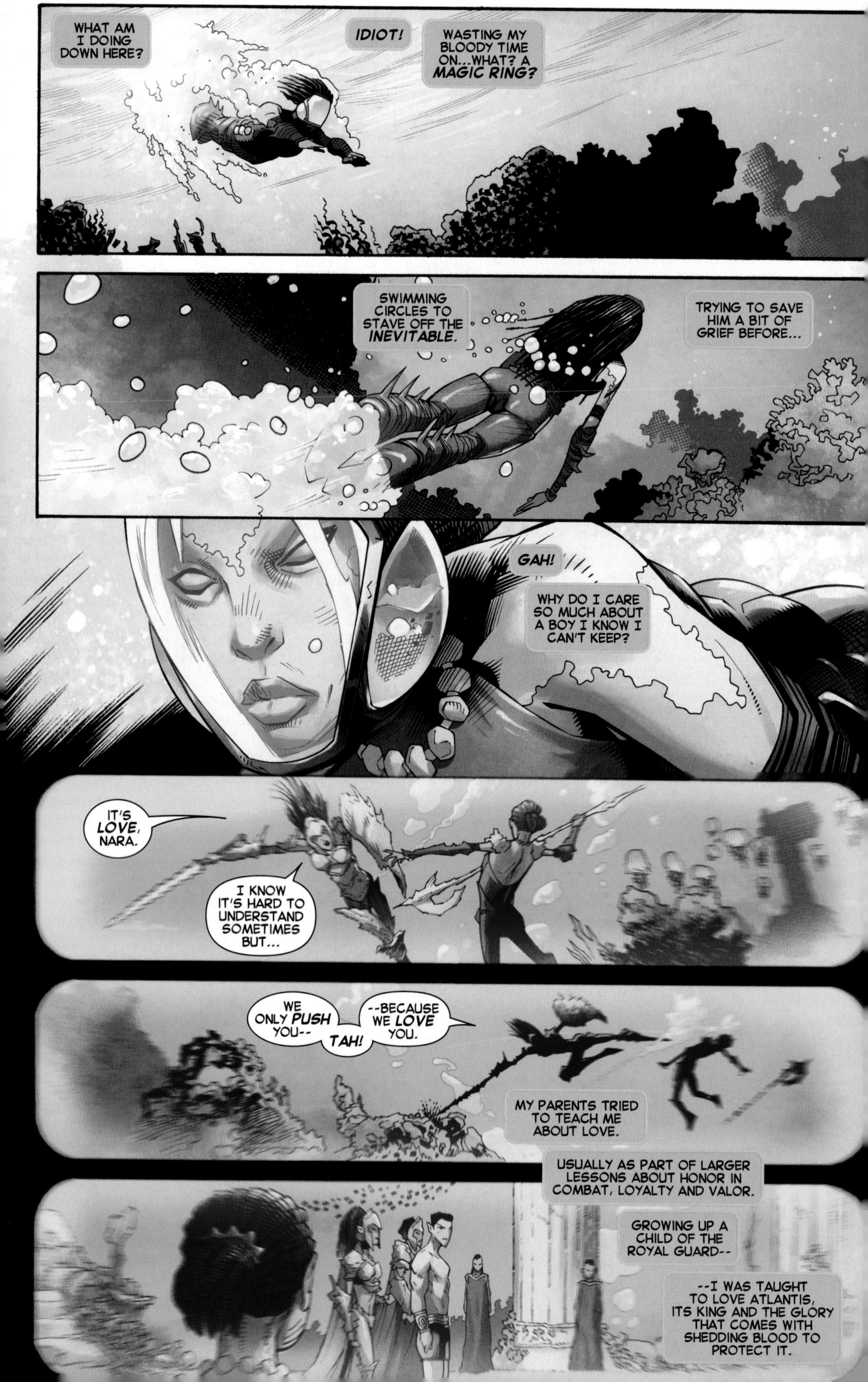
WHAT AM I DOING DOWN HERE?
IDIOT!
WASTING MY BLOODY TIME ON...WHAT? A MAGIC RING?
SWIMMING CIRCLES TO STAVE OFF THE INEVITABLE.
TRYING TO SAVE HIM A BIT OF GRIEF BEFORE...
GAH!
WHY DO I CARE SO MUCH ABOUT A BOY I KNOW I CAN'T KEEP?
IT'S LOVE, NARA.
I KNOW IT'S HARD TO UNDERSTAND SOMETIMES BUT...
WE ONLY PUSH YOU--
TAH!
--BECAUSE WE LOVE YOU.
MY PARENTS TRIED TO TEACH ME ABOUT LOVE.
USUALLY AS PART OF LARGER LESSONS ABOUT HONOR IN COMBAT, LOYALTY AND VALOR.
GROWING UP A CHILD OF THE ROYAL GUARD--
--I WAS TAUGHT TO LOVE ATLANTIS, ITS KING AND THE GLORY THAT COMES WITH SHEDDING BLOOD TO PROTECT IT.

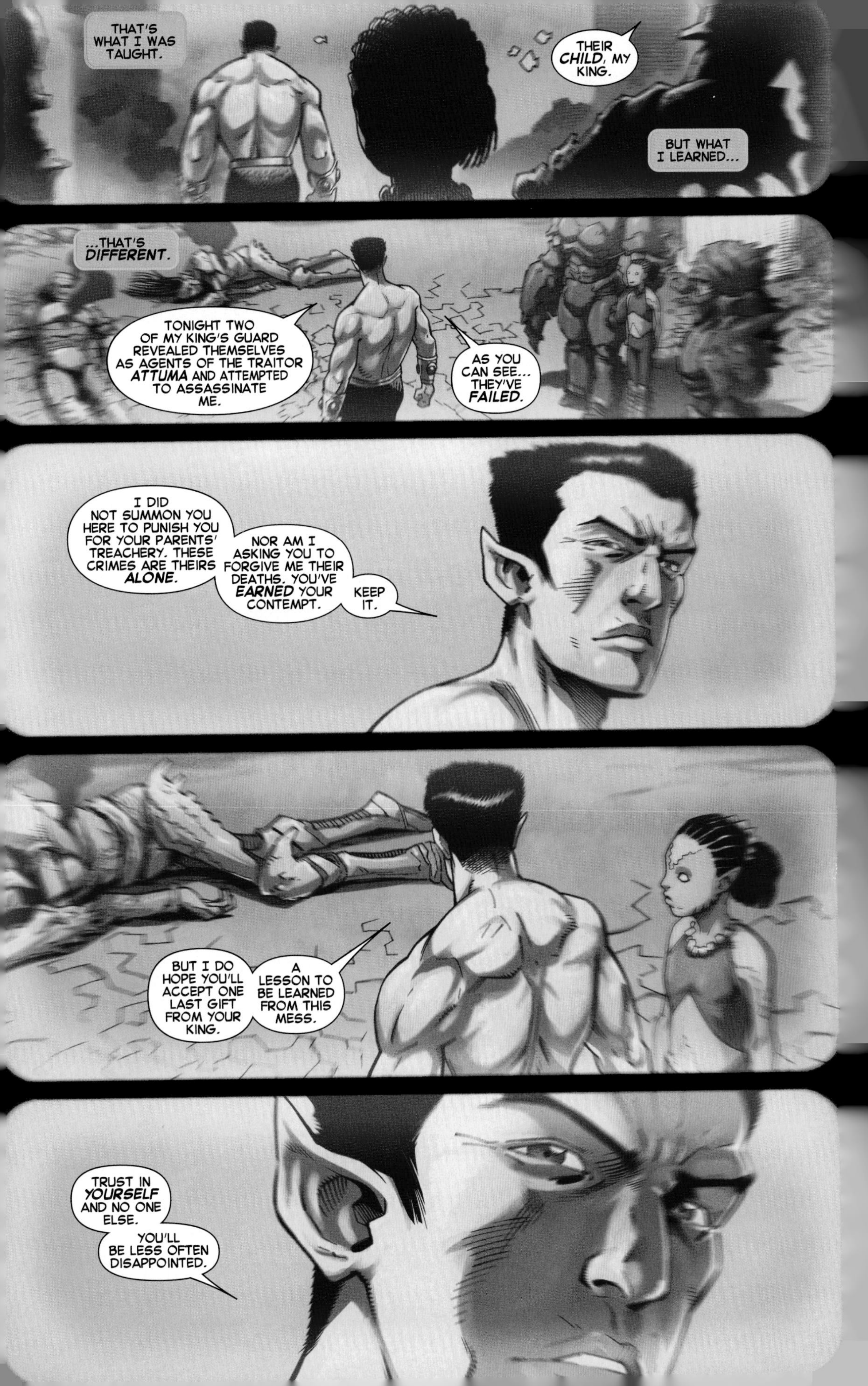
THAT'S WHAT I WAS TAUGHT.
THEIR CHILD, MY KING.
BUT WHAT I LEARNED...
...THAT'S DIFFERENT.
TONIGHT TWO OF MY KING'S GUARD REVEALED THEMSELVES AS AGENTS OF THE TRAITOR ATTUMA AND ATTEMPTED TO ASSASSINATE ME.
AS YOU CAN SEE... THEY'VE FAILED.
I DID NOT SUMMON YOU HERE TO PUNISH YOU FOR YOUR PARENTS' TREACHERY. THESE CRIMES ARE THEIRS ALONE.
NOR AM I ASKING YOU TO FORGIVE ME THEIR DEATHS. YOU'VE EARNED YOUR CONTEMPT.
KEEP IT.
BUT I DO HOPE YOU'LL ACCEPT ONE LAST GIFT FROM YOUR KING.
A LESSON TO BE LEARNED FROM THIS MESS.
TRUST IN YOURSELF AND NO ONE ELSE.
YOU'LL BE LESS OFTEN DISAPPOINTED.

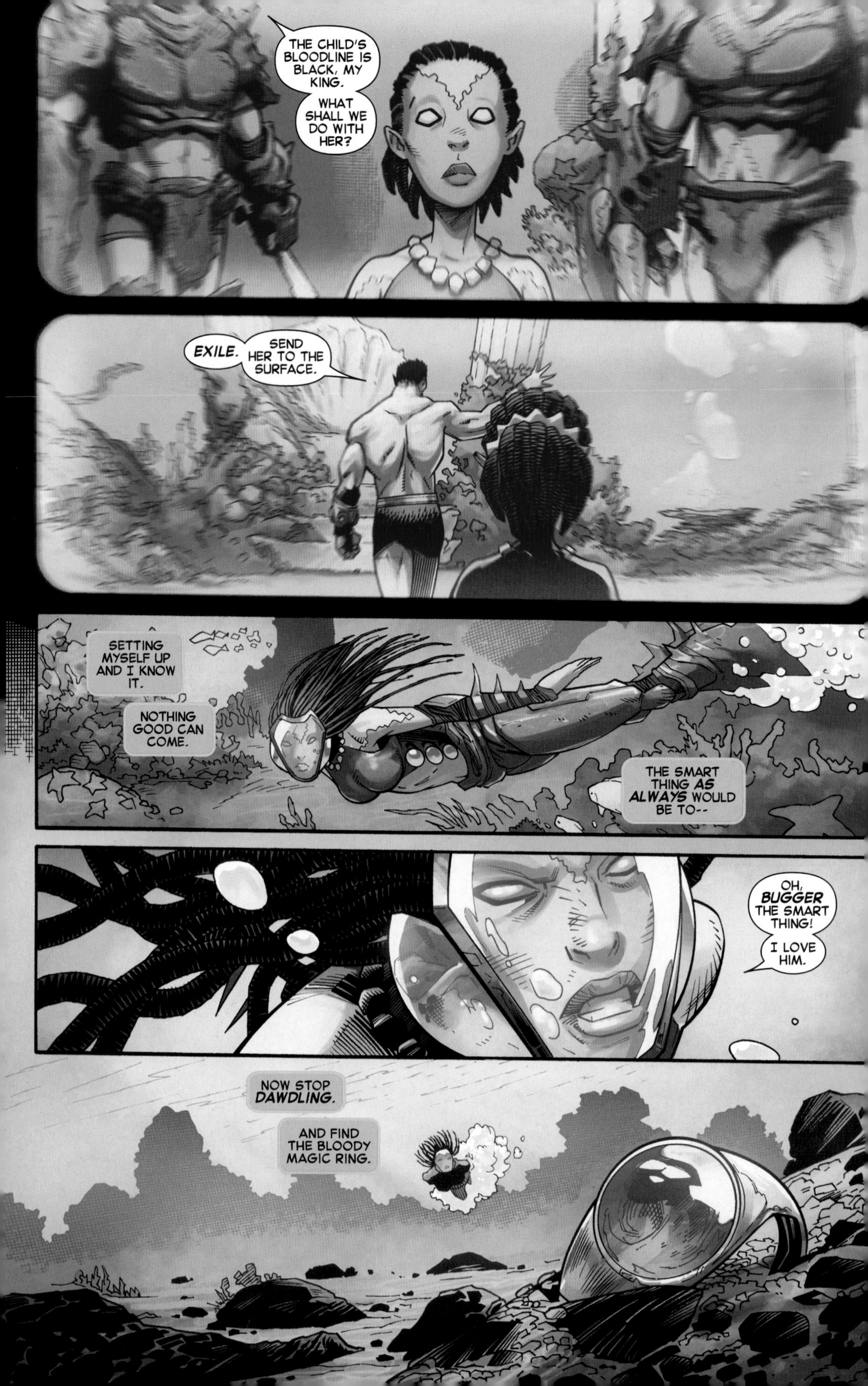
THE CHILD'S BLOODLINE IS BLACK, MY KING.
WHAT SHALL WE DO WITH HER?
EXILE.
SEND HER TO THE SURFACE.
SETTING MYSELF UP AND I KNOW IT.
NOTHING GOOD CAN COME.
THE SMART THING AS ALWAYS WOULD BE TO--
OH, BUGGER THE SMART THING!
I LOVE HIM.
NOW STOP DAWDLING.
AND FIND THE BLOODY MAGIC RING.

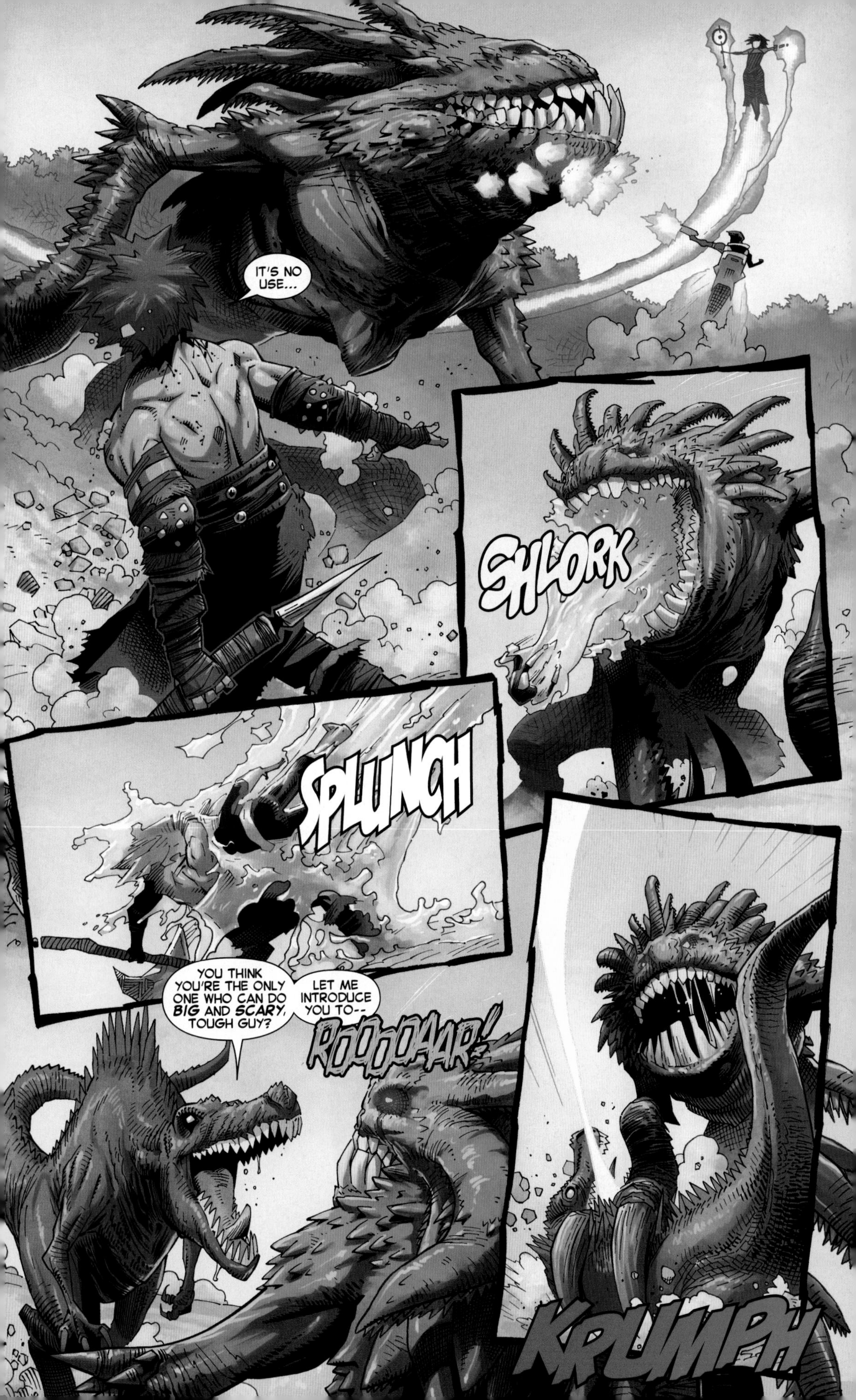
IT'S NO USE...
SHLORK
SPLUNCH
YOU THINK YOU'RE THE ONLY ONE WHO CAN DO BIG AND SCARY, TOUGH GUY?
LET ME INTRODUCE YOU TO--
ROOOOAAR!
KRUMPH

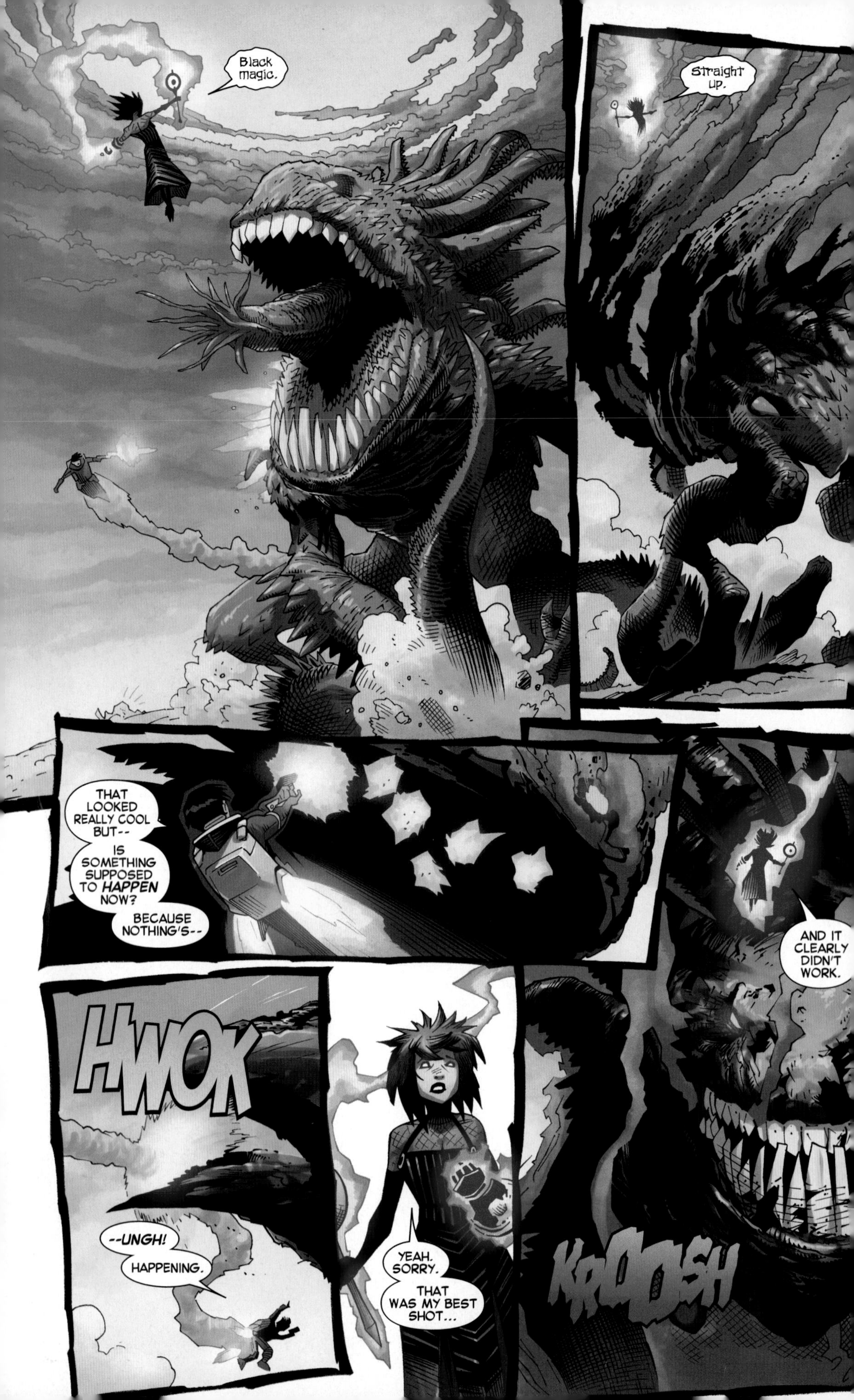
Black magic.
Straight up.
THAT LOOKED REALLY COOL BUT--
IS SOMETHING SUPPOSED TO *HAPPEN* NOW?
BECAUSE NOTHING'S--
AND IT CLEARLY DIDN'T WORK.
HWOK
--UNGH!
HAPPENING.
YEAH. SORRY.
THAT WAS MY BEST SHOT...
KROOSH

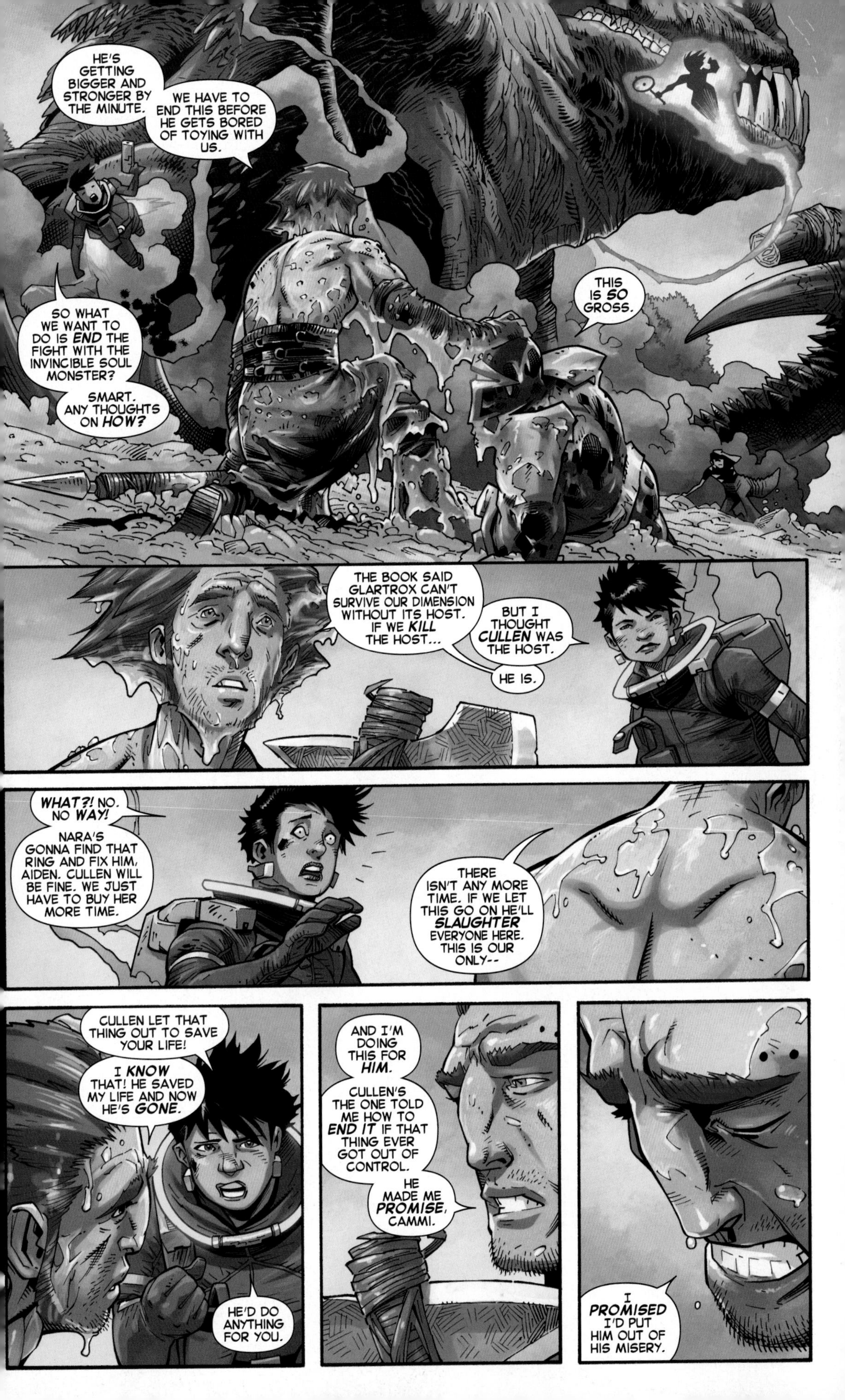
HE'S GETTING BIGGER AND STRONGER BY THE MINUTE.
WE HAVE TO END THIS BEFORE HE GETS BORED OF TOYING WITH US.
SO WHAT WE WANT TO DO IS END THE FIGHT WITH THE INVINCIBLE SOUL MONSTER?
SMART. ANY THOUGHTS ON HOW?
THIS IS SO GROSS.
THE BOOK SAID GLARTROX CAN'T SURVIVE OUR DIMENSION WITHOUT ITS HOST. IF WE KILL THE HOST...
BUT I THOUGHT CULLEN WAS THE HOST.
HE IS.
WHAT?! NO. NO WAY!
NARA'S GONNA FIND THAT RING AND FIX HIM, AIDEN. CULLEN WILL BE FINE. WE JUST HAVE TO BUY HER MORE TIME.
THERE ISN'T ANY MORE TIME. IF WE LET THIS GO ON HE'LL SLAUGHTER EVERYONE HERE. THIS IS OUR ONLY--
CULLEN LET THAT THING OUT TO SAVE YOUR LIFE!
I KNOW THAT! HE SAVED MY LIFE AND NOW HE'S GONE.
HE'D DO ANYTHING FOR YOU.
AND I'M DOING THIS FOR HIM.
CULLEN'S THE ONE TOLD ME HOW TO END IT IF THAT THING EVER GOT OUT OF CONTROL.
HE MADE ME PROMISE, CAMMI.
I PROMISED I'D PUT HIM OUT OF HIS MISERY.

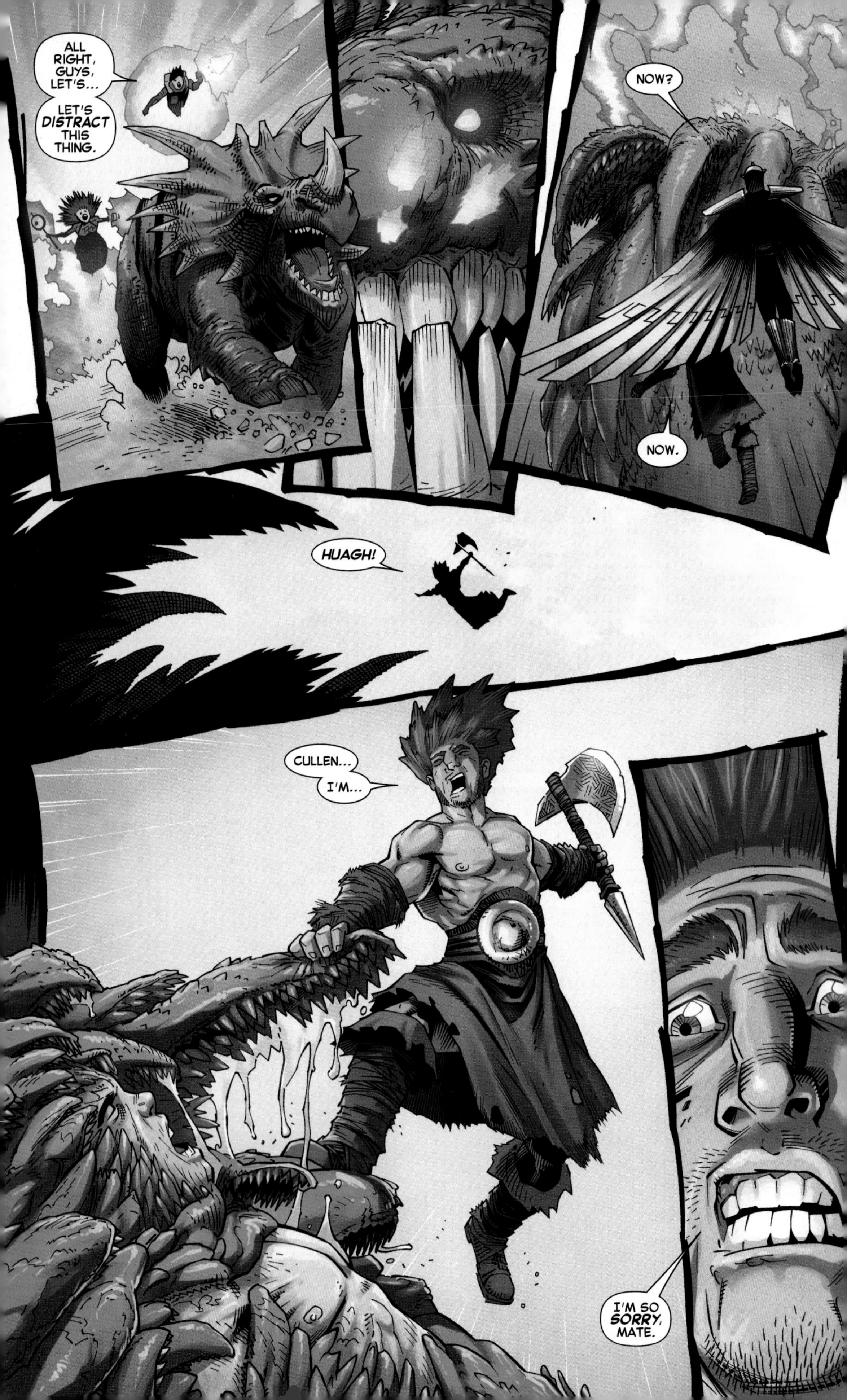
ALL RIGHT, GUYS, LET'S...
LET'S DISTRACT THIS THING.
NOW?
NOW.
HUAGH!
CULLEN... I'M...
I'M SO SORRY, MATE.

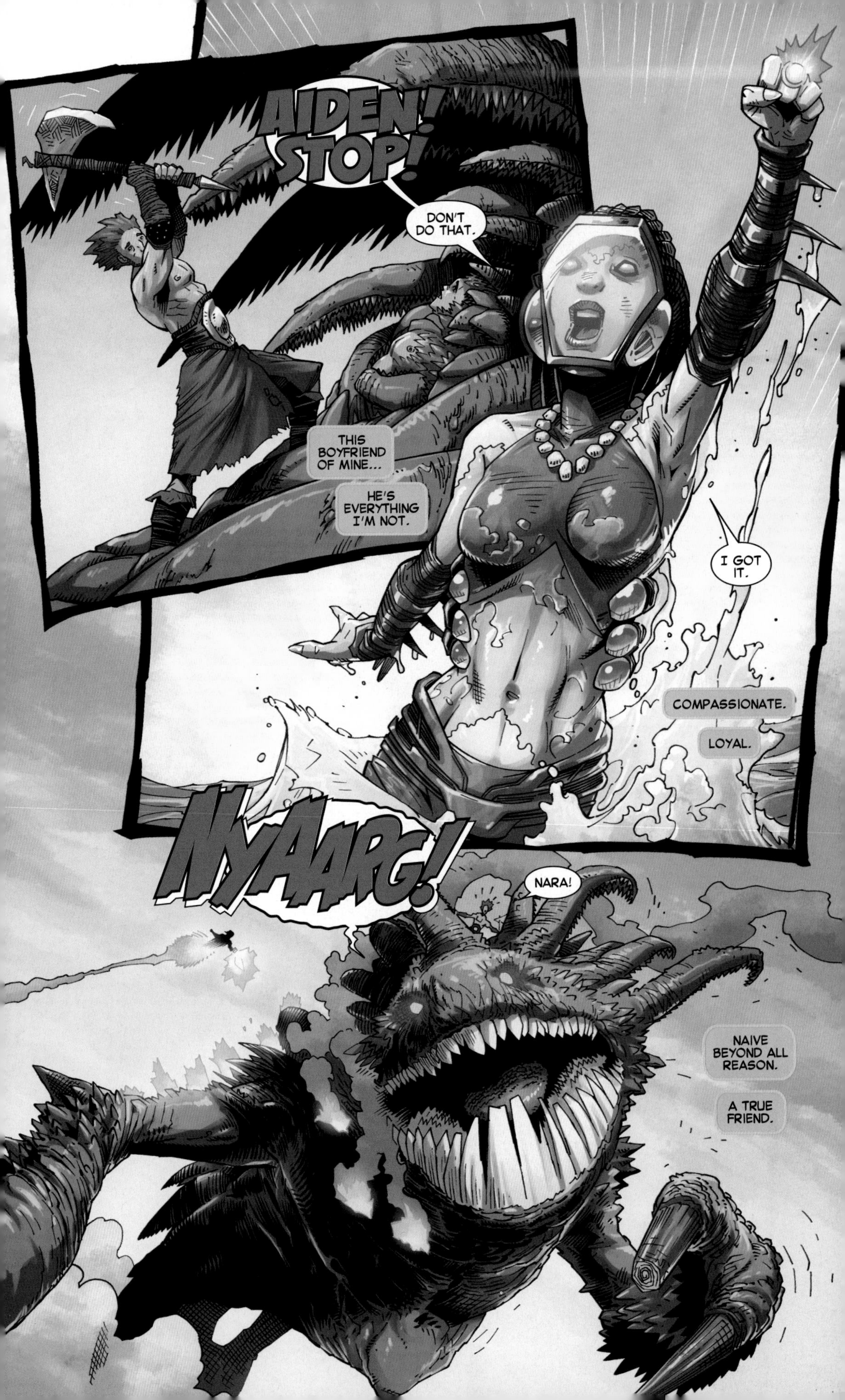

AIDEN! STOP!
DON'T DO THAT.
THIS BOYFRIEND OF MINE...
HE'S EVERYTHING I'M NOT.
I GOT IT.
COMPASSIONATE.
LOYAL.
NYAARG!
NARA!
NAIVE BEYOND ALL REASON.
A TRUE FRIEND.

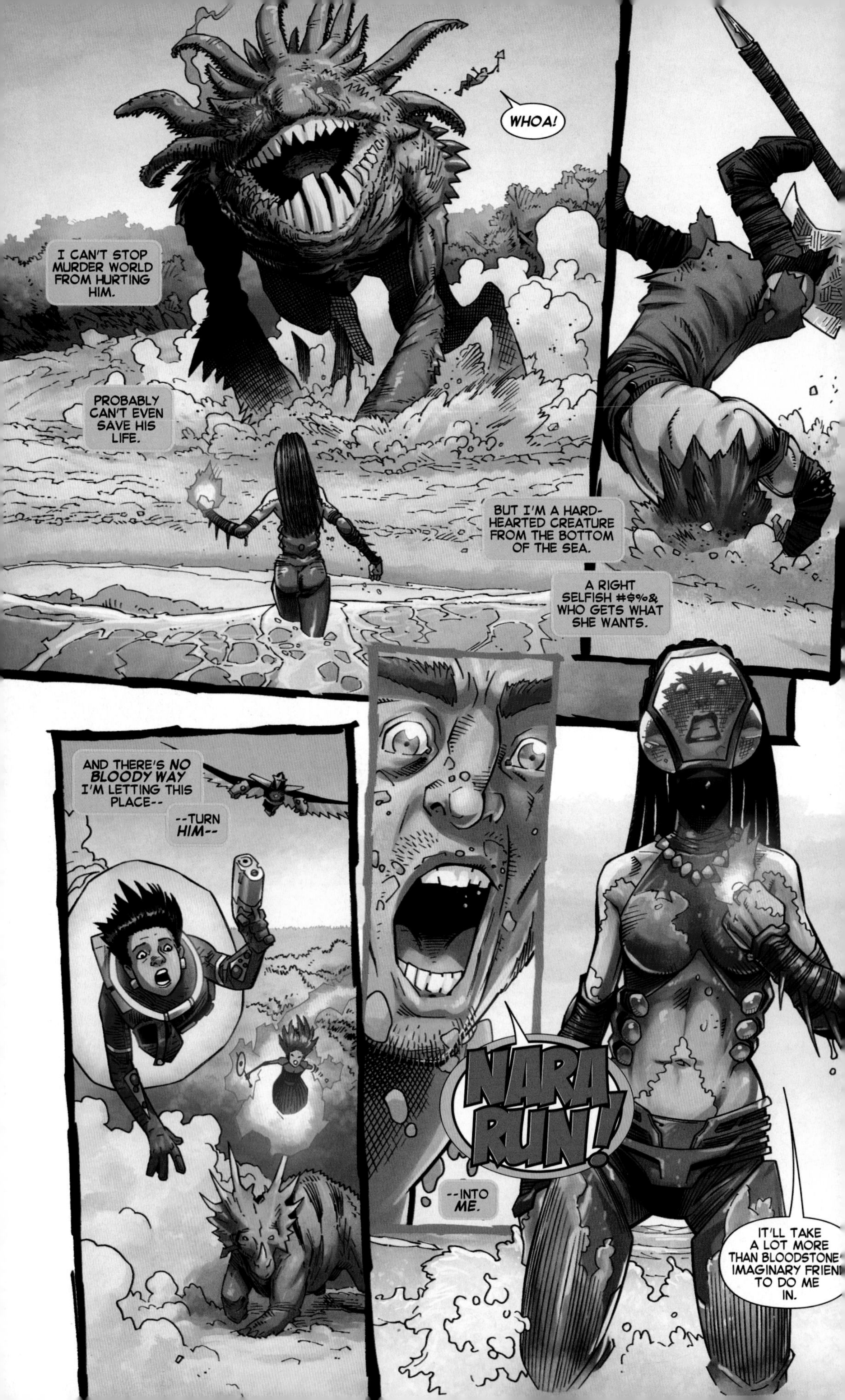
WHOA!
I CAN'T STOP MURDER WORLD FROM HURTING HIM.
PROBABLY CAN'T EVEN SAVE HIS LIFE.
BUT I'M A HARD-HEARTED CREATURE FROM THE BOTTOM OF THE SEA.
A RIGHT SELFISH #$%& WHO GETS WHAT SHE WANTS.
AND THERE'S NO BLOODY WAY I'M LETTING THIS PLACE--
--TURN HIM--
--INTO ME.
NARA RUN!
IT'LL TAKE A LOT MORE THAN BLOODSTONE' IMAGINARY FRIEN TO DO ME IN.

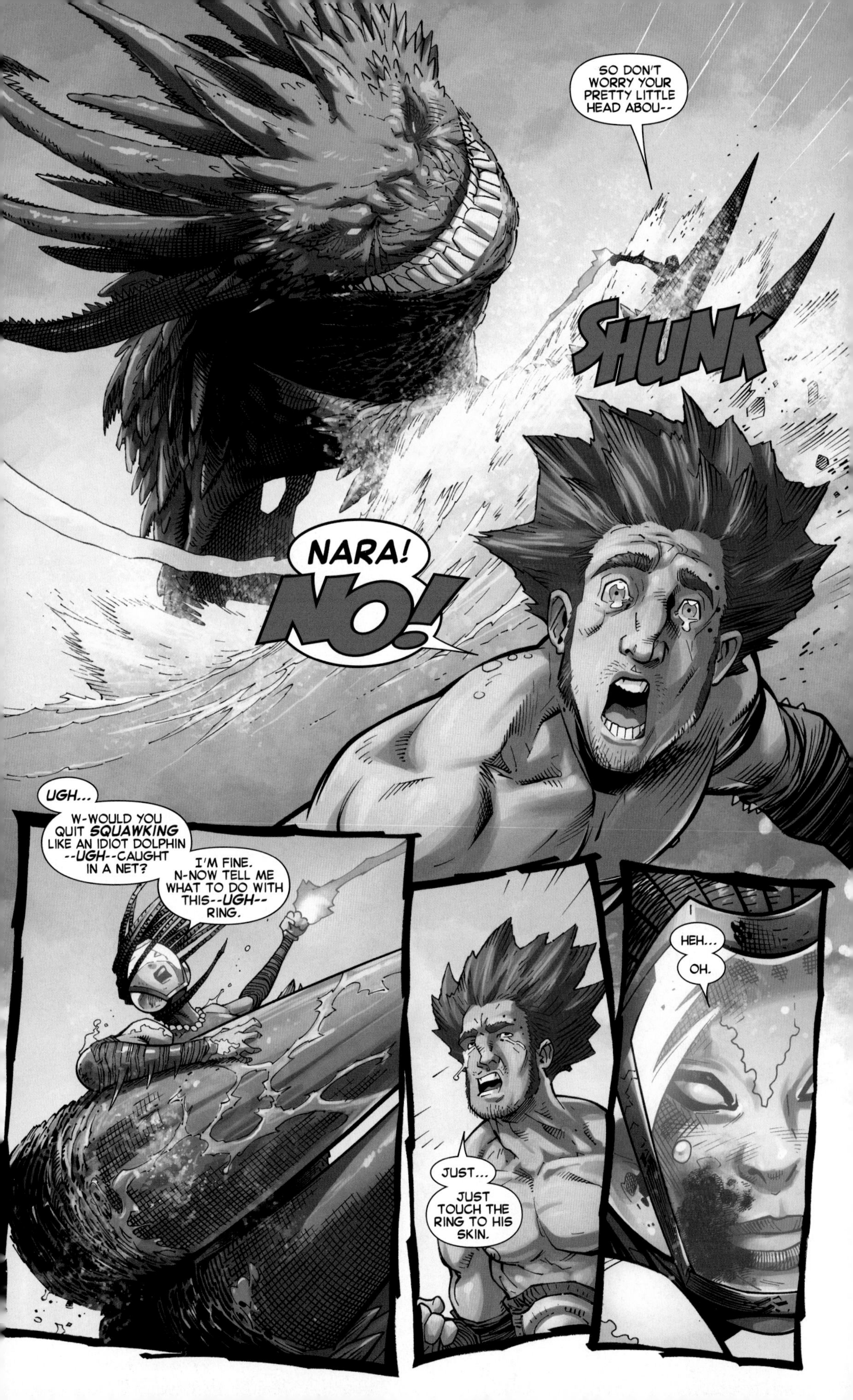

SO DON'T WORRY YOUR PRETTY LITTLE HEAD ABOU--
SHUNK
NARA! NO!
UGH...
W-WOULD YOU QUIT SQUAWKING LIKE AN IDIOT DOLPHIN --UGH--CAUGHT IN A NET?
I'M FINE. N-NOW TELL ME WHAT TO DO WITH THIS--UGH-- RING.
JUST...
JUST TOUCH THE RING TO HIS SKIN.
HEH...
OH.

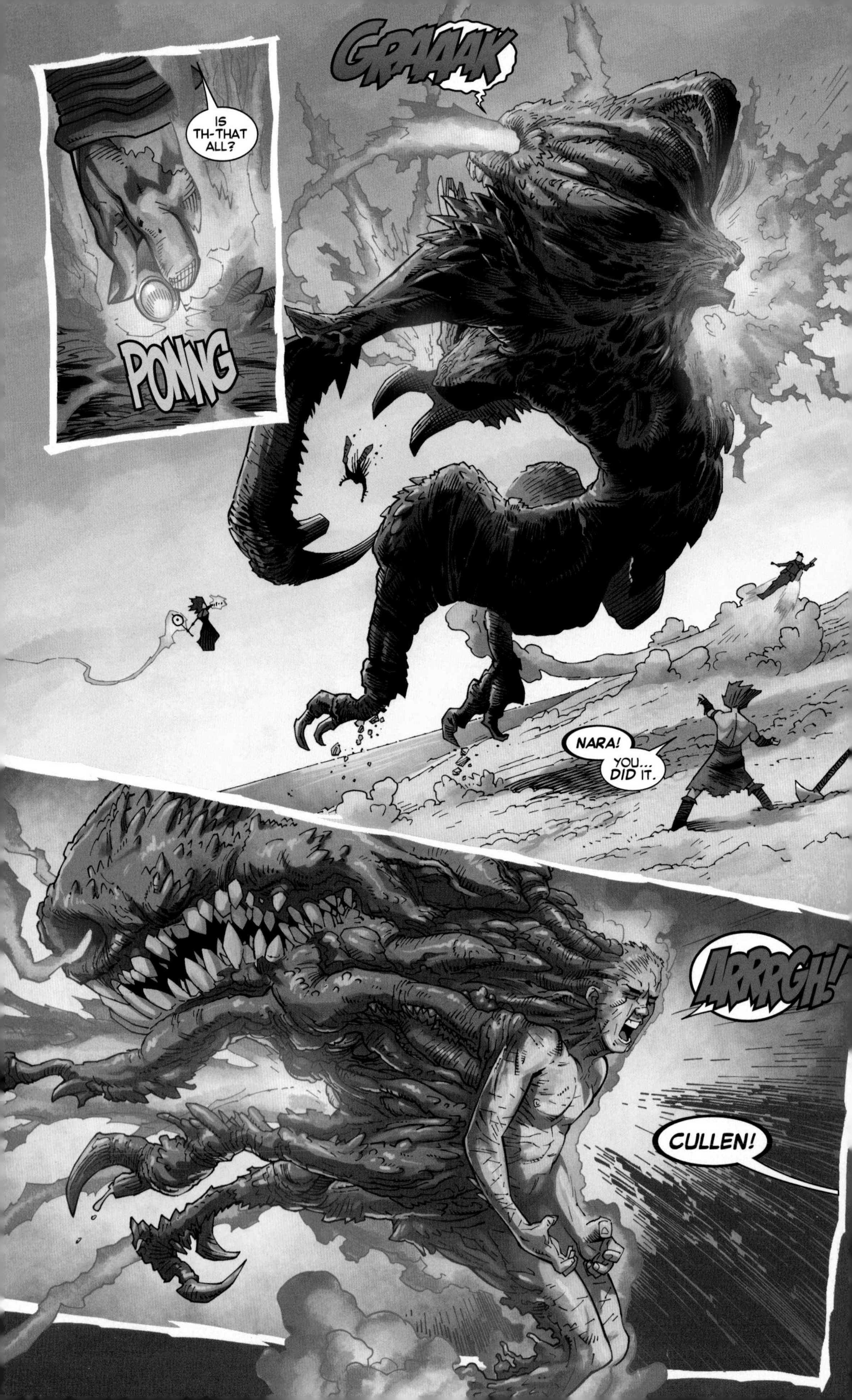
IS TH-THAT ALL?
PONNG
GRAAAK
NARA!
YOU... DID IT.
ARRRGH!
CULLEN!

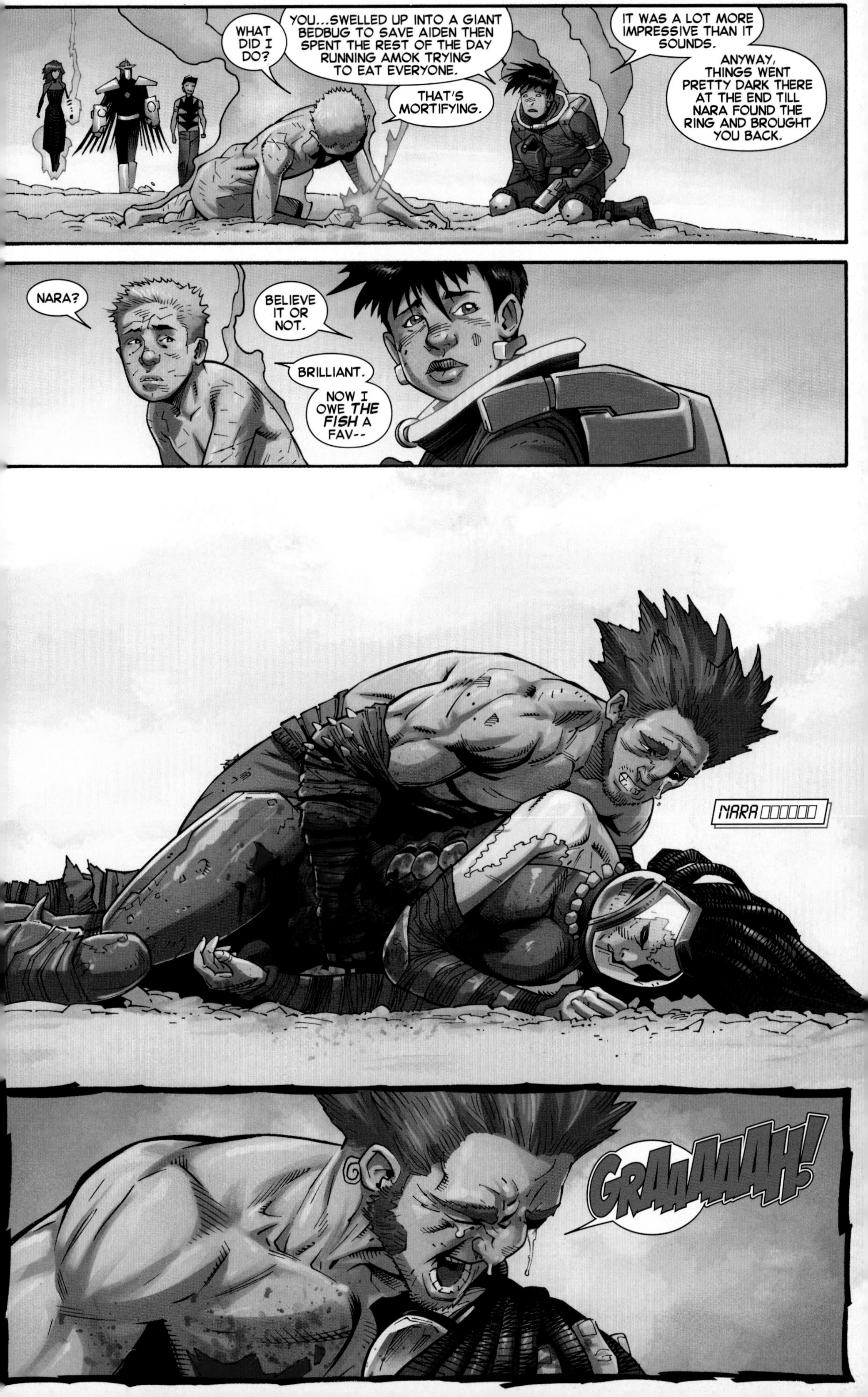

WHAT DID I DO?
YOU...SWELLED UP INTO A GIANT BEDBUG TO SAVE AIDEN THEN SPENT THE REST OF THE DAY RUNNING AMOK TRYING TO EAT EVERYONE.
THAT'S MORTIFYING.
IT WAS A LOT MORE IMPRESSIVE THAN IT SOUNDS.
ANYWAY, THINGS WENT PRETTY DARK THERE AT THE END TILL NARA FOUND THE RING AND BROUGHT YOU BACK.
NARA?
BELIEVE IT OR NOT.
BRILLIANT.
NOW I OWE THE FISH A FAV--
NARA
GRAAAAAH!

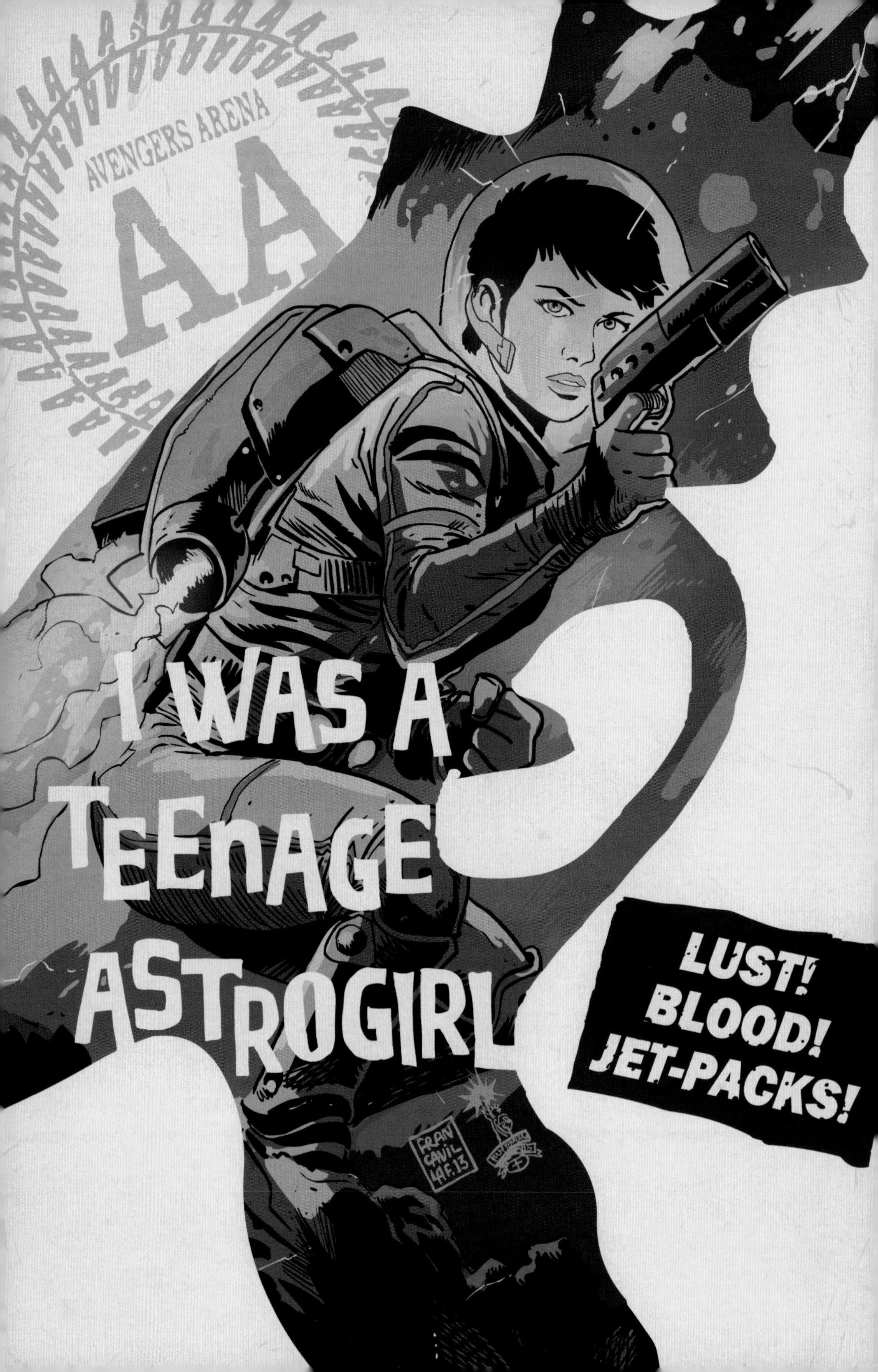
AVENGERS ARENA
AA
I WAS A TEENAGE ASTROGIRL
LUST! BLOOD! JET-PACKS!
FRAN CAVIL 14F.13

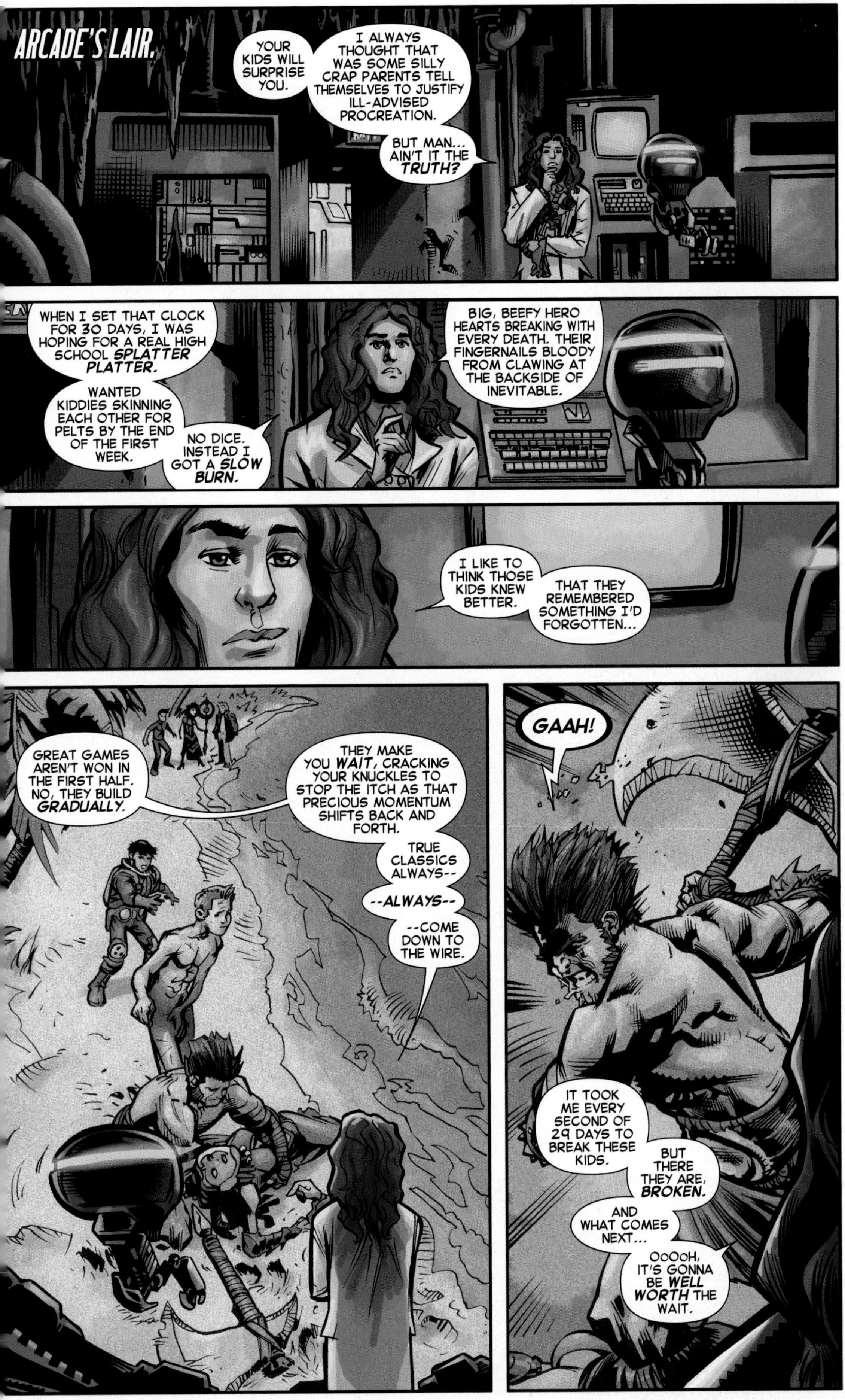

ARCADE'S LAIR.
YOUR KIDS WILL SURPRISE YOU.
I ALWAYS THOUGHT THAT WAS SOME SILLY CRAP PARENTS TELL THEMSELVES TO JUSTIFY ILL-ADVISED PROCREATION.
BUT MAN... AIN'T IT THE TRUTH?
WHEN I SET THAT CLOCK FOR 30 DAYS, I WAS HOPING FOR A REAL HIGH SCHOOL SPLATTER PLATTER.
WANTED KIDDIES SKINNING EACH OTHER FOR PELTS BY THE END OF THE FIRST WEEK.
NO DICE. INSTEAD I GOT A SLOW BURN.
BIG, BEEFY HERO HEARTS BREAKING WITH EVERY DEATH. THEIR FINGERNAILS BLOODY FROM CLAWING AT THE BACKSIDE OF INEVITABLE.
I LIKE TO THINK THOSE KIDS KNEW BETTER.
THAT THEY REMEMBERED SOMETHING I'D FORGOTTEN...
GREAT GAMES AREN'T WON IN THE FIRST HALF. NO, THEY BUILD GRADUALLY.
THEY MAKE YOU WAIT, CRACKING YOUR KNUCKLES TO STOP THE ITCH AS THAT PRECIOUS MOMENTUM SHIFTS BACK AND FORTH.
TRUE CLASSICS ALWAYS--
--ALWAYS--
--COME DOWN TO THE WIRE.
GAAH!
IT TOOK ME EVERY SECOND OF 29 DAYS TO BREAK THESE KIDS.
BUT THERE THEY ARE, BROKEN.
AND WHAT COMES NEXT...
OOOOH, IT'S GONNA BE WELL WORTH THE WAIT.

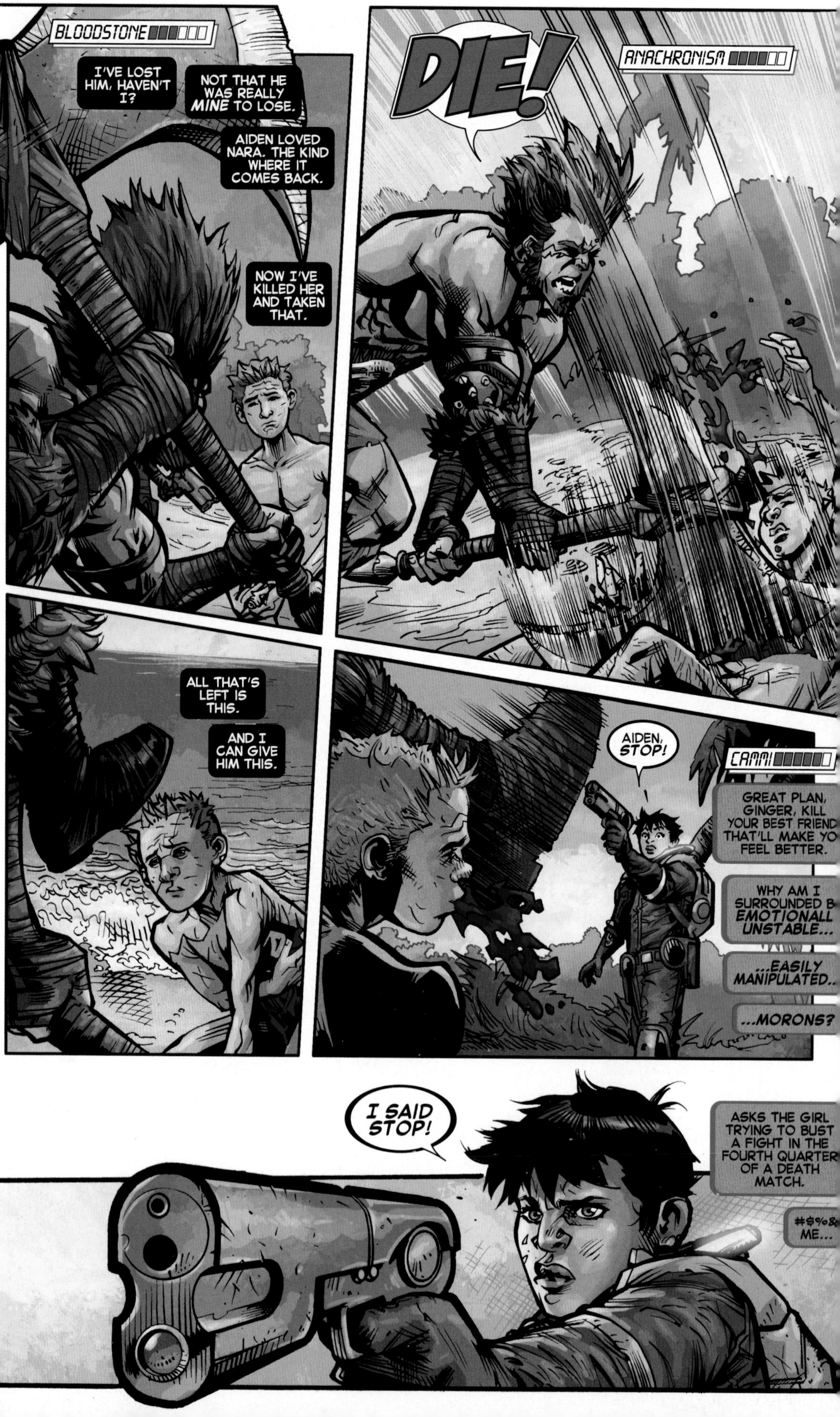

BLOODSTONE
I'VE LOST HIM, HAVEN'T I?
NOT THAT HE WAS REALLY *MINE* TO LOSE.
AIDEN LOVED NARA. THE KIND WHERE IT COMES BACK.
NOW I'VE KILLED HER AND TAKEN THAT.
DIE!
ANACHRONISM
ALL THAT'S LEFT IS THIS.
AND I CAN GIVE HIM THIS.
AIDEN, STOP!
CAMMI
GREAT PLAN, GINGER, KILL YOUR BEST FRIEND THAT'LL MAKE YO FEEL BETTER.
WHY AM I SURROUNDED B *EMOTIONALL UNSTABLE...*
...EASILY MANIPULATED..
...MORONS?
I SAID STOP!
ASKS THE GIRL TRYING TO BUST A FIGHT IN THE FOURTH QUARTER OF A DEATH MATCH.
#$%& ME...

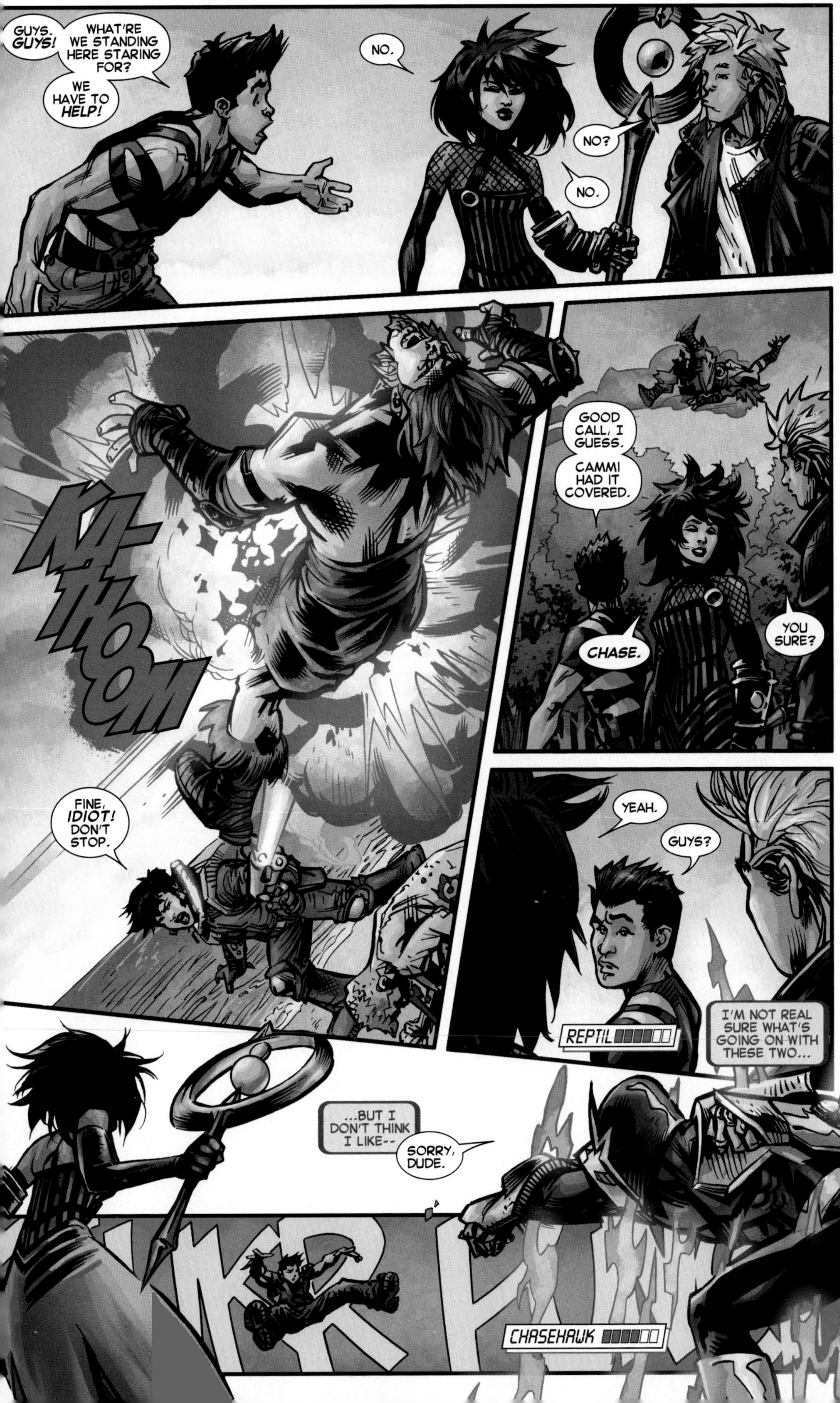
GUYS. GUYS!
WHAT'RE WE STANDING HERE STARING FOR?
WE HAVE TO HELP!
NO.
NO?
NO.
KA-THOOM
FINE, IDIOT! DON'T STOP.
GOOD CALL, I GUESS.
CAMMI HAD IT COVERED.
CHASE.
YOU SURE?
YEAH.
GUYS?
REPTIL
I'M NOT REAL SURE WHAT'S GOING ON WITH THESE TWO...
...BUT I DON'T THINK I LIKE--
SORRY, DUDE.
CHASEHAWK

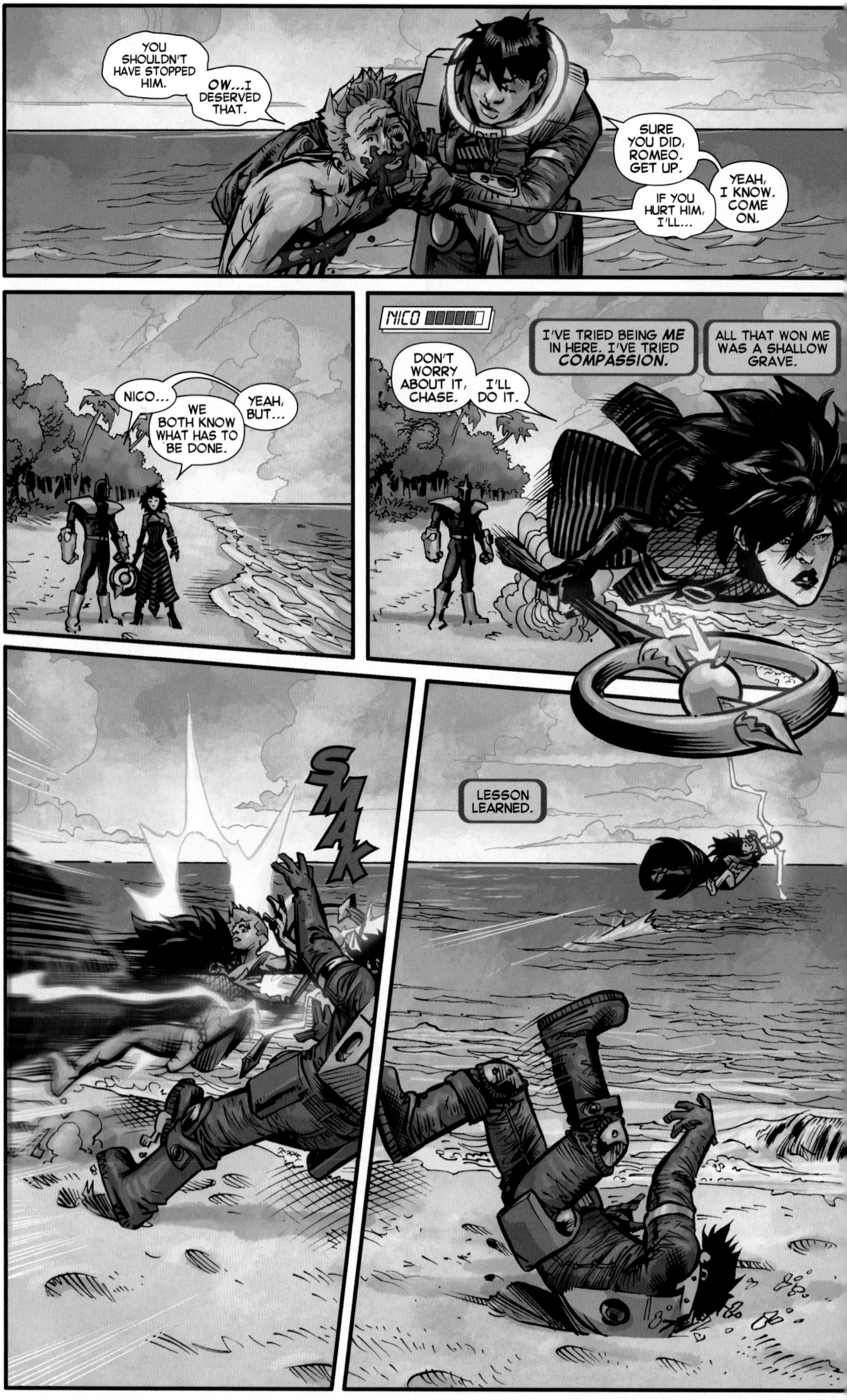
YOU SHOULDN'T HAVE STOPPED HIM.
OW...I DESERVED THAT.
SURE YOU DID, ROMEO. GET UP.
IF YOU HURT HIM, I'LL...
YEAH, I KNOW. COME ON.
NICO...
WE BOTH KNOW WHAT HAS TO BE DONE.
YEAH, BUT...
NICO
DON'T WORRY ABOUT IT, CHASE.
I'LL DO IT.
I'VE TRIED BEING ME IN HERE. I'VE TRIED COMPASSION.
ALL THAT WON ME WAS A SHALLOW GRAVE.
SMAK
LESSON LEARNED.

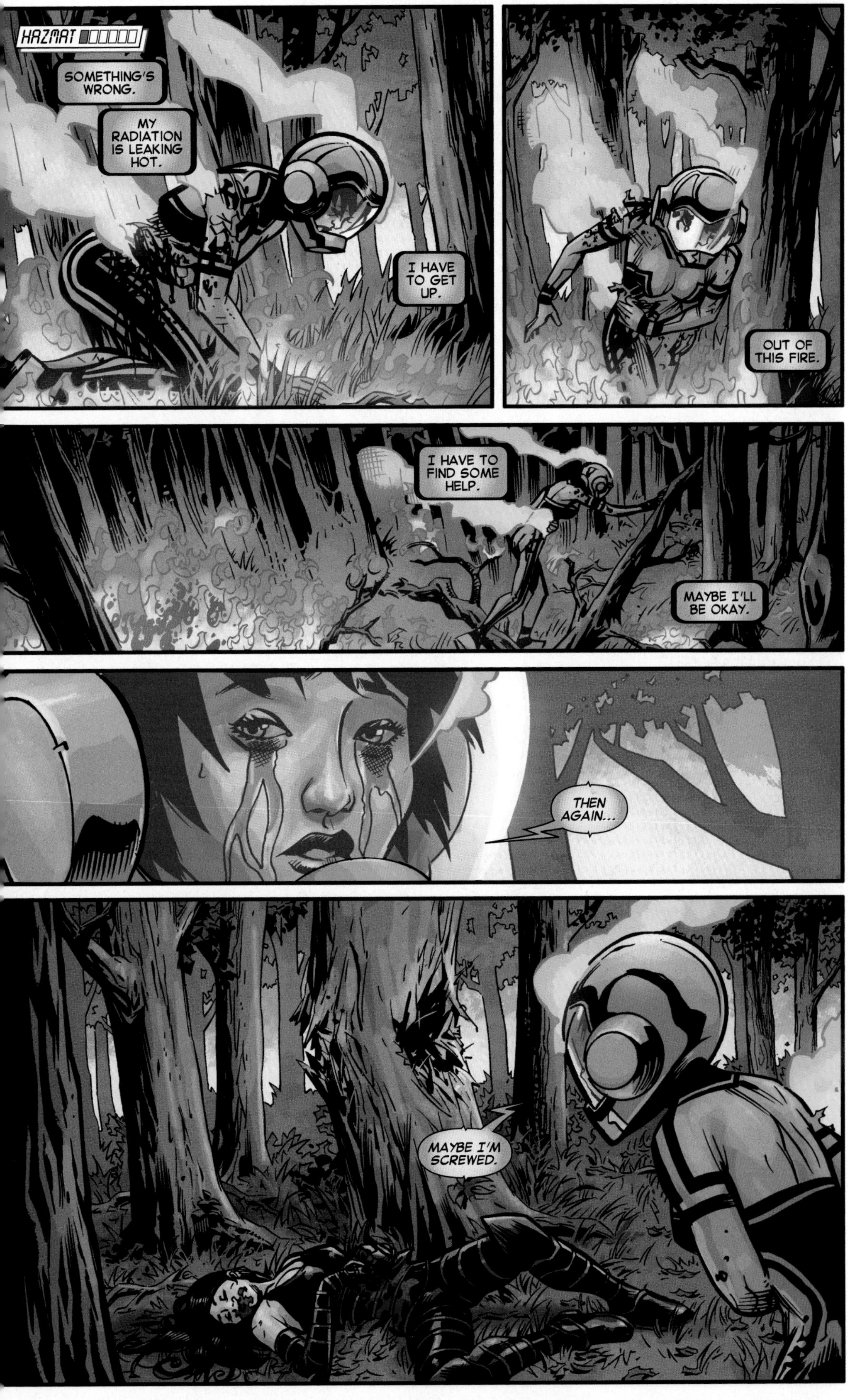
HAZMAT
SOMETHING'S WRONG.
MY RADIATION IS LEAKING HOT.
I HAVE TO GET UP.
OUT OF THIS FIRE.
I HAVE TO FIND SOME HELP.
MAYBE I'LL BE OKAY.
THEN AGAIN...
MAYBE I'M SCREWED.

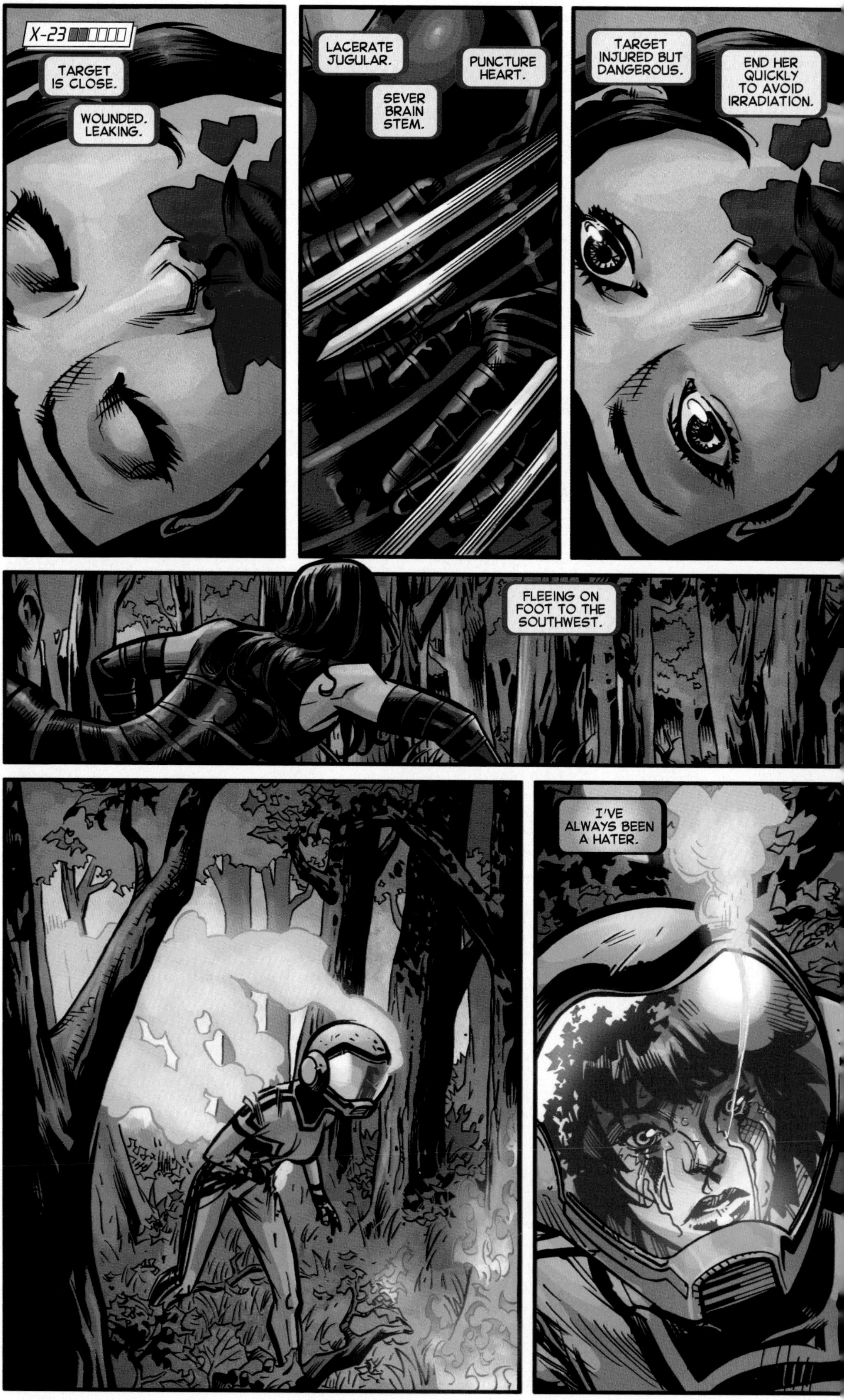
X-23
TARGET IS CLOSE.
WOUNDED. LEAKING.
LACERATE JUGULAR.
SEVER BRAIN STEM.
PUNCTURE HEART.
TARGET INJURED BUT DANGEROUS.
END HER QUICKLY TO AVOID IRRADIATION.
FLEEING ON FOOT TO THE SOUTHWEST.
I'VE ALWAYS BEEN A HATER.

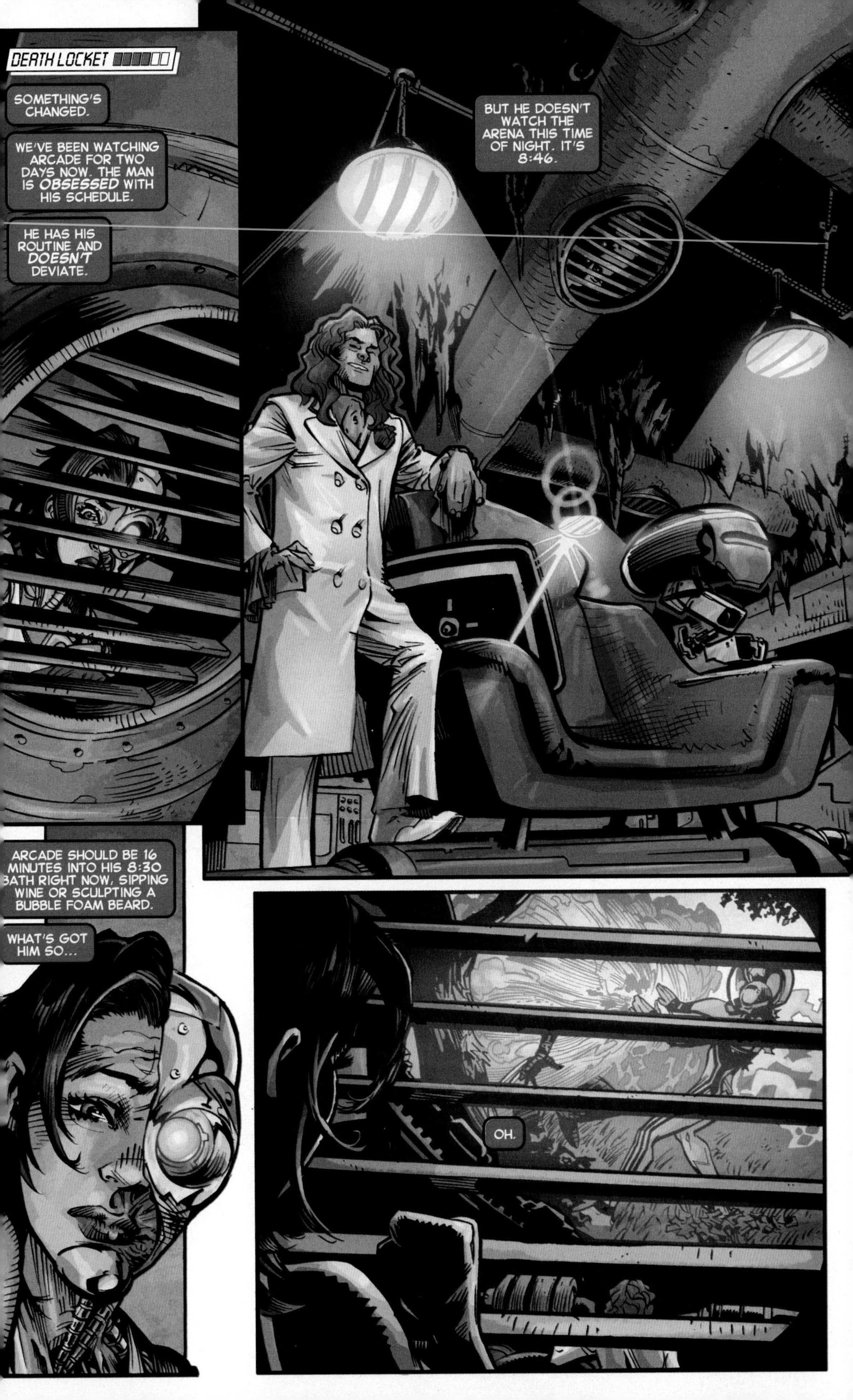
DEATH LOCKET
SOMETHING'S CHANGED.
WE'VE BEEN WATCHING ARCADE FOR TWO DAYS NOW. THE MAN IS OBSESSED WITH HIS SCHEDULE.
HE HAS HIS ROUTINE AND DOESN'T DEVIATE.
BUT HE DOESN'T WATCH THE ARENA THIS TIME OF NIGHT. IT'S 8:46.
ARCADE SHOULD BE 16 MINUTES INTO HIS 8:30 BATH RIGHT NOW, SIPPING WINE OR SCULPTING A BUBBLE FOAM BEARD.
WHAT'S GOT HIM SO...
OH.

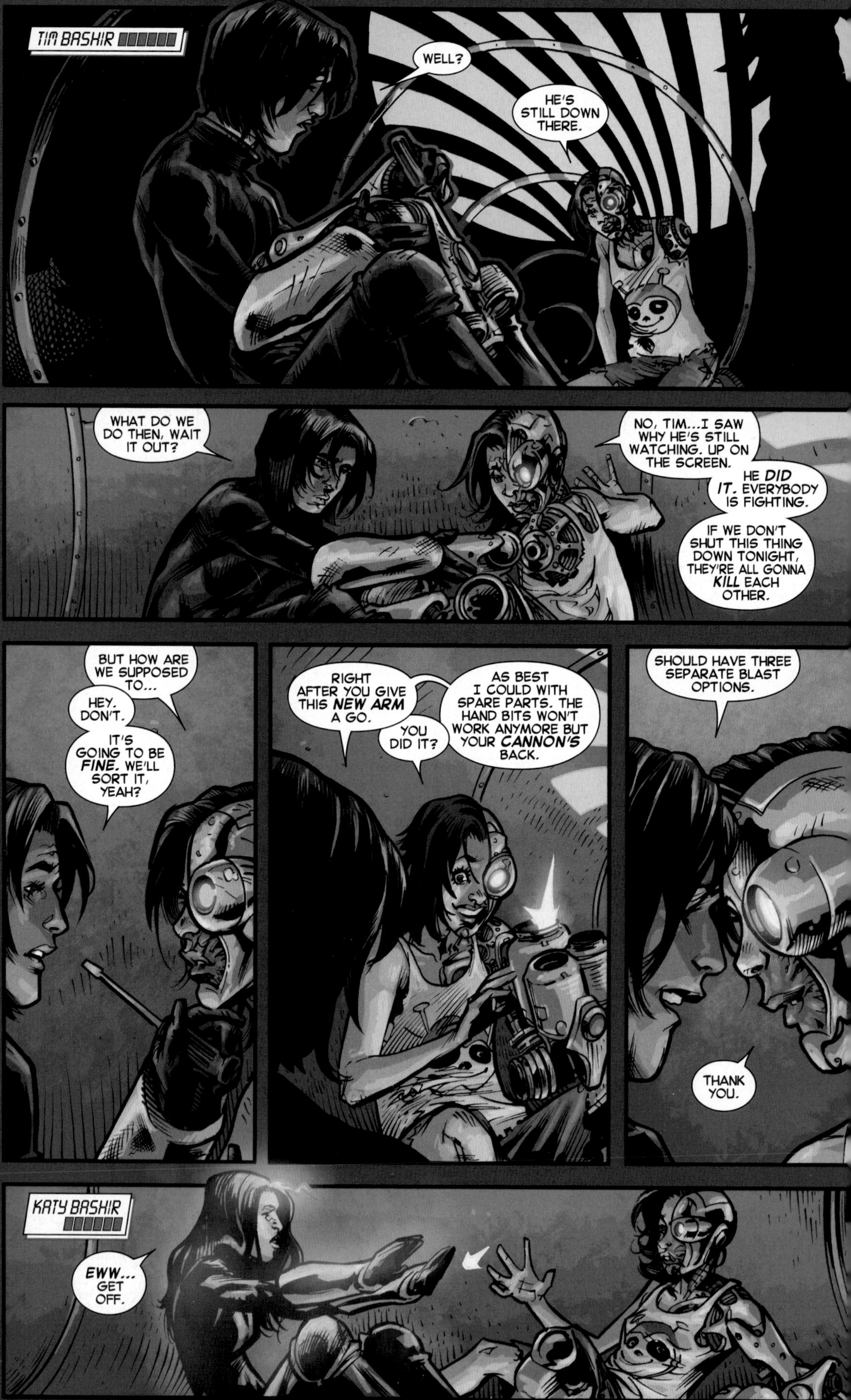
TIM BASHIR
WELL?
HE'S STILL DOWN THERE.
WHAT DO WE DO THEN, WAIT IT OUT?
NO, TIM...I SAW WHY HE'S STILL WATCHING. UP ON THE SCREEN.
HE DID IT. EVERYBODY IS FIGHTING.
IF WE DON'T SHUT THIS THING DOWN TONIGHT, THEY'RE ALL GONNA KILL EACH OTHER.
BUT HOW ARE WE SUPPOSED TO...
HEY. DON'T.
IT'S GOING TO BE FINE. WE'LL SORT IT, YEAH?
RIGHT AFTER YOU GIVE THIS NEW ARM A GO.
YOU DID IT?
AS BEST I COULD WITH SPARE PARTS. THE HAND BITS WON'T WORK ANYMORE BUT YOUR CANNON'S BACK.
SHOULD HAVE THREE SEPARATE BLAST OPTIONS.
THANK YOU.
KATY BASHIR
EWW... GET OFF.

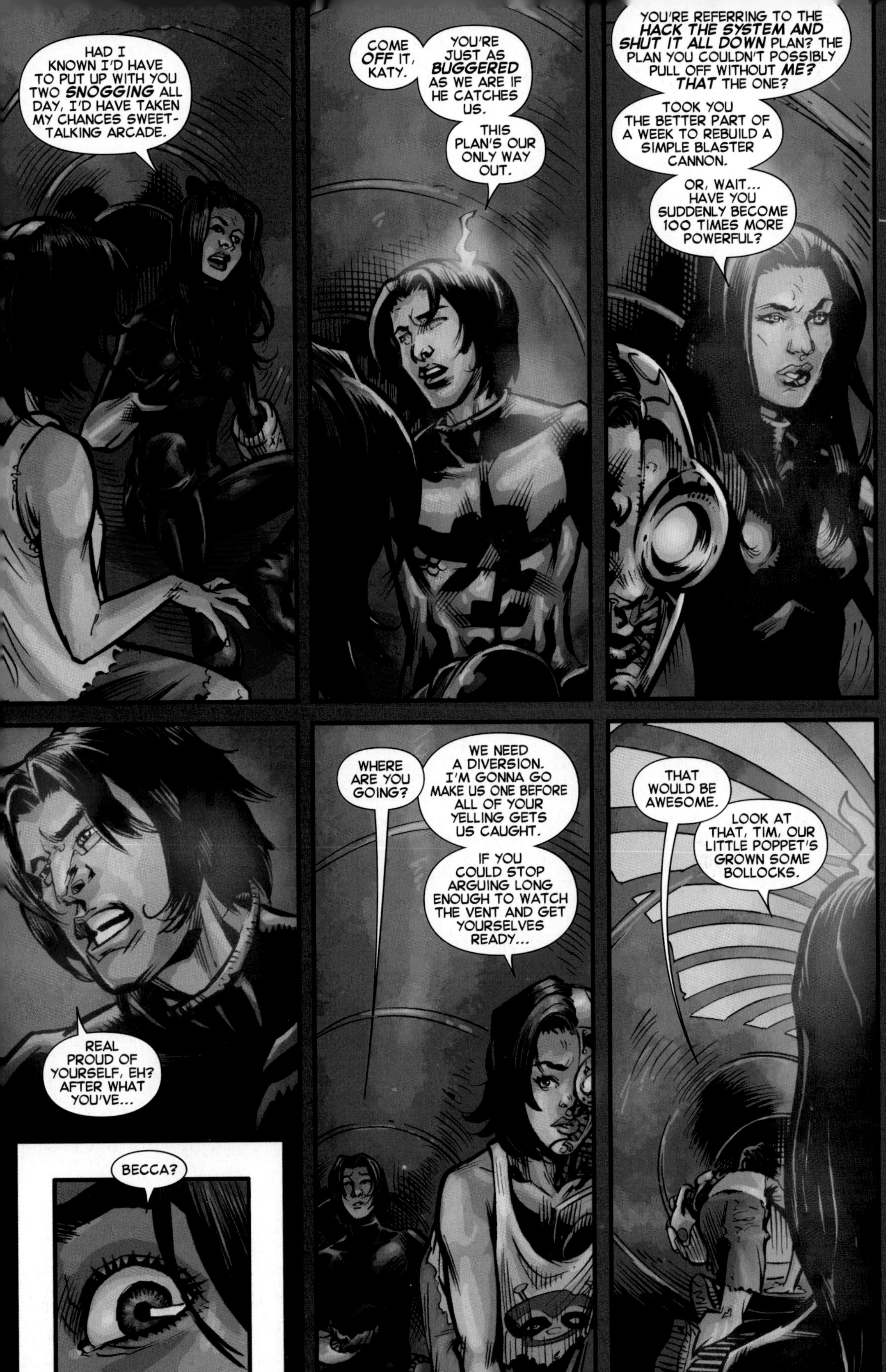
HAD I KNOWN I'D HAVE TO PUT UP WITH YOU TWO SNOGGING ALL DAY, I'D HAVE TAKEN MY CHANCES SWEET-TALKING ARCADE.
COME OFF IT, KATY.
YOU'RE JUST AS BUGGERED AS WE ARE IF HE CATCHES US.
THIS PLAN'S OUR ONLY WAY OUT.
YOU'RE REFERRING TO THE HACK THE SYSTEM AND SHUT IT ALL DOWN PLAN? THE PLAN YOU COULDN'T POSSIBLY PULL OFF WITHOUT ME? THAT THE ONE?
TOOK YOU THE BETTER PART OF A WEEK TO REBUILD A SIMPLE BLASTER CANNON.
OR, WAIT... HAVE YOU SUDDENLY BECOME 100 TIMES MORE POWERFUL?
REAL PROUD OF YOURSELF, EH? AFTER WHAT YOU'VE...
BECCA?
WHERE ARE YOU GOING?
WE NEED A DIVERSION. I'M GONNA GO MAKE US ONE BEFORE ALL OF YOUR YELLING GETS US CAUGHT.
IF YOU COULD STOP ARGUING LONG ENOUGH TO WATCH THE VENT AND GET YOURSELVES READY...
THAT WOULD BE AWESOME.
LOOK AT THAT, TIM, OUR LITTLE POPPET'S GROWN SOME BOLLOCKS.

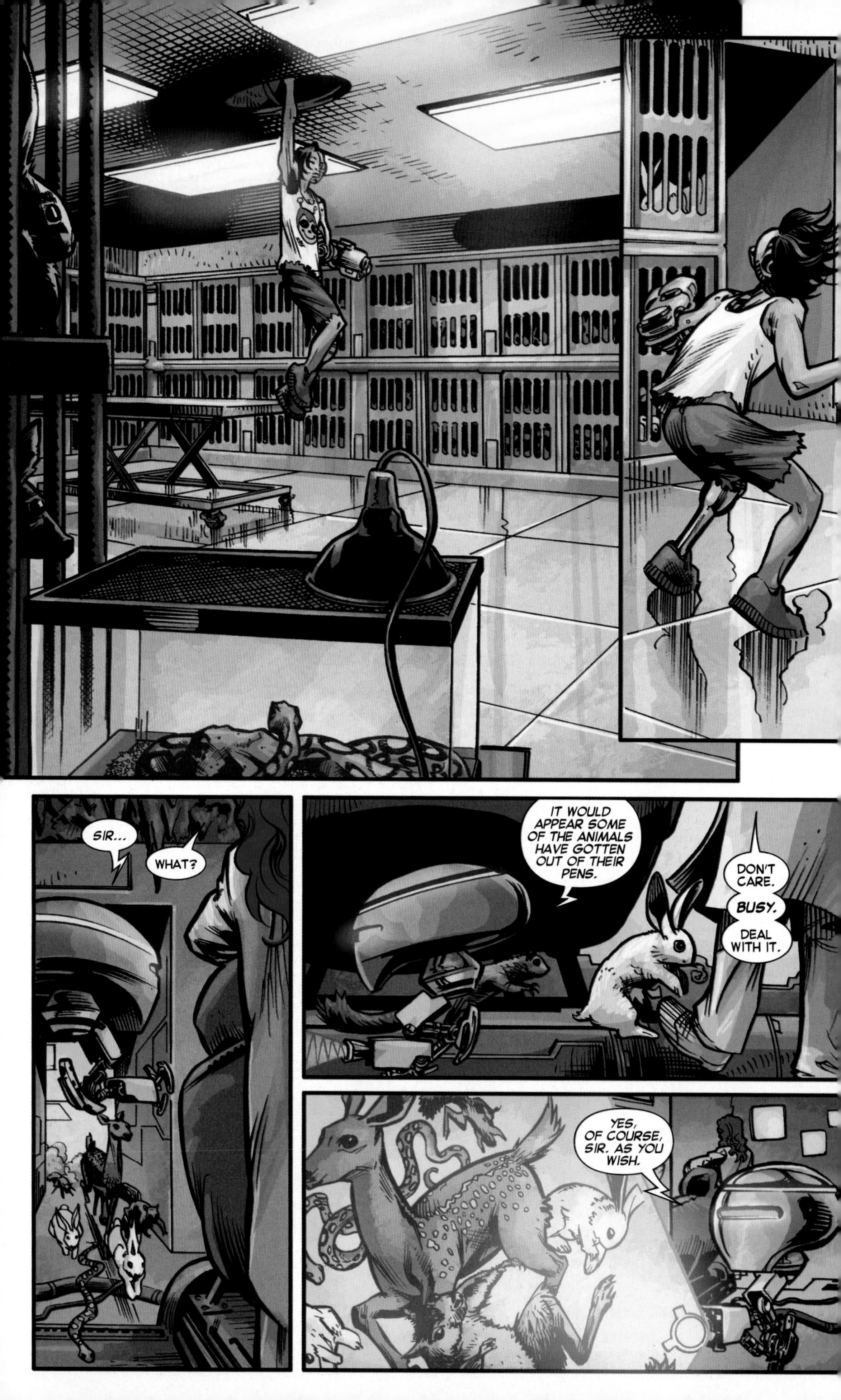
SIR...
WHAT?
IT WOULD APPEAR SOME OF THE ANIMALS HAVE GOTTEN OUT OF THEIR PENS.
DON'T CARE.
BUSY.
DEAL WITH IT.
YES, OF COURSE, SIR. AS YOU WISH.

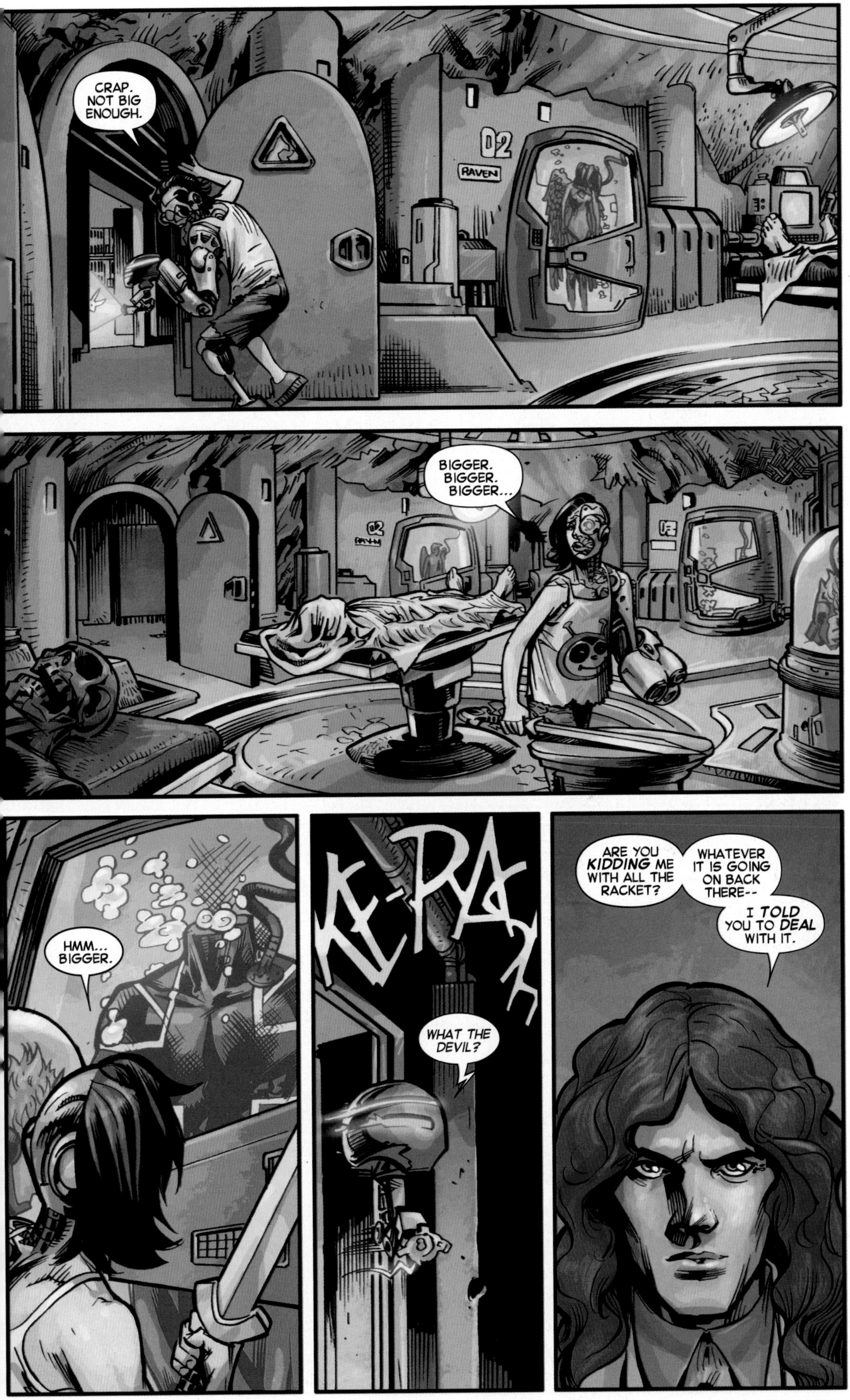
CRAP. NOT BIG ENOUGH.
RAVEN
BIGGER. BIGGER. BIGGER...
HMM... BIGGER.
KE-RASH
WHAT THE DEVIL?
ARE YOU KIDDING ME WITH ALL THE RACKET?
WHATEVER IT IS GOING ON BACK THERE--
I TOLD YOU TO DEAL WITH IT.

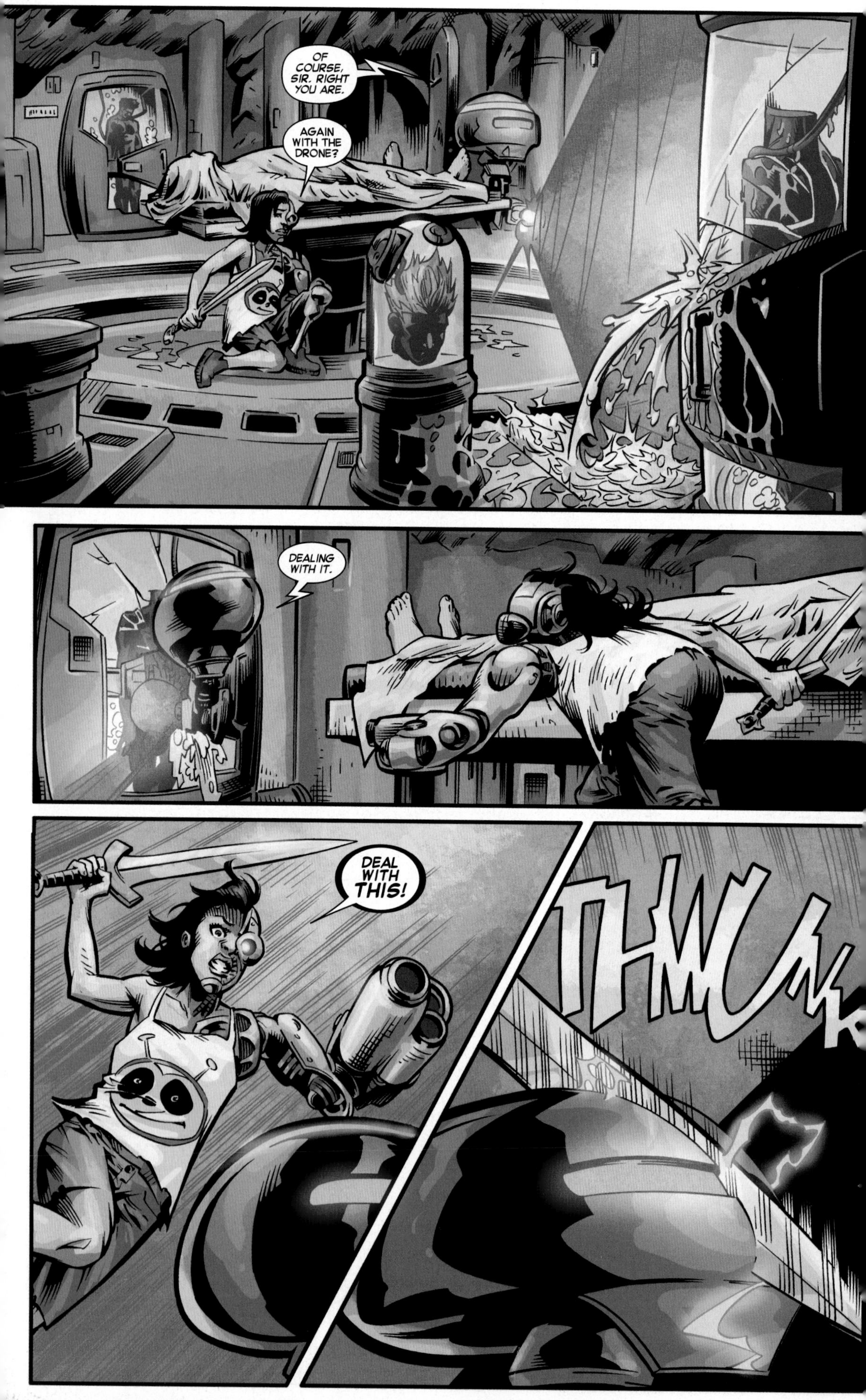
OF COURSE, SIR. RIGHT YOU ARE.
AGAIN WITH THE DRONE?
DEALING WITH IT.
DEAL WITH THIS!
THWAK

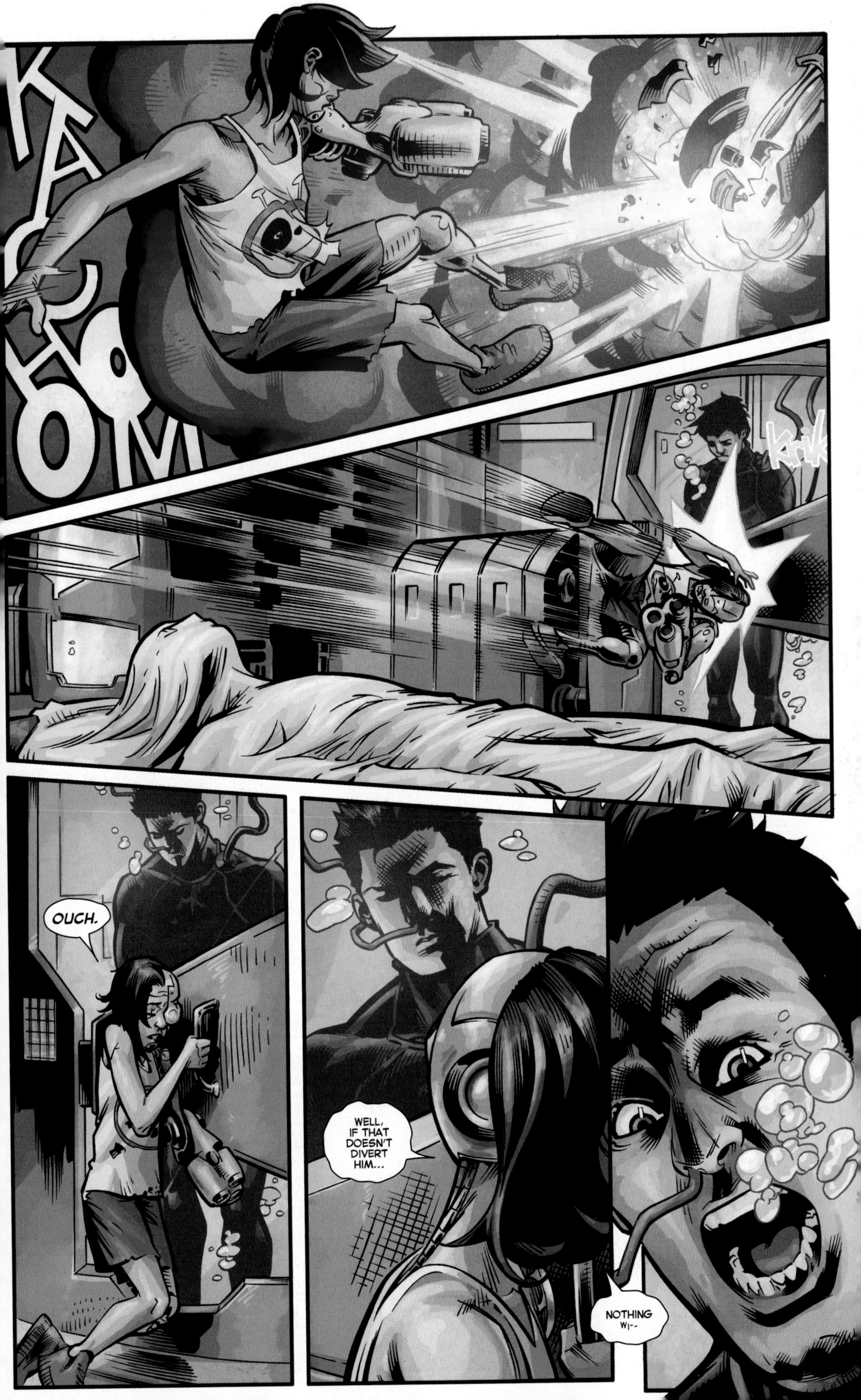
KACHOOM
KRIK
OUCH.
WELL, IF THAT DOESN'T DIVERT HIM...
NOTHING WI--

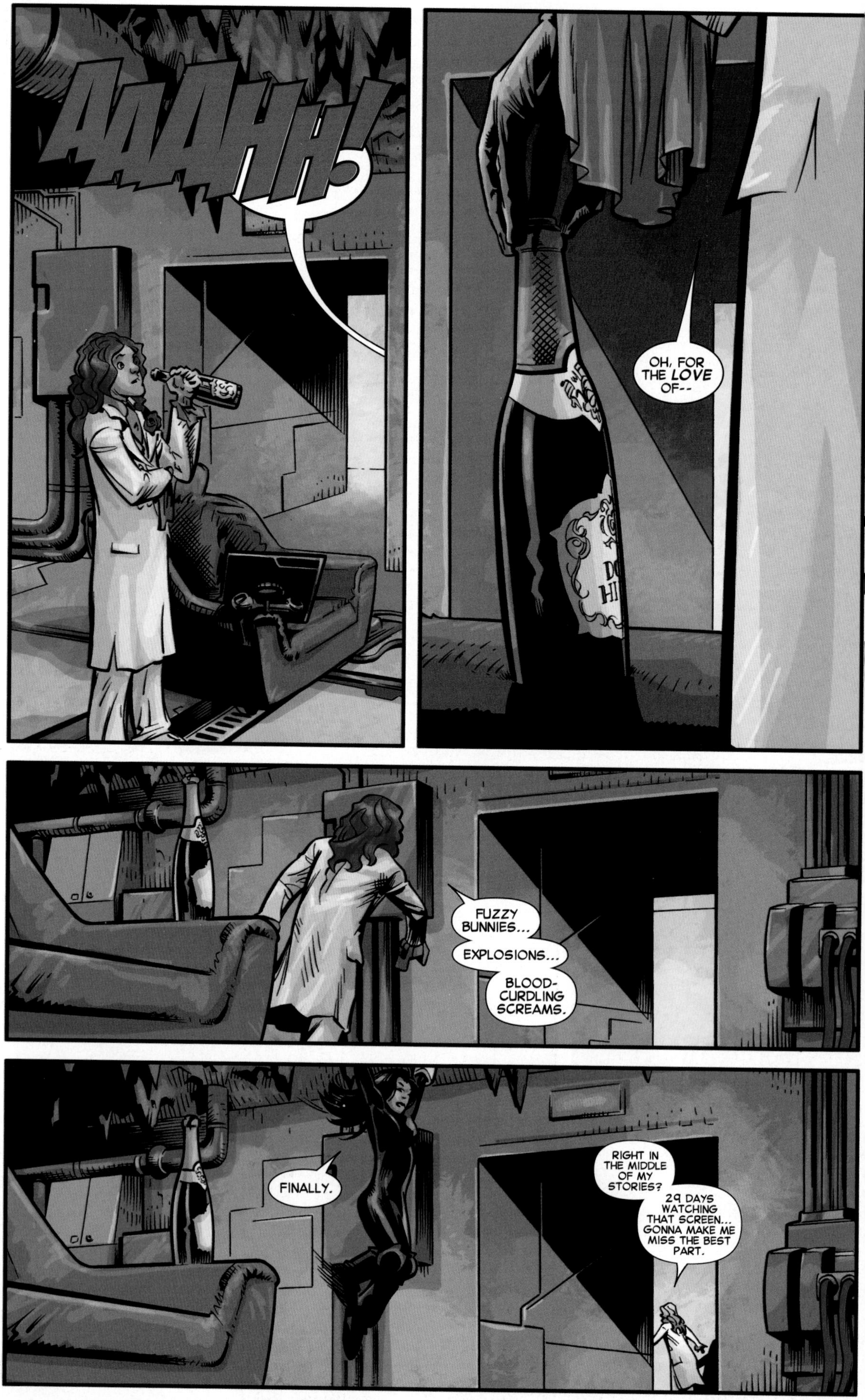
AAAHH!
OH, FOR THE LOVE OF--
FUZZY BUNNIES...
EXPLOSIONS...
BLOOD-CURDLING SCREAMS.
FINALLY.
RIGHT IN THE MIDDLE OF MY STORIES?
29 DAYS WATCHING THAT SCREEN... GONNA MAKE ME MISS THE BEST PART.

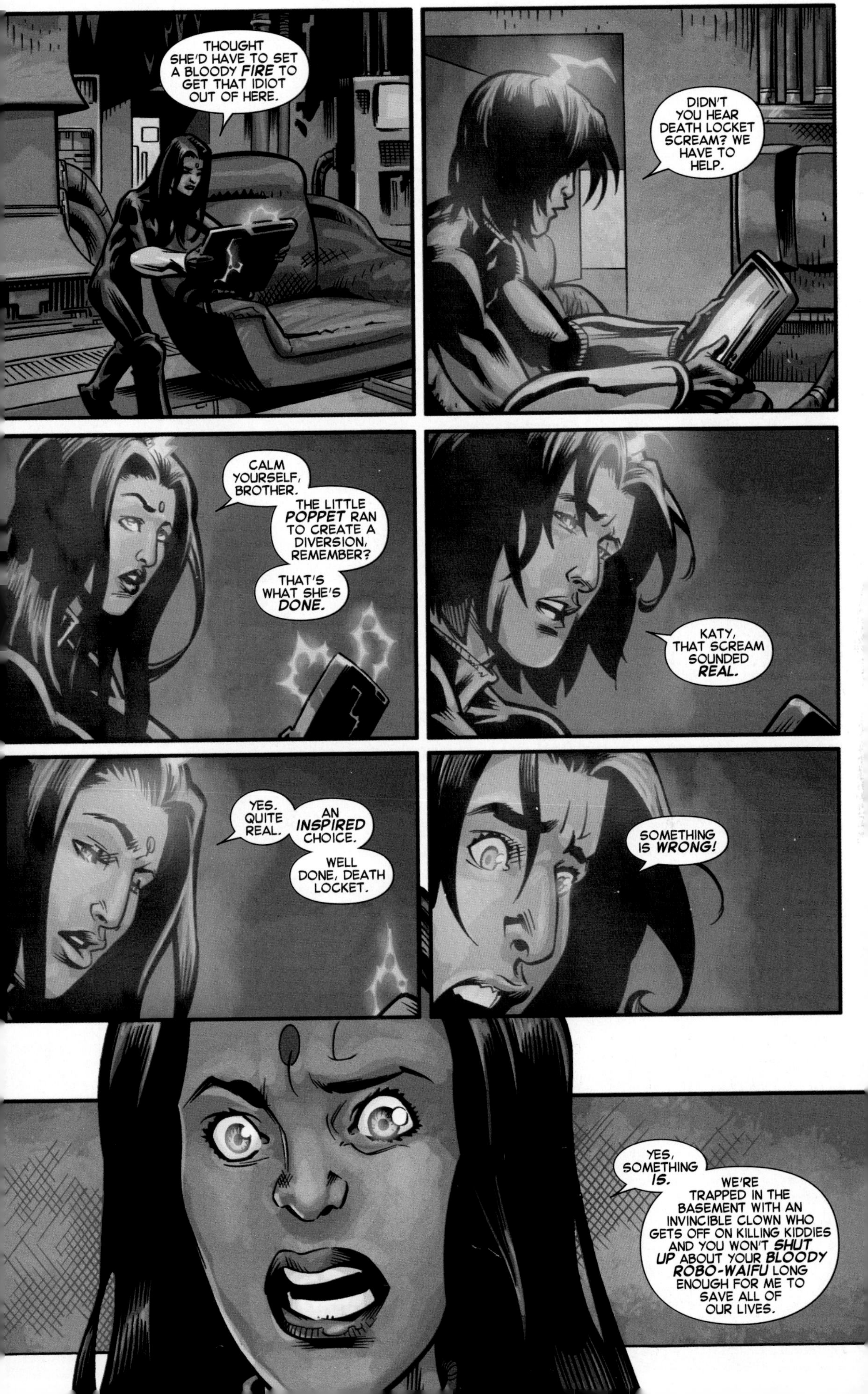
THOUGHT SHE'D HAVE TO SET A BLOODY FIRE TO GET THAT IDIOT OUT OF HERE.
DIDN'T YOU HEAR DEATH LOCKET SCREAM? WE HAVE TO HELP.
CALM YOURSELF, BROTHER.
THE LITTLE POPPET RAN TO CREATE A DIVERSION, REMEMBER?
THAT'S WHAT SHE'S DONE.
KATY, THAT SCREAM SOUNDED REAL.
YES. QUITE REAL.
AN INSPIRED CHOICE.
WELL DONE, DEATH LOCKET.
SOMETHING IS WRONG!
YES, SOMETHING IS.
WE'RE TRAPPED IN THE BASEMENT WITH AN INVINCIBLE CLOWN WHO GETS OFF ON KILLING KIDDIES AND YOU WON'T SHUT UP ABOUT YOUR BLOODY ROBO-WAIFU LONG ENOUGH FOR ME TO SAVE ALL OF OUR LIVES.

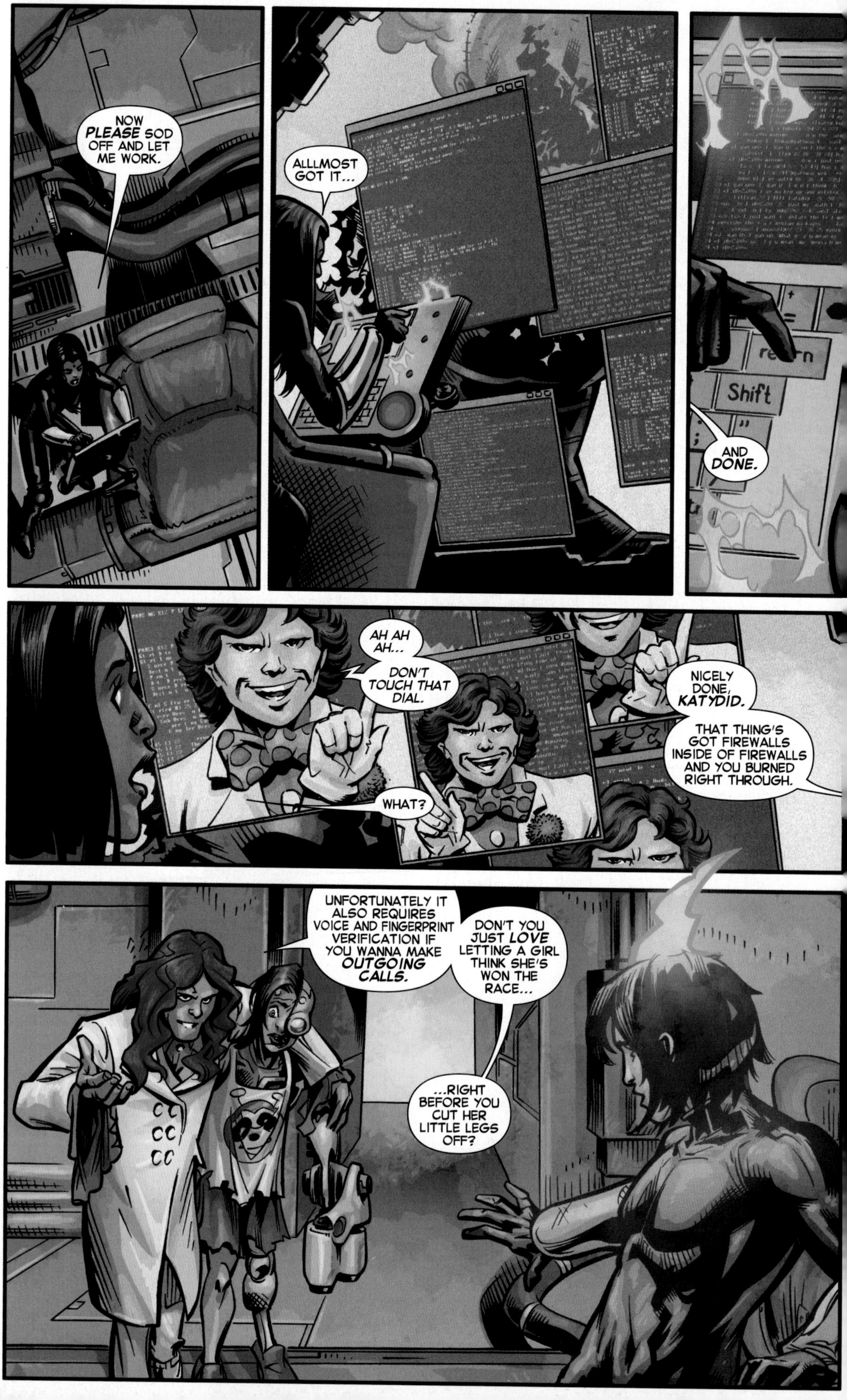
NOW PLEASE SOD OFF AND LET ME WORK.
ALLLMOST GOT IT...
AND DONE.
AH AH AH...
DON'T TOUCH THAT DIAL.
WHAT?
NICELY DONE, KATYDID.
THAT THING'S GOT FIREWALLS INSIDE OF FIREWALLS AND YOU BURNED RIGHT THROUGH.
UNFORTUNATELY IT ALSO REQUIRES VOICE AND FINGERPRINT VERIFICATION IF YOU WANNA MAKE OUTGOING CALLS.
DON'T YOU JUST LOVE LETTING A GIRL THINK SHE'S WON THE RACE...
...RIGHT BEFORE YOU CUT HER LITTLE LEGS OFF?

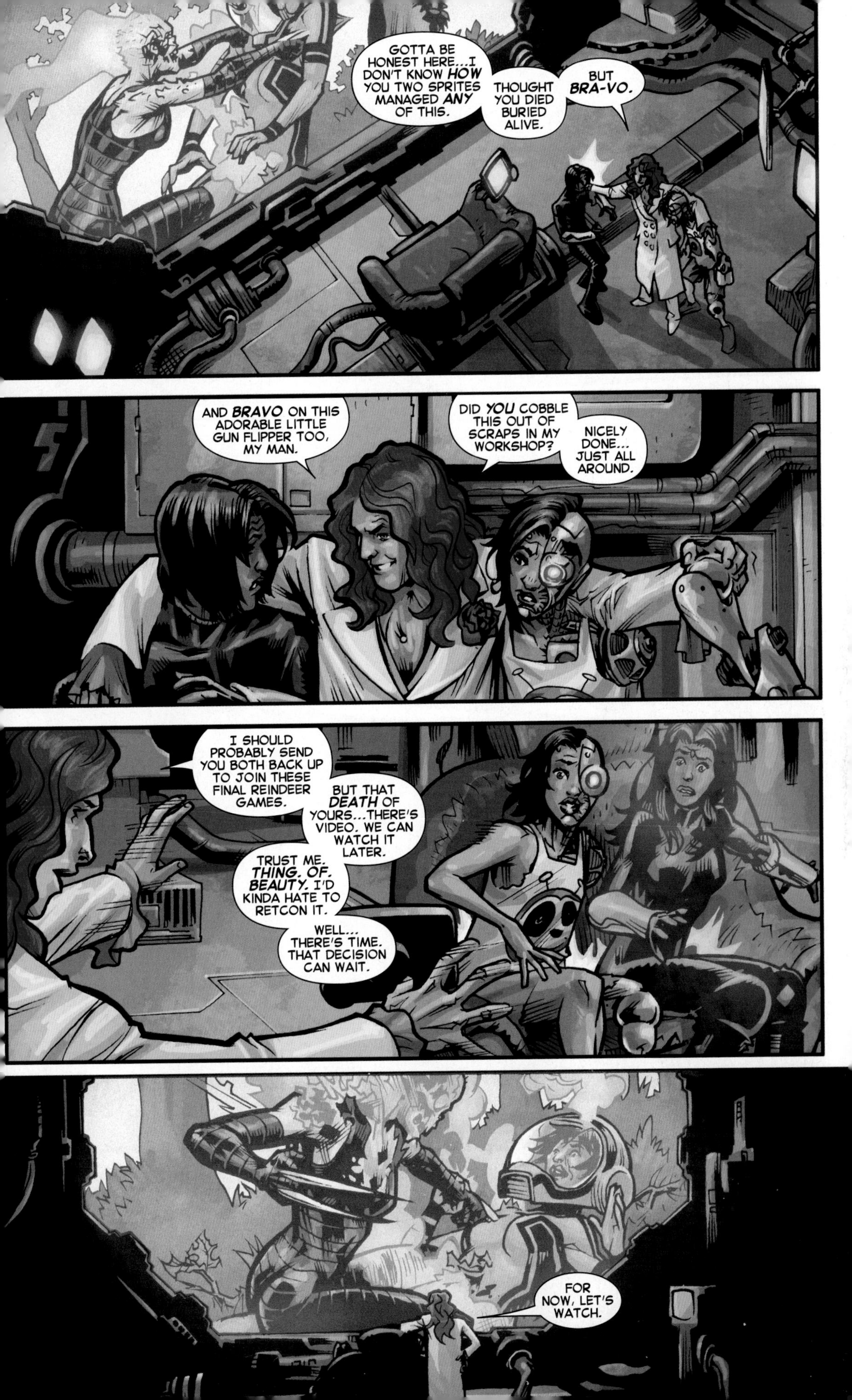
GOTTA BE HONEST HERE...I DON'T KNOW HOW YOU TWO SPRITES MANAGED ANY OF THIS.
THOUGHT YOU DIED BURIED ALIVE.
BUT BRA-VO.
AND BRAVO ON THIS ADORABLE LITTLE GUN FLIPPER TOO, MY MAN.
DID YOU COBBLE THIS OUT OF SCRAPS IN MY WORKSHOP?
NICELY DONE... JUST ALL AROUND.
I SHOULD PROBABLY SEND YOU BOTH BACK UP TO JOIN THESE FINAL REINDEER GAMES.
BUT THAT DEATH OF YOURS...THERE'S VIDEO. WE CAN WATCH IT LATER.
TRUST ME. THING. OF. BEAUTY. I'D KINDA HATE TO RETCON IT.
WELL... THERE'S TIME. THAT DECISION CAN WAIT.
FOR NOW, LET'S WATCH.

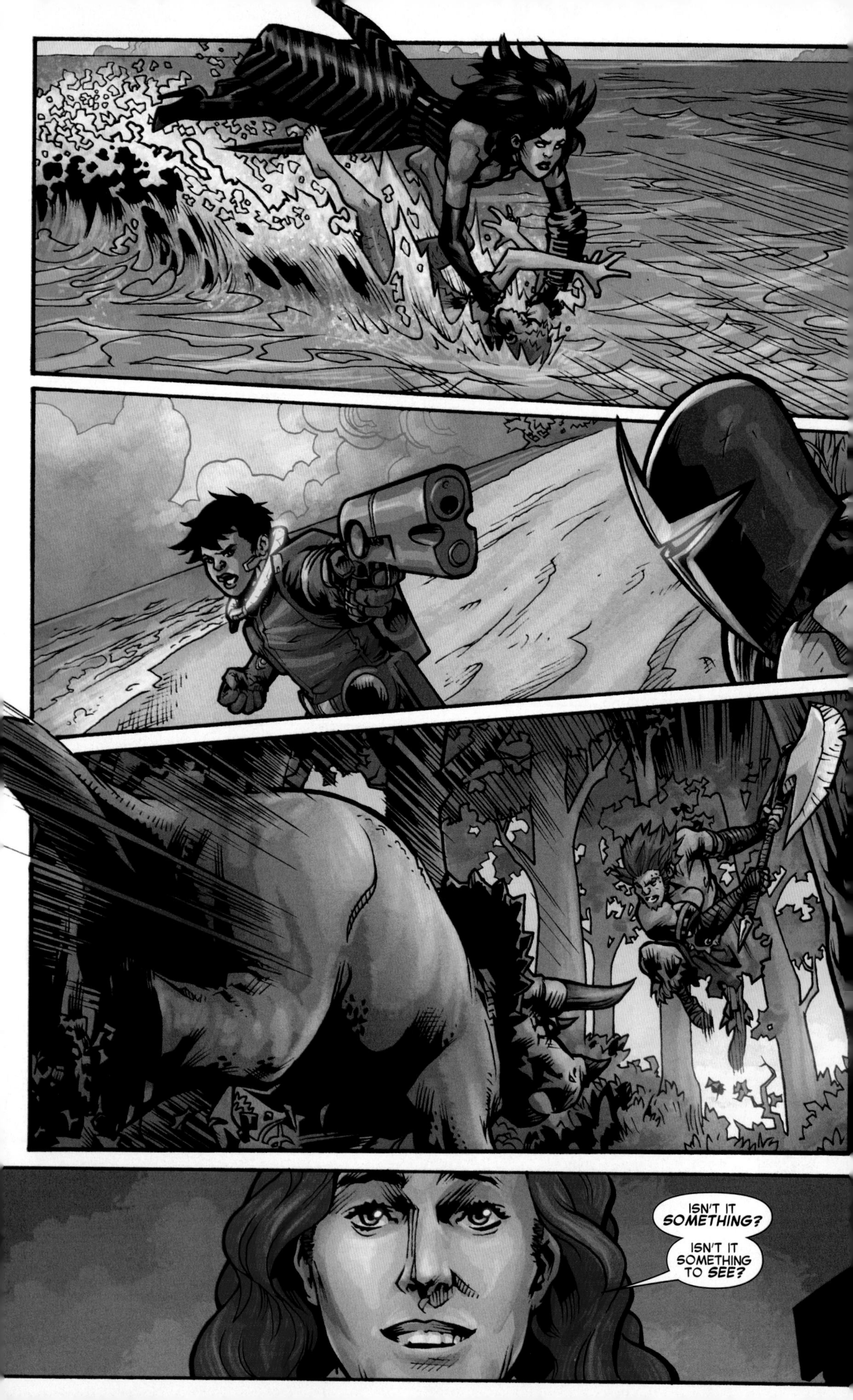
ISN'T IT SOMETHING?
ISN'T IT SOMETHING TO SEE?

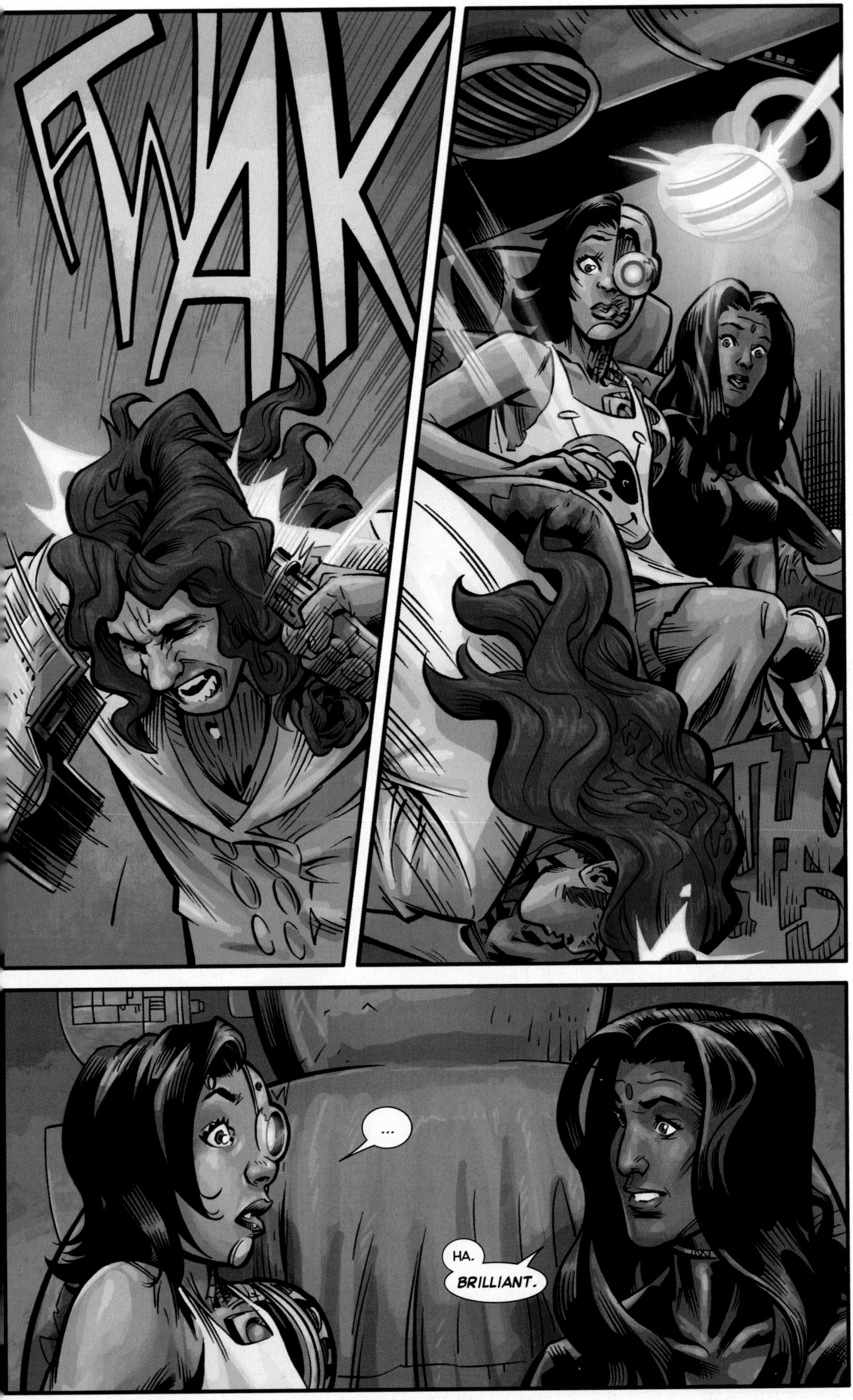
FWAK
THUD
...
HA.
BRILLIANT.

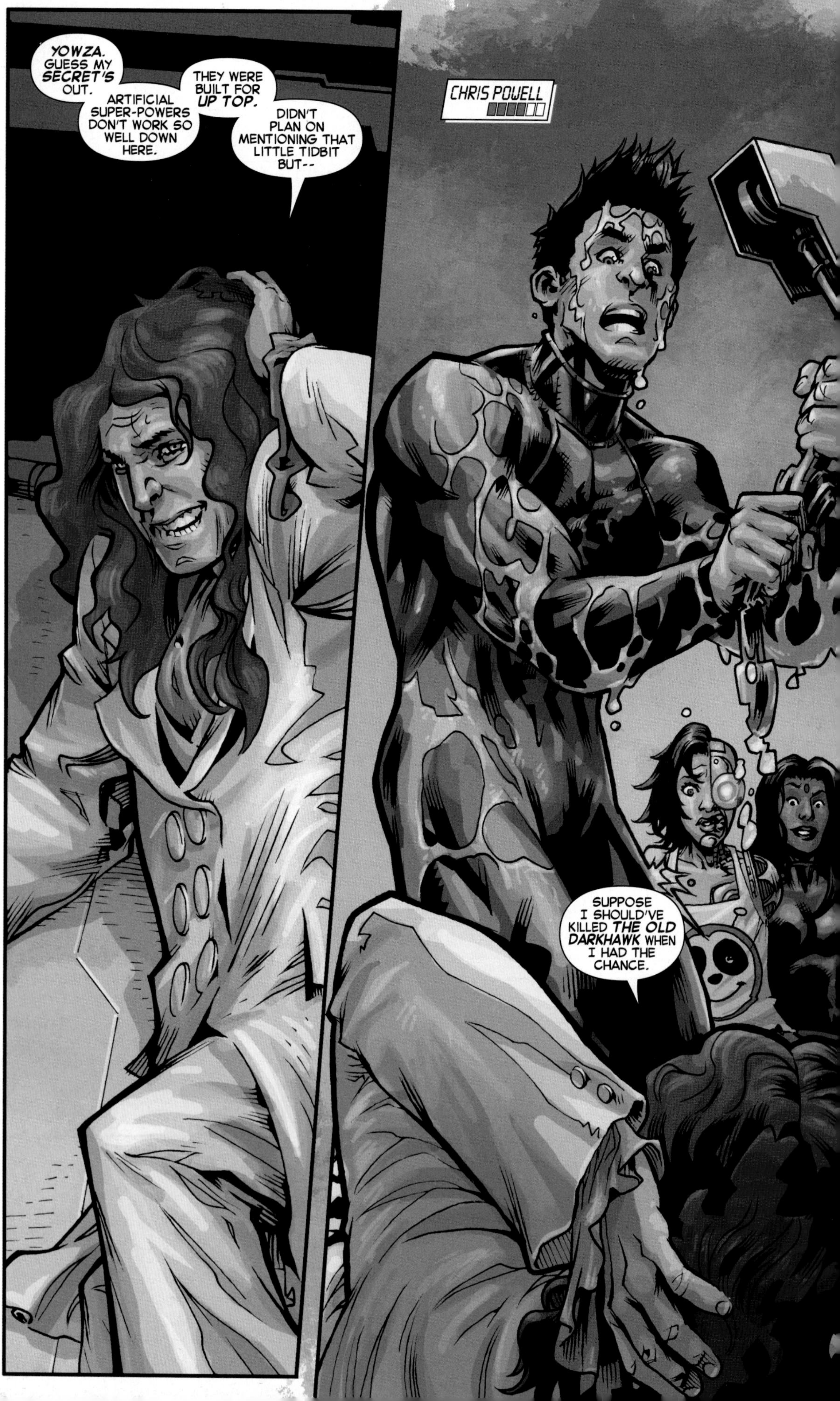
YOWZA. GUESS MY SECRET'S OUT.
ARTIFICIAL SUPER-POWERS DON'T WORK SO WELL DOWN HERE.
THEY WERE BUILT FOR UP TOP.
DIDN'T PLAN ON MENTIONING THAT LITTLE TIDBIT BUT--
CHRIS POWELL
SUPPOSE I SHOULD'VE KILLED THE OLD DARKHAWK WHEN I HAD THE CHANCE.

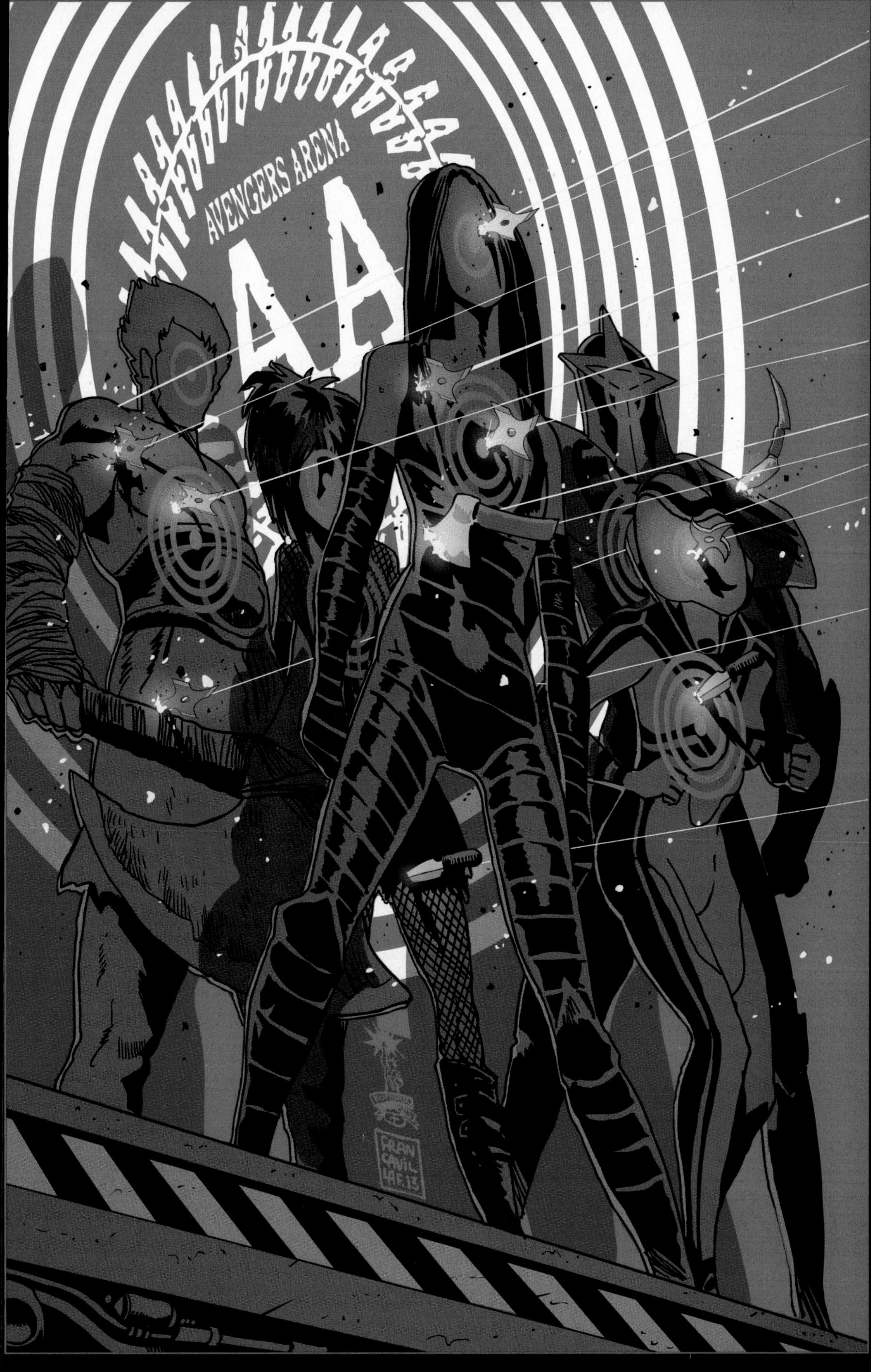
AAAAAAAAAAAAGGGGGGGGGGGGHHHH
AVENGERS ARENA
AA
FRAN
CAVIL
LAF.13

17: BOSS LEVEL PART 4

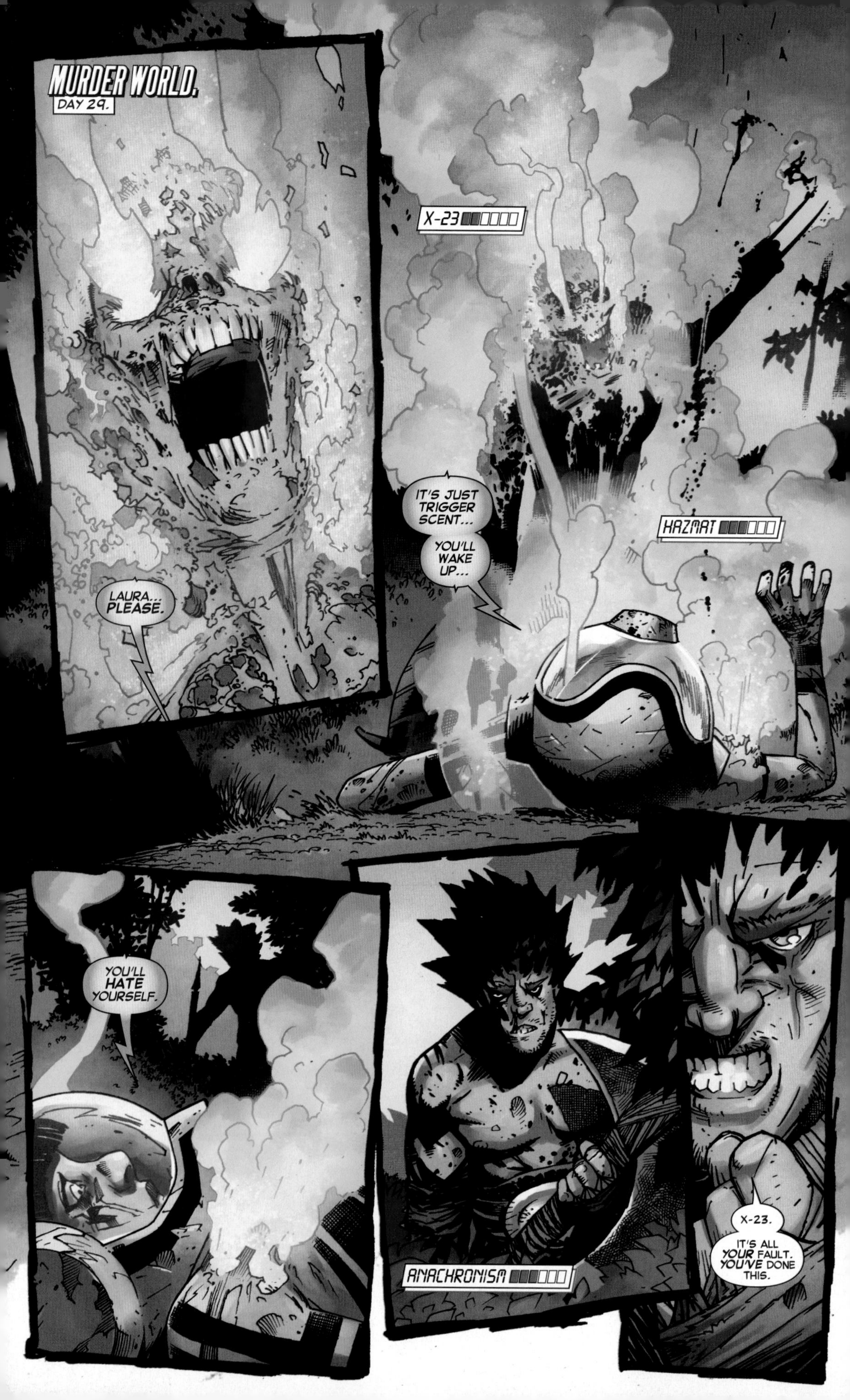
MURDER WORLD.
DAY 29.
X-23
LAURA... PLEASE.
IT'S JUST TRIGGER SCENT...
YOU'LL WAKE UP...
HAZMAT
YOU'LL HATE YOURSELF.
ANACHRONISM
X-23.
IT'S ALL YOUR FAULT. YOU'VE DONE THIS.

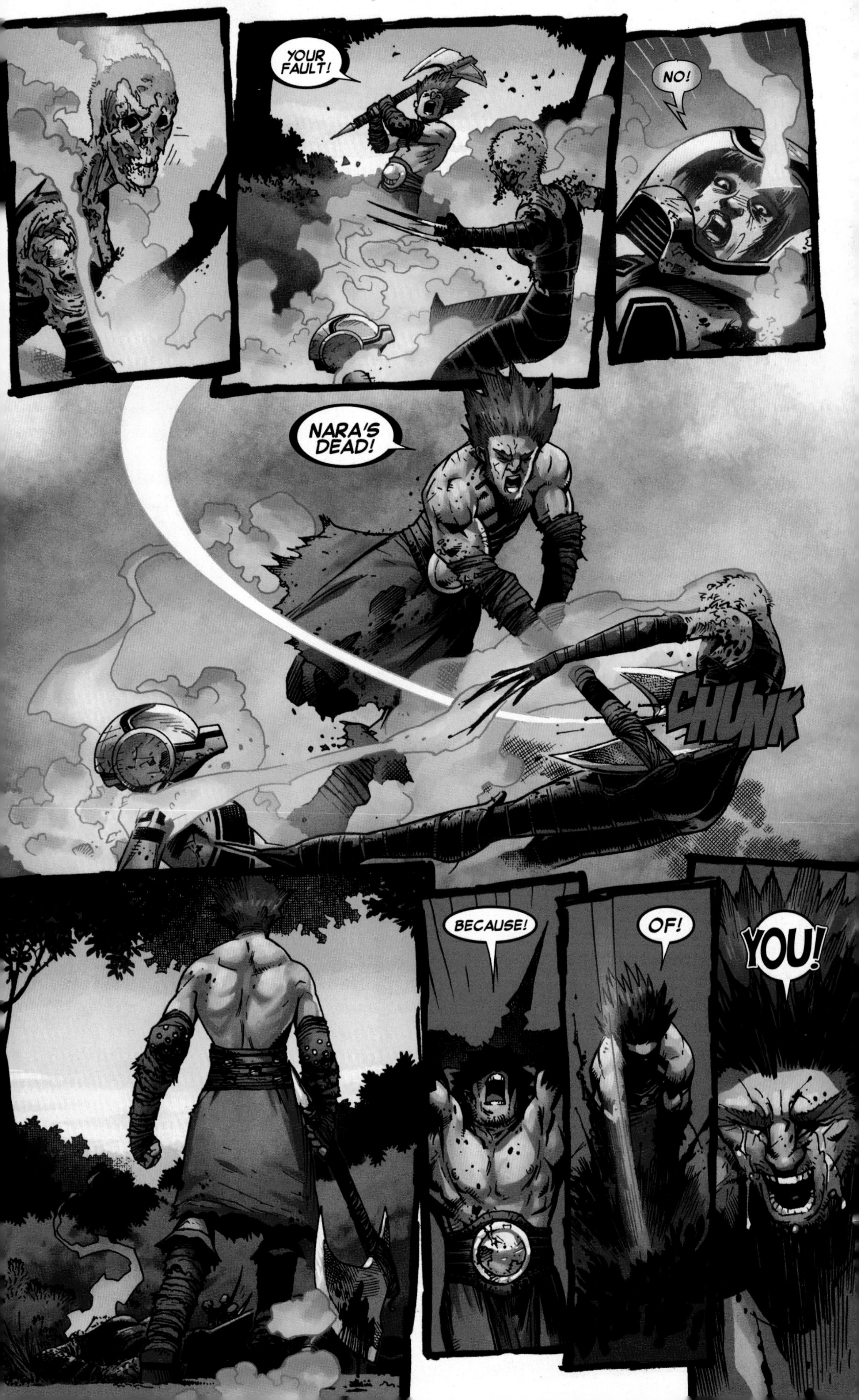
YOUR FAULT!
NO!
NARA'S DEAD!
CHUNK
BECAUSE!
OF!
YOU!

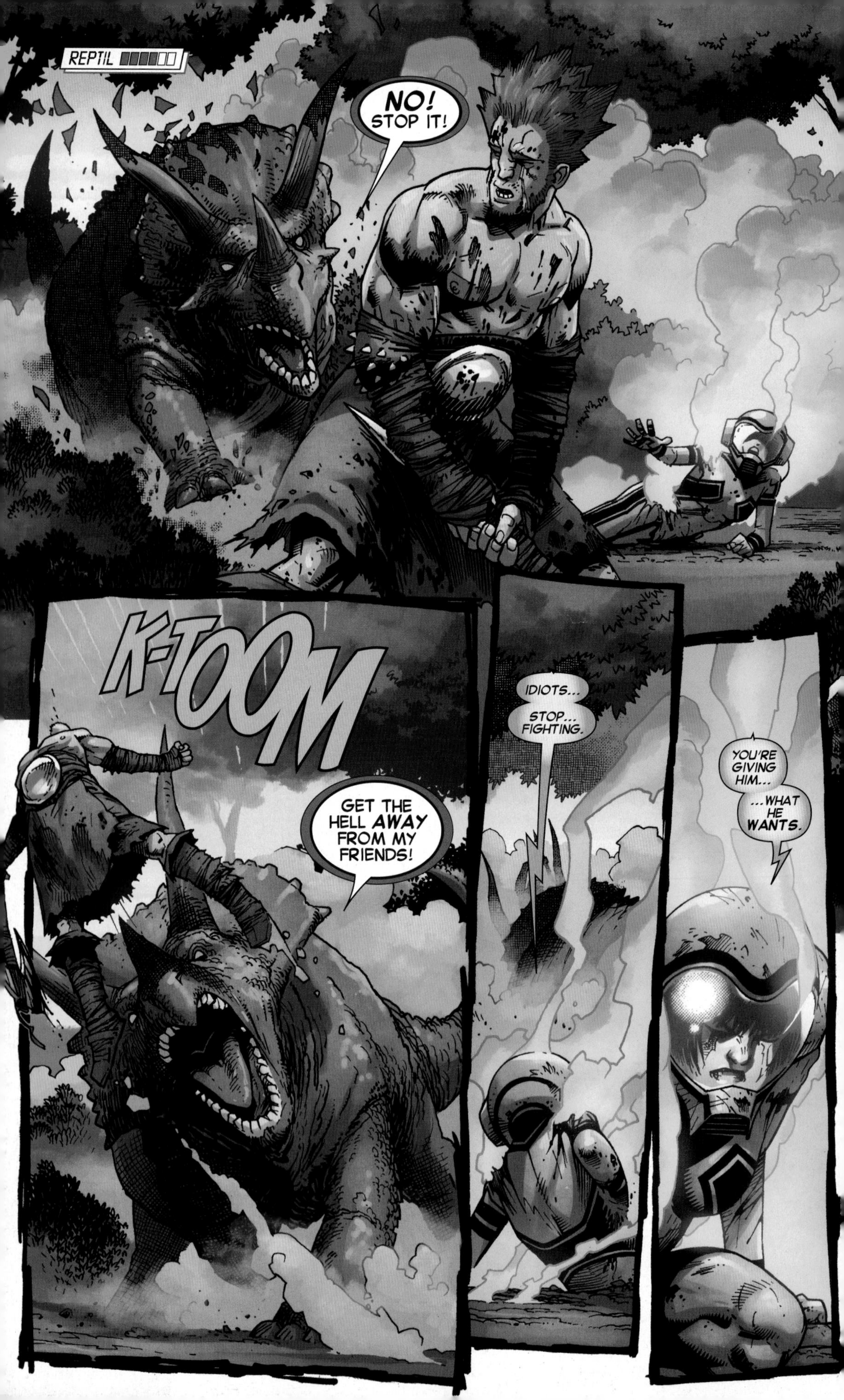
REPTIL
NO! STOP IT!
K-TOOOM
GET THE HELL AWAY FROM MY FRIENDS!
IDIOTS...
STOP... FIGHTING.
YOU'RE GIVING HIM...
...WHAT HE WANTS.

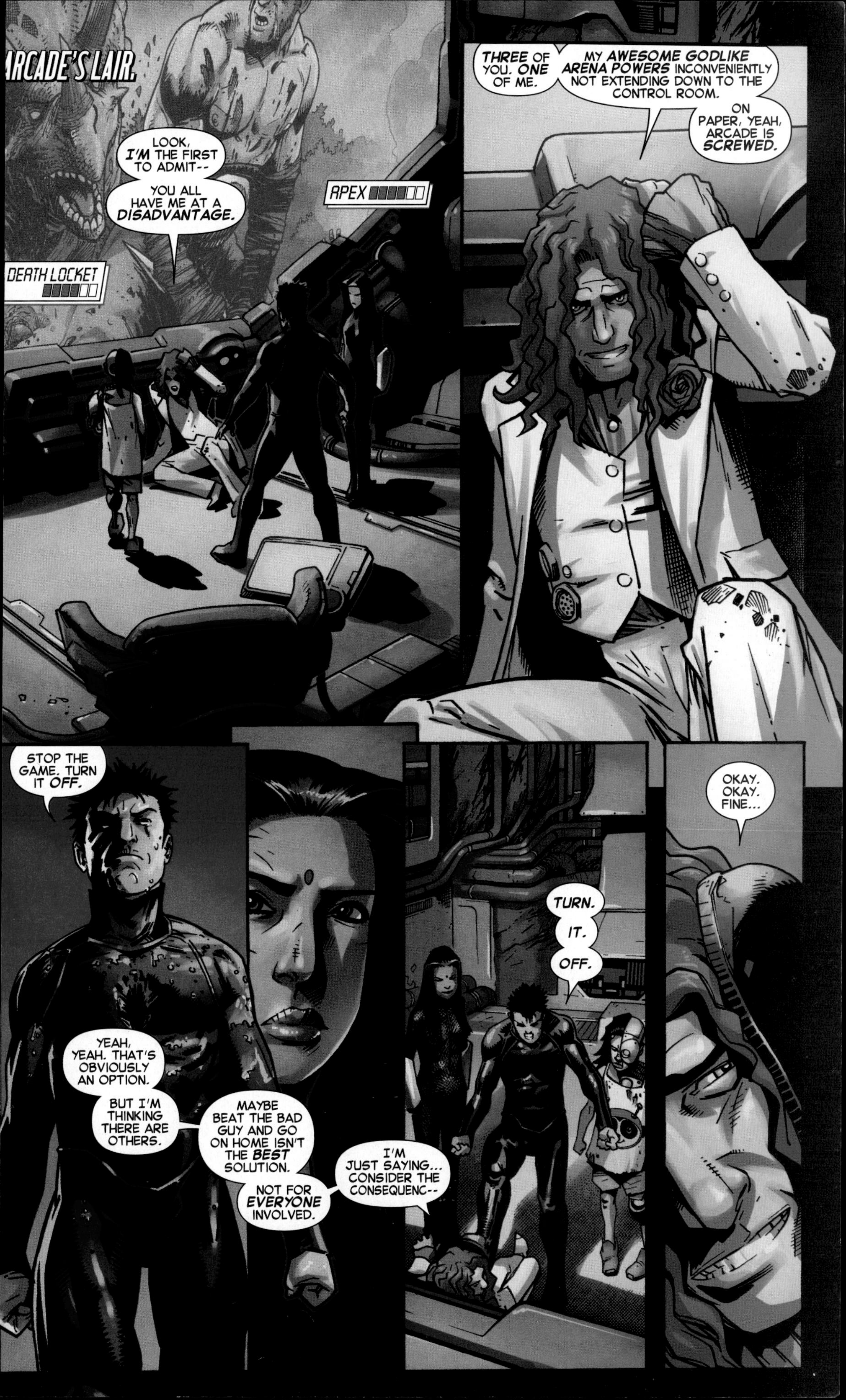
ARCADE'S LAIR.
LOOK, I'M THE FIRST TO ADMIT--
YOU ALL HAVE ME AT A DISADVANTAGE.
APEX
DEATH LOCKET
THREE OF YOU. ONE OF ME.
MY AWESOME GODLIKE ARENA POWERS INCONVENIENTLY NOT EXTENDING DOWN TO THE CONTROL ROOM.
ON PAPER, YEAH, ARCADE IS SCREWED.
STOP THE GAME. TURN IT OFF.
TURN. IT. OFF.
OKAY. OKAY. FINE...
YEAH, YEAH. THAT'S OBVIOUSLY AN OPTION.
BUT I'M THINKING THERE ARE OTHERS.
MAYBE BEAT THE BAD GUY AND GO ON HOME ISN'T THE BEST SOLUTION.
NOT FOR EVERYONE INVOLVED.
I'M JUST SAYING... CONSIDER THE CONSEQUENC--

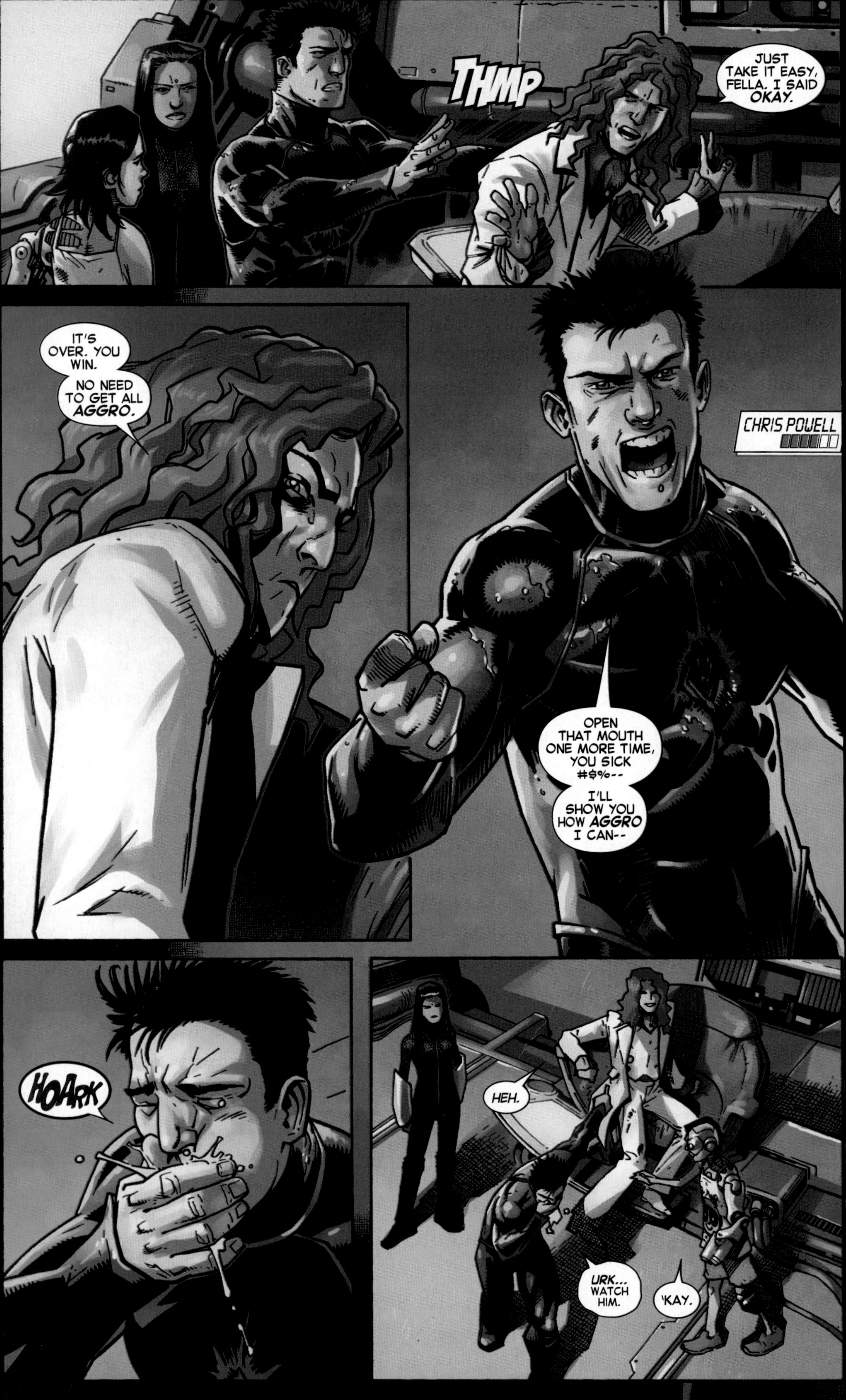
THMP
JUST TAKE IT EASY, FELLA. I SAID OKAY.
IT'S OVER. YOU WIN.
NO NEED TO GET ALL AGGRO.
CHRIS POWELL
OPEN THAT MOUTH ONE MORE TIME, YOU SICK #$%--
I'LL SHOW YOU HOW AGGRO I CAN--
HOARK
HEH.
URK... WATCH HIM.
'KAY.

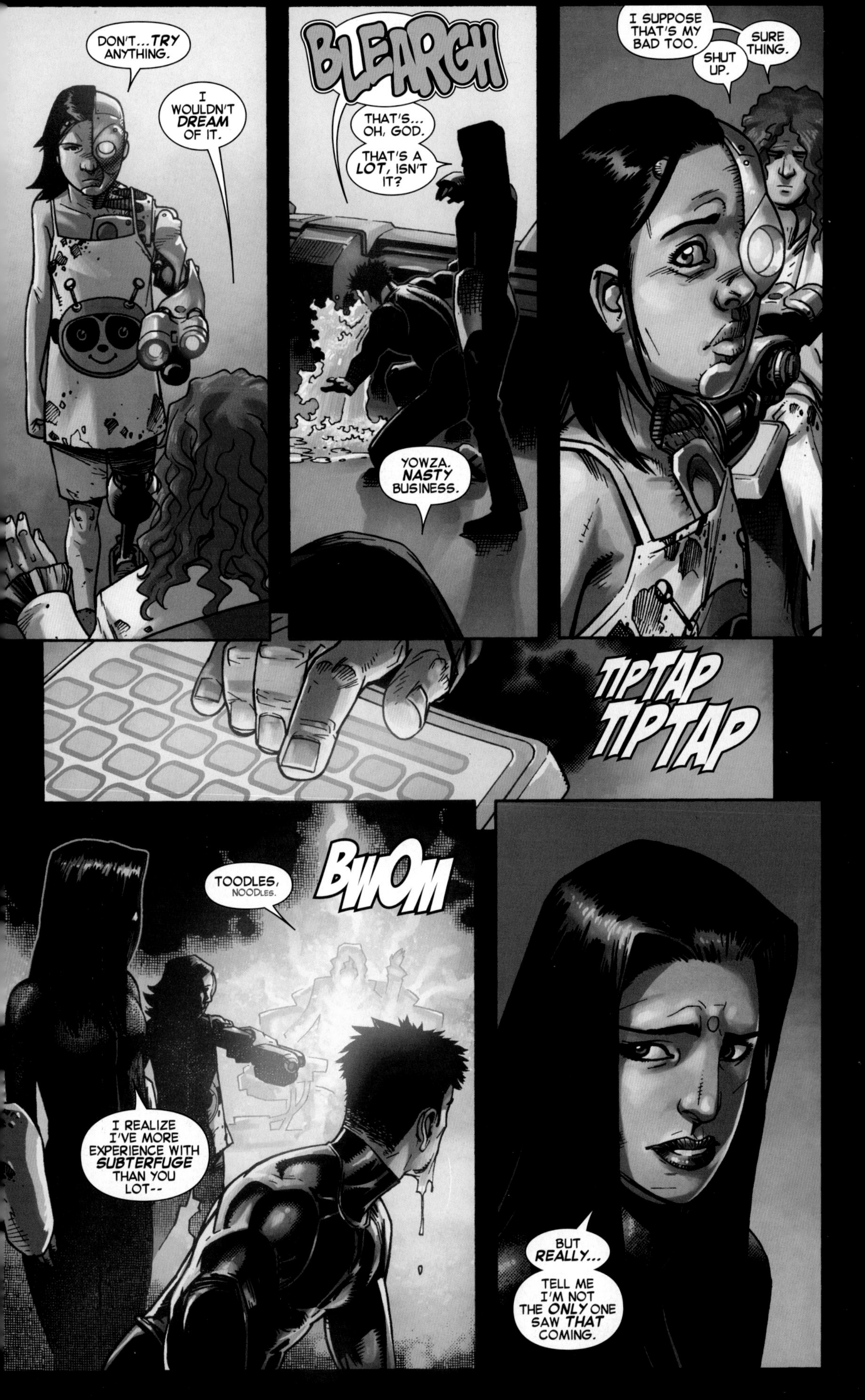
DON'T...TRY ANYTHING.
I WOULDN'T DREAM OF IT.
BLEARGH
THAT'S... OH, GOD.
THAT'S A LOT, ISN'T IT?
YOWZA. NASTY BUSINESS.
I SUPPOSE THAT'S MY BAD TOO.
SURE THING.
SHUT UP.
TIPTAP TIPTAP
TOODLES, NOODLES.
BWOM
I REALIZE I'VE MORE EXPERIENCE WITH SUBTERFUGE THAN YOU LOT--
BUT REALLY...
TELL ME I'M NOT THE ONLY ONE SAW THAT COMING.

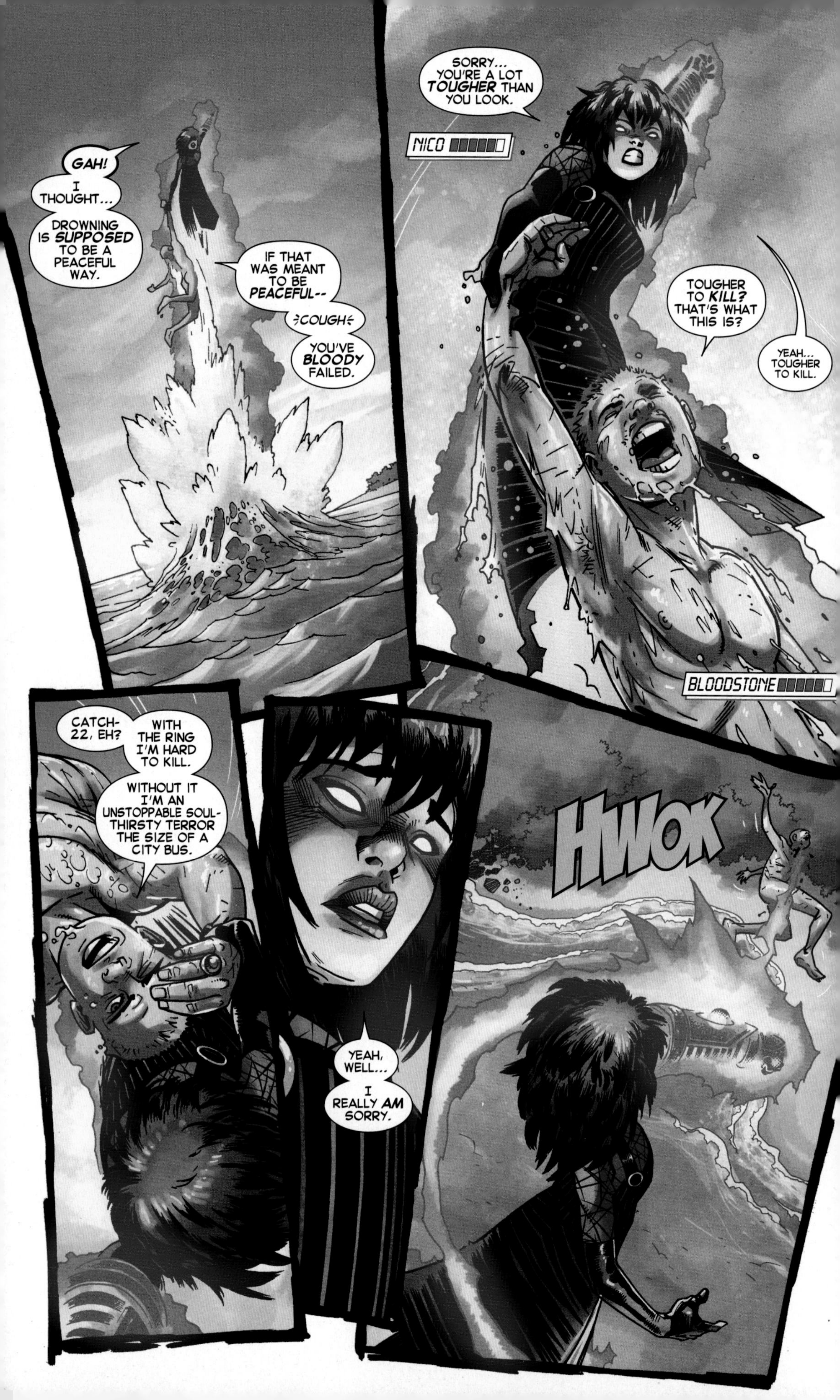

GAH!
I THOUGHT...
DROWNING IS SUPPOSED TO BE A PEACEFUL WAY.
IF THAT WAS MEANT TO BE PEACEFUL--
COUGH
YOU'VE BLOODY FAILED.
SORRY... YOU'RE A LOT TOUGHER THAN YOU LOOK.
NICO
TOUGHER TO KILL? THAT'S WHAT THIS IS?
YEAH... TOUGHER TO KILL.
BLOODSTONE
CATCH-22, EH?
WITH THE RING I'M HARD TO KILL.
WITHOUT IT I'M AN UNSTOPPABLE SOUL-THIRSTY TERROR THE SIZE OF A CITY BUS.
YEAH, WELL...
I REALLY AM SORRY.
HWOK

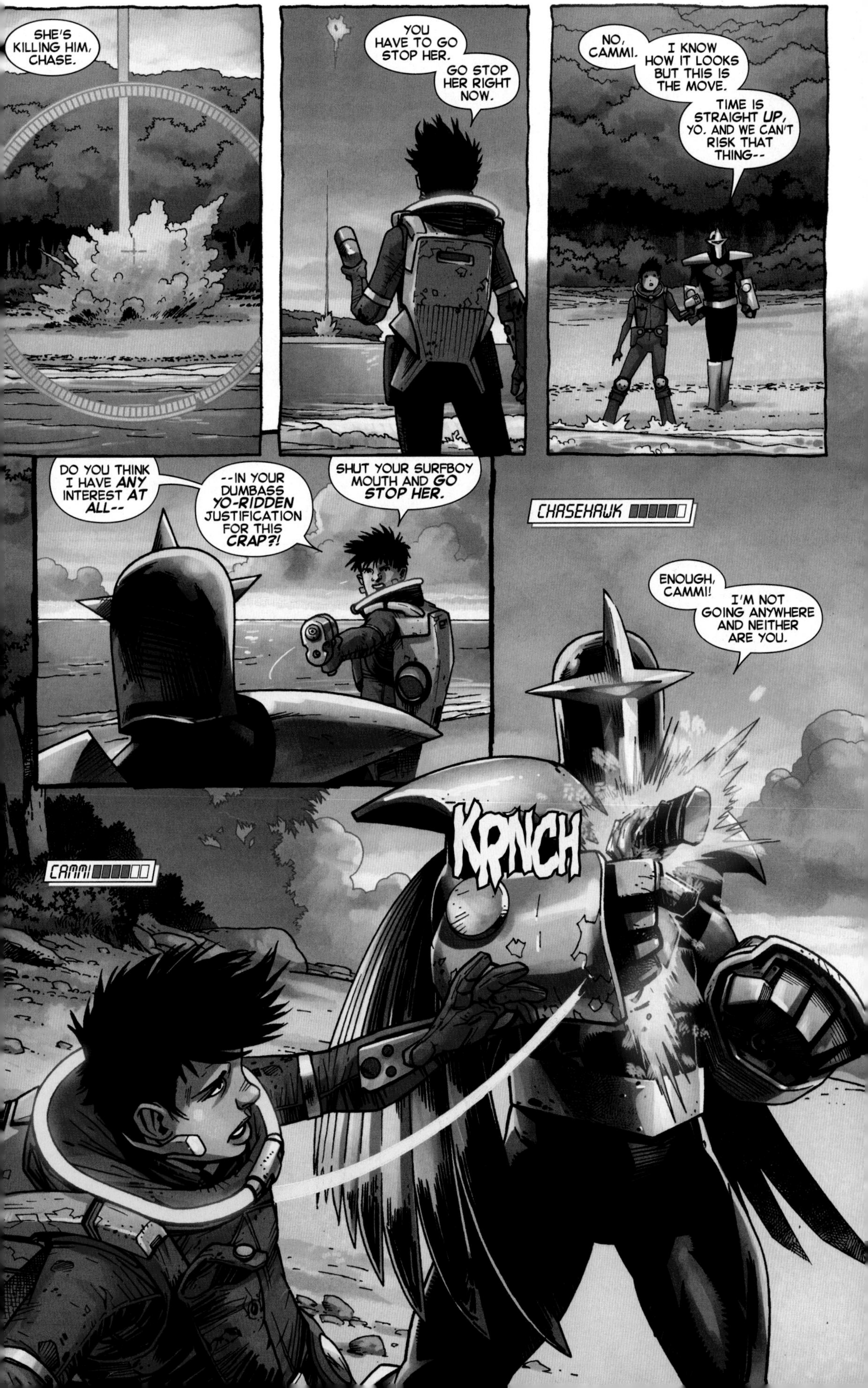
SHE'S KILLING HIM, CHASE.
YOU HAVE TO GO STOP HER.
GO STOP HER RIGHT NOW.
NO, CAMMI.
I KNOW HOW IT LOOKS BUT THIS IS THE MOVE.
TIME IS STRAIGHT UP, YO. AND WE CAN'T RISK THAT THING--
DO YOU THINK I HAVE ANY INTEREST AT ALL--
--IN YOUR DUMBASS YO-RIDDEN JUSTIFICATION FOR THIS CRAP?!
SHUT YOUR SURFBOY MOUTH AND GO STOP HER.
CHASEHAWK
ENOUGH, CAMMI!
I'M NOT GOING ANYWHERE AND NEITHER ARE YOU.
KRNCH
CAMMI

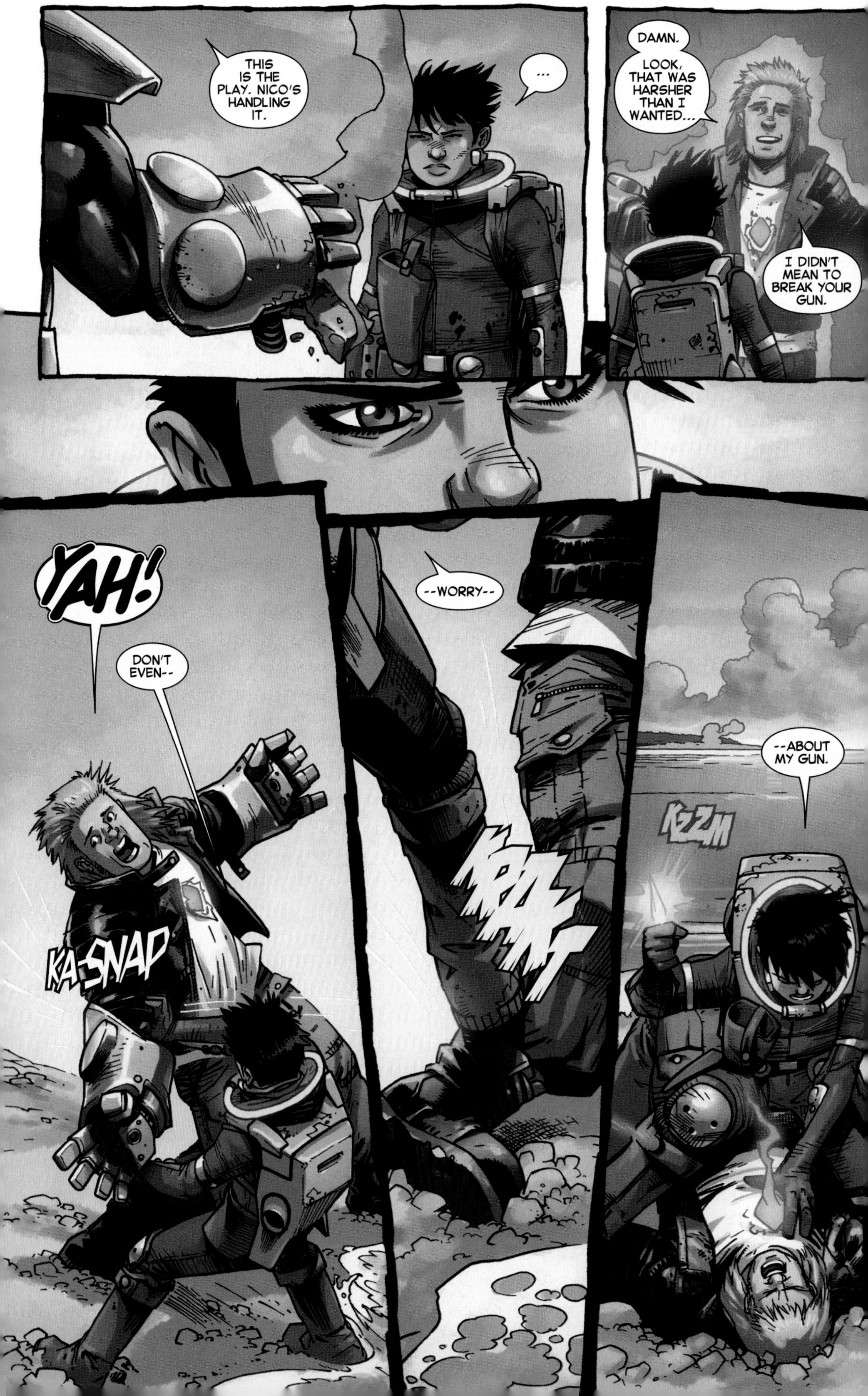
THIS IS THE PLAY. NICO'S HANDLING IT.
...
DAMN.
LOOK, THAT WAS HARSHER THAN I WANTED...
I DIDN'T MEAN TO BREAK YOUR GUN.
YAH!
DON'T EVEN--
KA-SNAP
--WORRY--
--ABOUT MY GUN.
KZZM

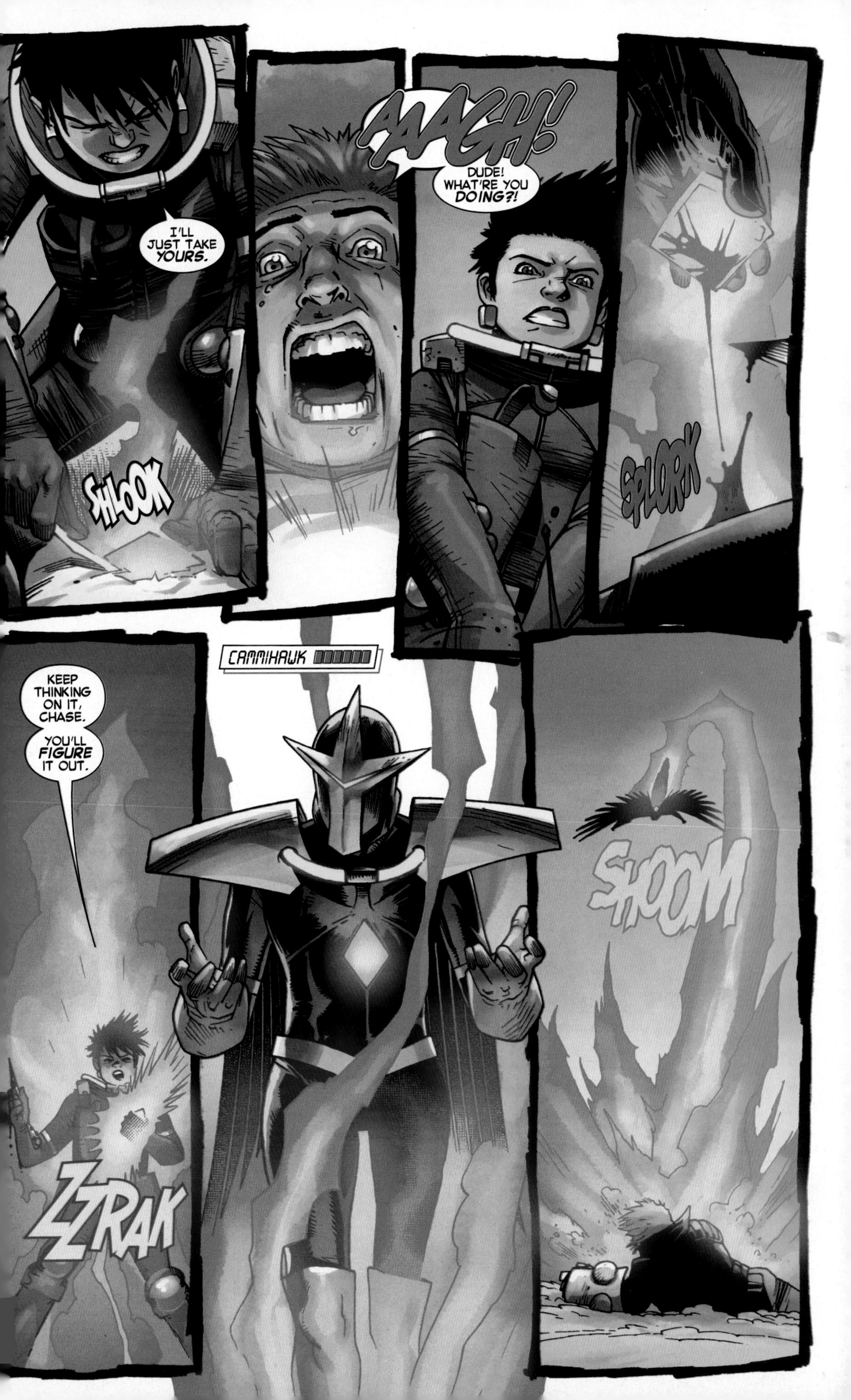
I'LL JUST TAKE YOURS.
SHLOOK
AAAGH!
DUDE! WHAT'RE YOU DOING?!
SPLORK
CAMMIHAWK
KEEP THINKING ON IT, CHASE.
YOU'LL FIGURE IT OUT.
ZZRAK
SHOOM

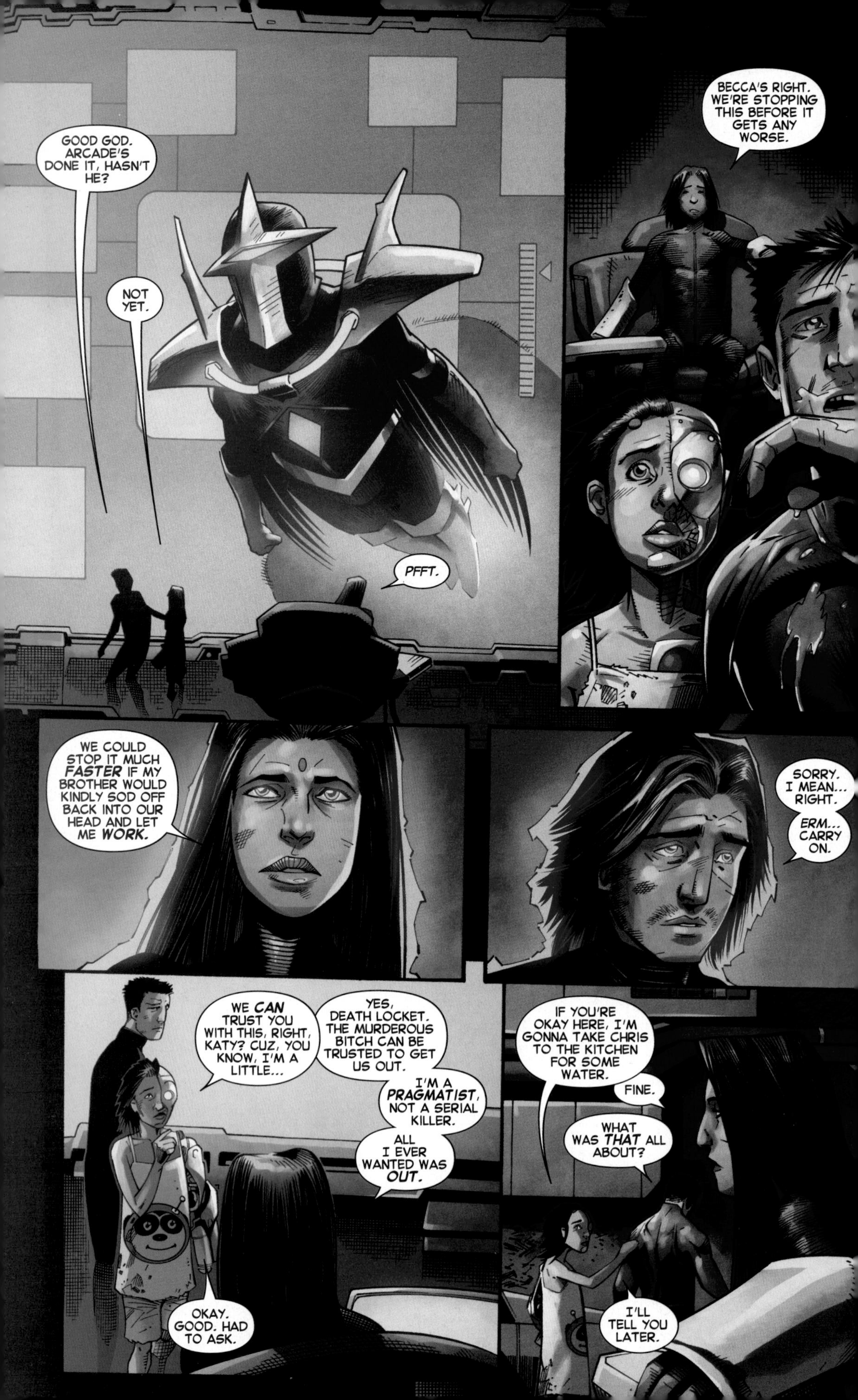
GOOD GOD. ARCADE'S DONE IT, HASN'T HE?
NOT YET.
PFFT.
BECCA'S RIGHT. WE'RE STOPPING THIS BEFORE IT GETS ANY WORSE.
WE COULD STOP IT MUCH FASTER IF MY BROTHER WOULD KINDLY SOD OFF BACK INTO OUR HEAD AND LET ME WORK.
SORRY. I MEAN... RIGHT.
ERM... CARRY ON.
WE CAN TRUST YOU WITH THIS, RIGHT, KATY? CUZ, YOU KNOW, I'M A LITTLE...
YES, DEATH LOCKET. THE MURDEROUS BITCH CAN BE TRUSTED TO GET US OUT.
I'M A PRAGMATIST, NOT A SERIAL KILLER.
ALL I EVER WANTED WAS OUT.
OKAY. GOOD. HAD TO ASK.
IF YOU'RE OKAY HERE, I'M GONNA TAKE CHRIS TO THE KITCHEN FOR SOME WATER.
FINE.
WHAT WAS THAT ALL ABOUT?
I'LL TELL YOU LATER.

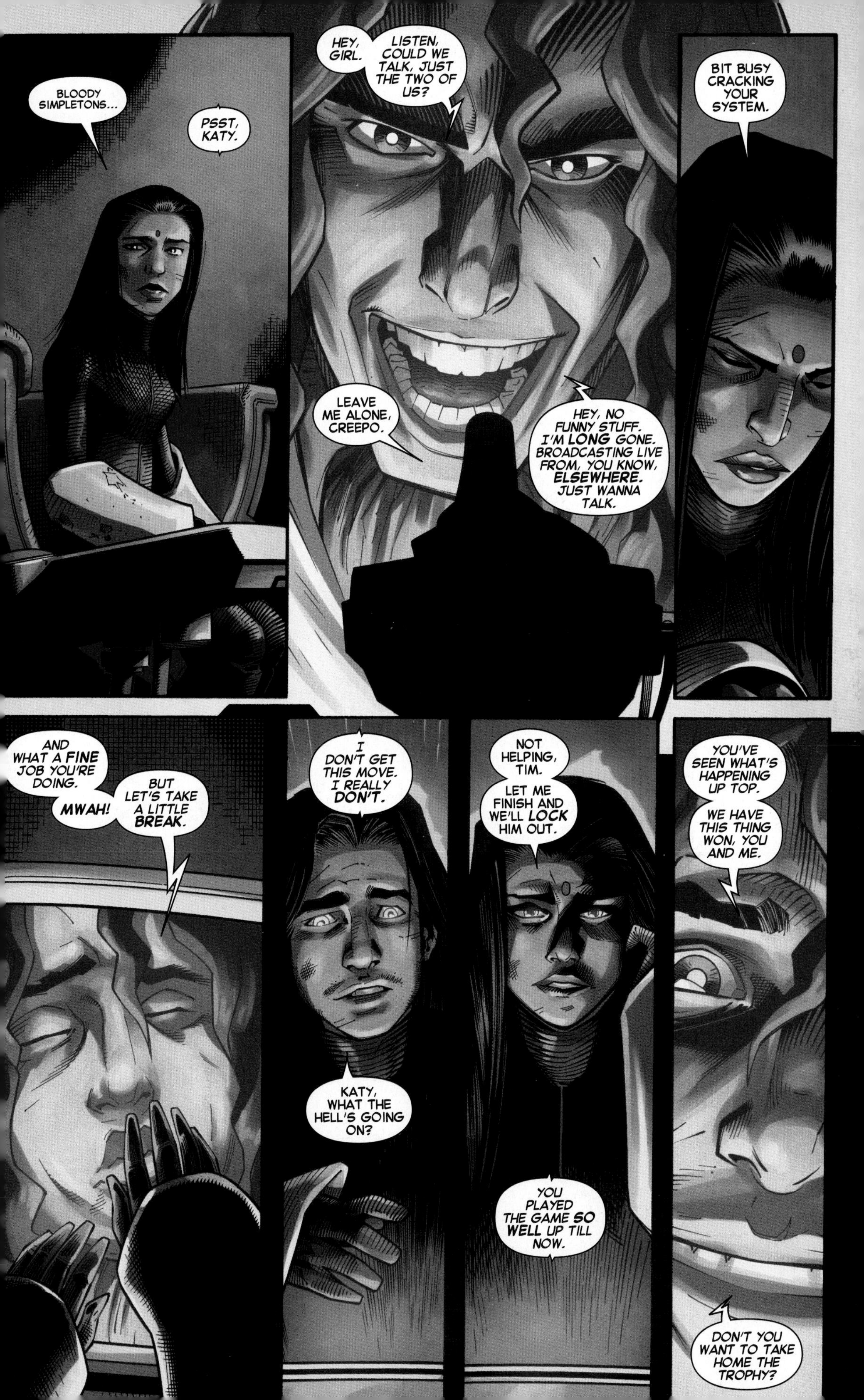
BLOODY SIMPLETONS...
PSST, KATY.
HEY, GIRL.
LISTEN, COULD WE TALK, JUST THE TWO OF US?
BIT BUSY CRACKING YOUR SYSTEM.
LEAVE ME ALONE, CREEPO.
HEY, NO FUNNY STUFF. I'M **LONG** GONE. BROADCASTING LIVE FROM, YOU KNOW, **ELSEWHERE.** JUST WANNA TALK.
AND WHAT A **FINE** JOB YOU'RE DOING.
MWAH!
BUT LET'S TAKE A LITTLE **BREAK.**
I DON'T GET THIS MOVE. I REALLY **DON'T.**
KATY, WHAT THE HELL'S GOING ON?
NOT HELPING, TIM.
LET ME FINISH AND WE'LL **LOCK** HIM OUT.
YOU PLAYED THE GAME **SO WELL** UP TILL NOW.
YOU'VE SEEN WHAT'S HAPPENING UP TOP.
WE HAVE THIS THING WON, YOU AND ME.
DON'T YOU WANT TO TAKE HOME THE TROPHY?

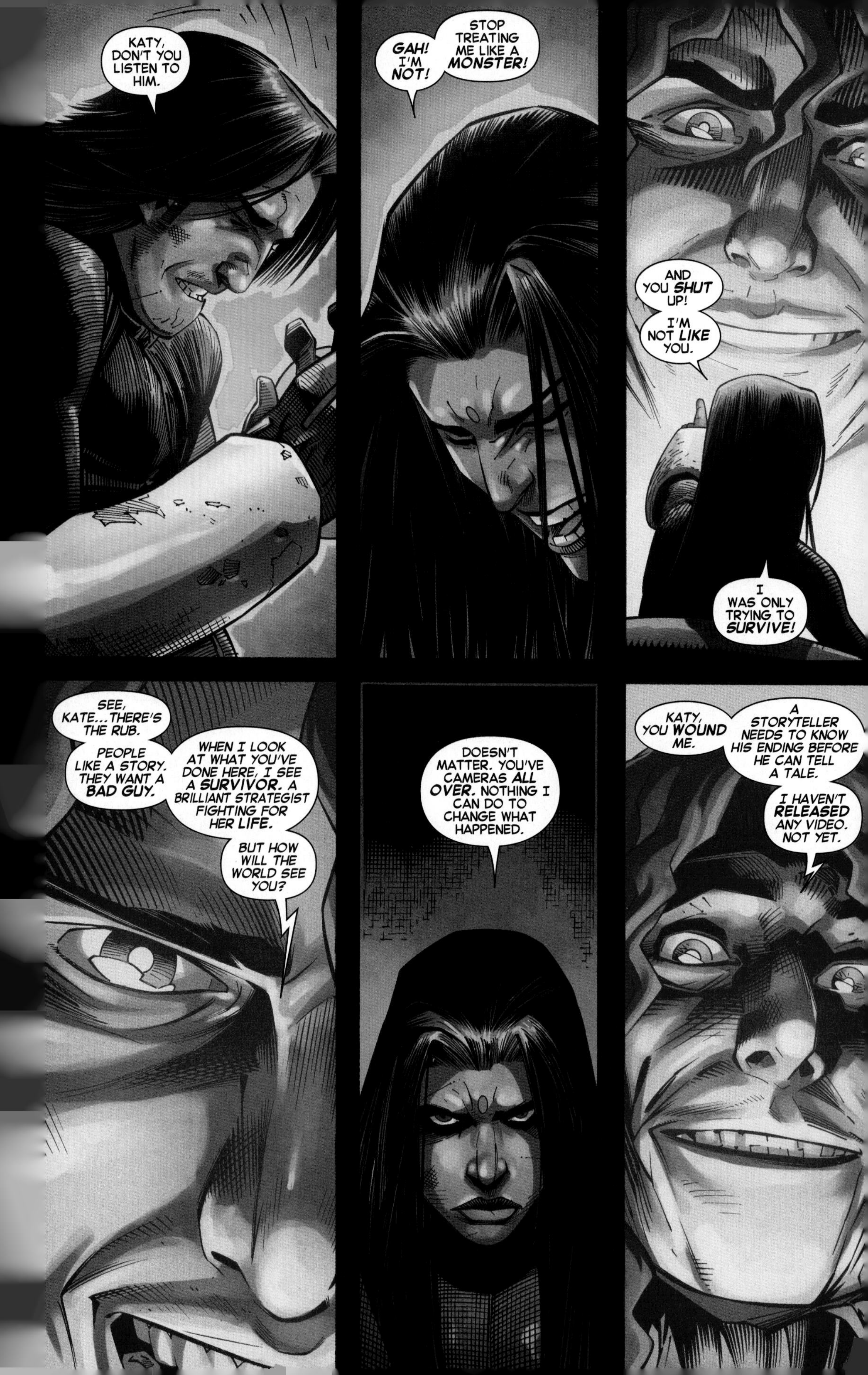
KATY, DON'T YOU LISTEN TO HIM.
GAH! I'M NOT!
STOP TREATING ME LIKE A MONSTER!
AND YOU SHUT UP!
I'M NOT LIKE YOU.
I WAS ONLY TRYING TO SURVIVE!
SEE, KATE...THERE'S THE RUB.
PEOPLE LIKE A STORY. THEY WANT A BAD GUY.
WHEN I LOOK AT WHAT YOU'VE DONE HERE, I SEE A SURVIVOR. A BRILLIANT STRATEGIST FIGHTING FOR HER LIFE.
BUT HOW WILL THE WORLD SEE YOU?
DOESN'T MATTER. YOU'VE CAMERAS ALL OVER. NOTHING I CAN DO TO CHANGE WHAT HAPPENED.
KATY, YOU WOUND ME.
A STORYTELLER NEEDS TO KNOW HIS ENDING BEFORE HE CAN TELL A TALE.
I HAVEN'T RELEASED ANY VIDEO. NOT YET.

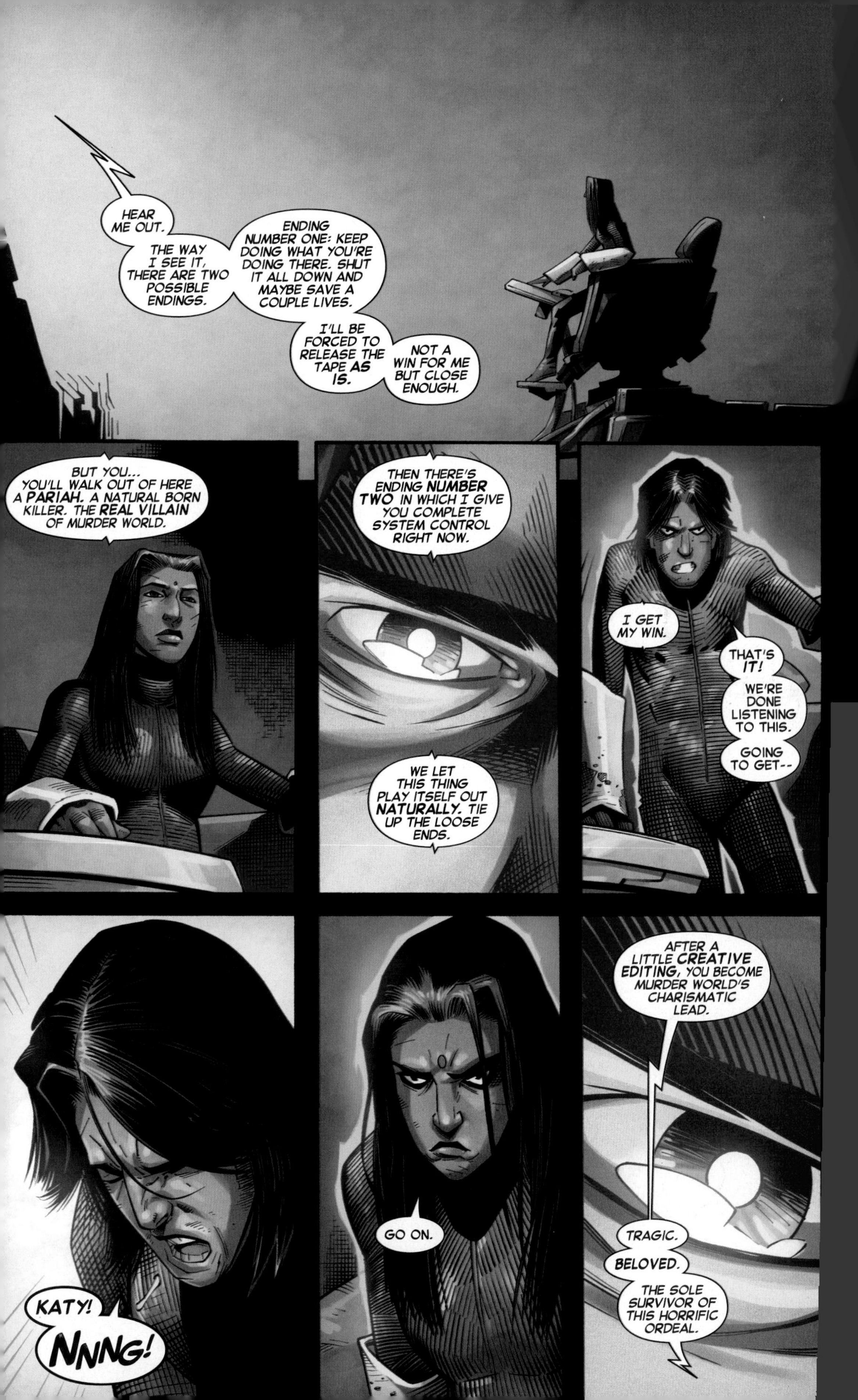
HEAR ME OUT.
THE WAY I SEE IT, THERE ARE TWO POSSIBLE ENDINGS.
ENDING NUMBER ONE: KEEP DOING WHAT YOU'RE DOING THERE. SHUT IT ALL DOWN AND MAYBE SAVE A COUPLE LIVES.
I'LL BE FORCED TO RELEASE THE TAPE AS IS.
NOT A WIN FOR ME BUT CLOSE ENOUGH.
BUT YOU... YOU'LL WALK OUT OF HERE A PARIAH. A NATURAL BORN KILLER. THE REAL VILLAIN OF MURDER WORLD.
THEN THERE'S ENDING NUMBER TWO IN WHICH I GIVE YOU COMPLETE SYSTEM CONTROL RIGHT NOW.
WE LET THIS THING PLAY ITSELF OUT NATURALLY. TIE UP THE LOOSE ENDS.
I GET MY WIN.
THAT'S IT!
WE'RE DONE LISTENING TO THIS.
GOING TO GET--
KATY!
NNNG!
GO ON.
AFTER A LITTLE CREATIVE EDITING, YOU BECOME MURDER WORLD'S CHARISMATIC LEAD.
TRAGIC.
BELOVED.
THE SOLE SURVIVOR OF THIS HORRIFIC ORDEAL.

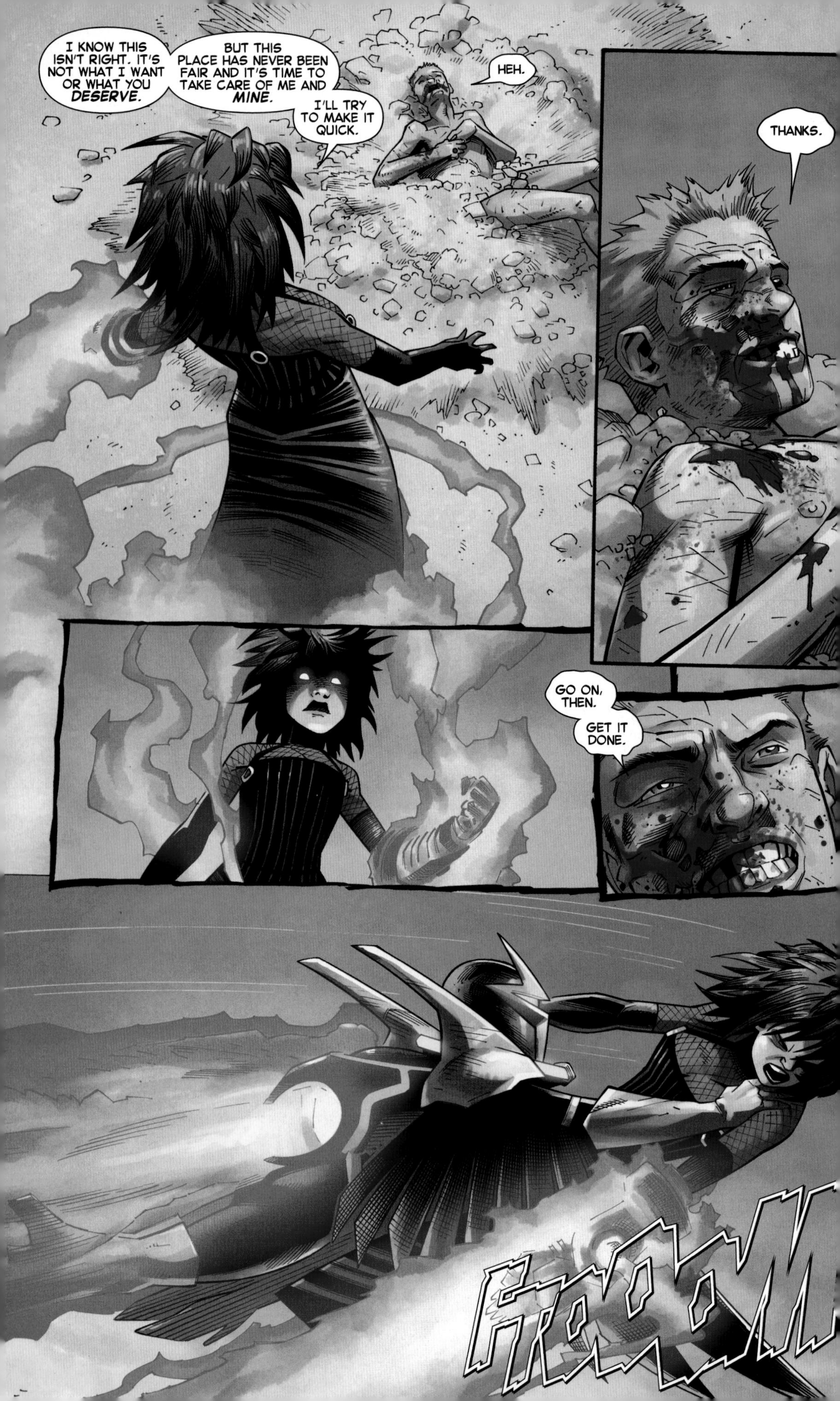
I KNOW THIS ISN'T RIGHT. IT'S NOT WHAT I WANT OR WHAT YOU *DESERVE.*
BUT THIS PLACE HAS NEVER BEEN FAIR AND IT'S TIME TO TAKE CARE OF ME AND *MINE.*
HEH.
I'LL TRY TO MAKE IT QUICK.
THANKS.
GO ON, THEN.
GET IT DONE.
FRAOOM

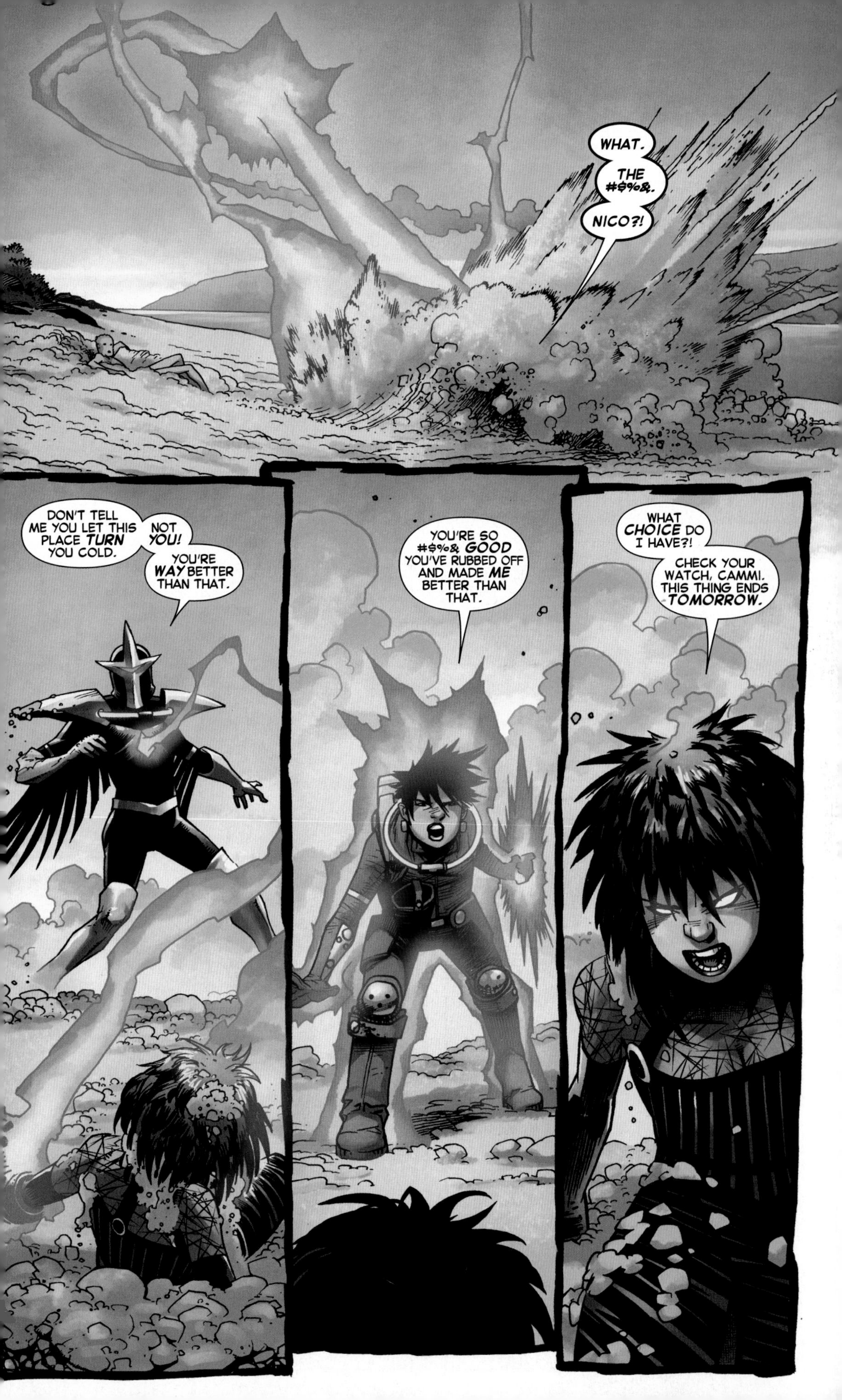
WHAT.
THE #$%&.
NICO?!
DON'T TELL ME YOU LET THIS PLACE TURN YOU COLD.
NOT YOU!
YOU'RE WAY BETTER THAN THAT.
YOU'RE SO #$%& GOOD YOU'VE RUBBED OFF AND MADE ME BETTER THAN THAT.
WHAT CHOICE DO I HAVE?!
CHECK YOUR WATCH, CAMMI. THIS THING ENDS TOMORROW.

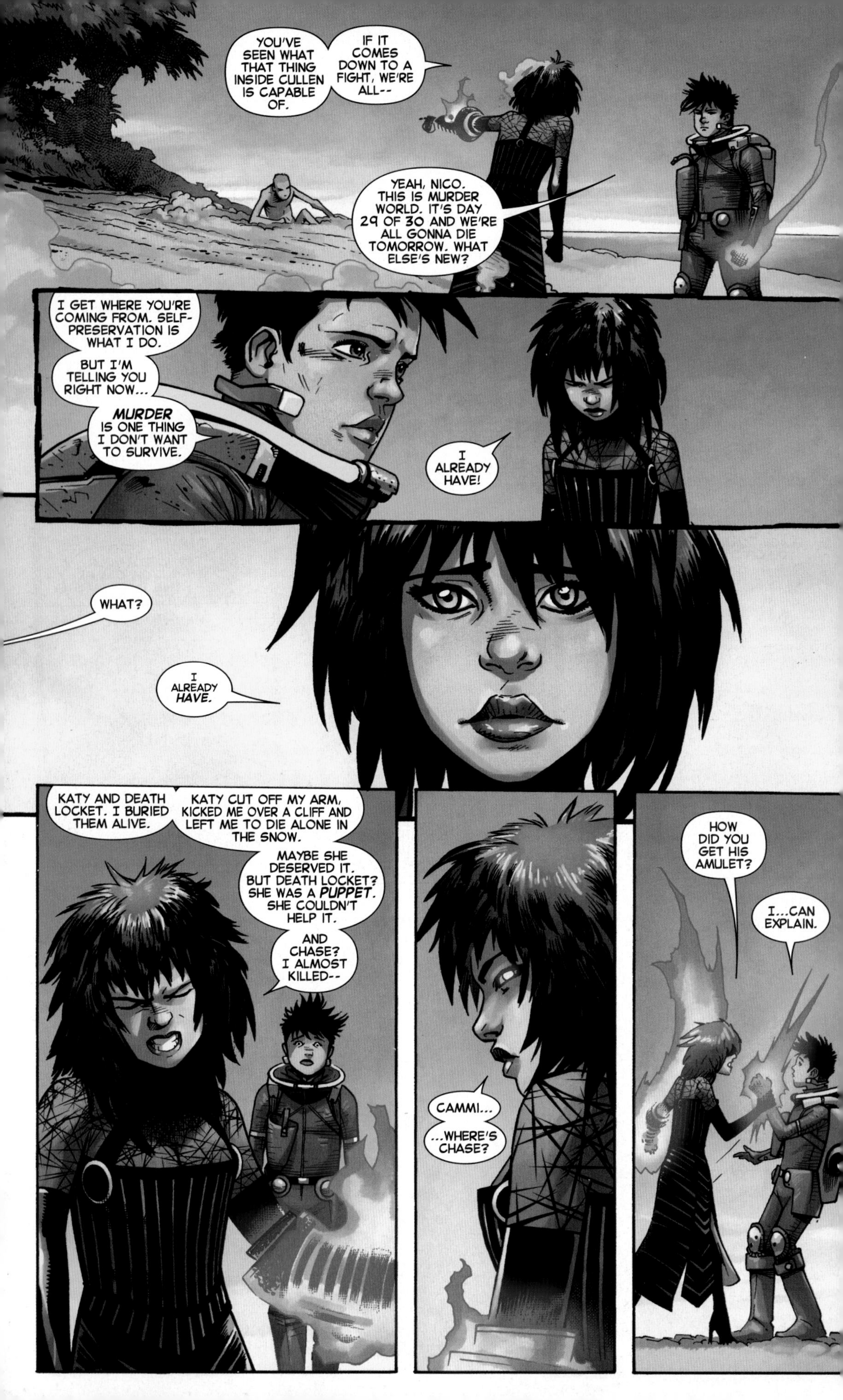

YOU'VE SEEN WHAT THAT THING INSIDE CULLEN IS CAPABLE OF.
IF IT COMES DOWN TO A FIGHT, WE'RE ALL--
YEAH, NICO. THIS IS MURDER WORLD. IT'S DAY 29 OF 30 AND WE'RE ALL GONNA DIE TOMORROW. WHAT ELSE'S NEW?
I GET WHERE YOU'RE COMING FROM. SELF-PRESERVATION IS WHAT I DO.
BUT I'M TELLING YOU RIGHT NOW...
MURDER IS ONE THING I DON'T WANT TO SURVIVE.
I ALREADY HAVE!
WHAT?
I ALREADY HAVE.
KATY AND DEATH LOCKET. I BURIED THEM ALIVE.
KATY CUT OFF MY ARM, KICKED ME OVER A CLIFF AND LEFT ME TO DIE ALONE IN THE SNOW.
MAYBE SHE DESERVED IT. BUT DEATH LOCKET? SHE WAS A PUPPET. SHE COULDN'T HELP IT.
AND CHASE? I ALMOST KILLED--
CAMMI...
...WHERE'S CHASE?
HOW DID YOU GET HIS AMULET?
I...CAN EXPLAIN.

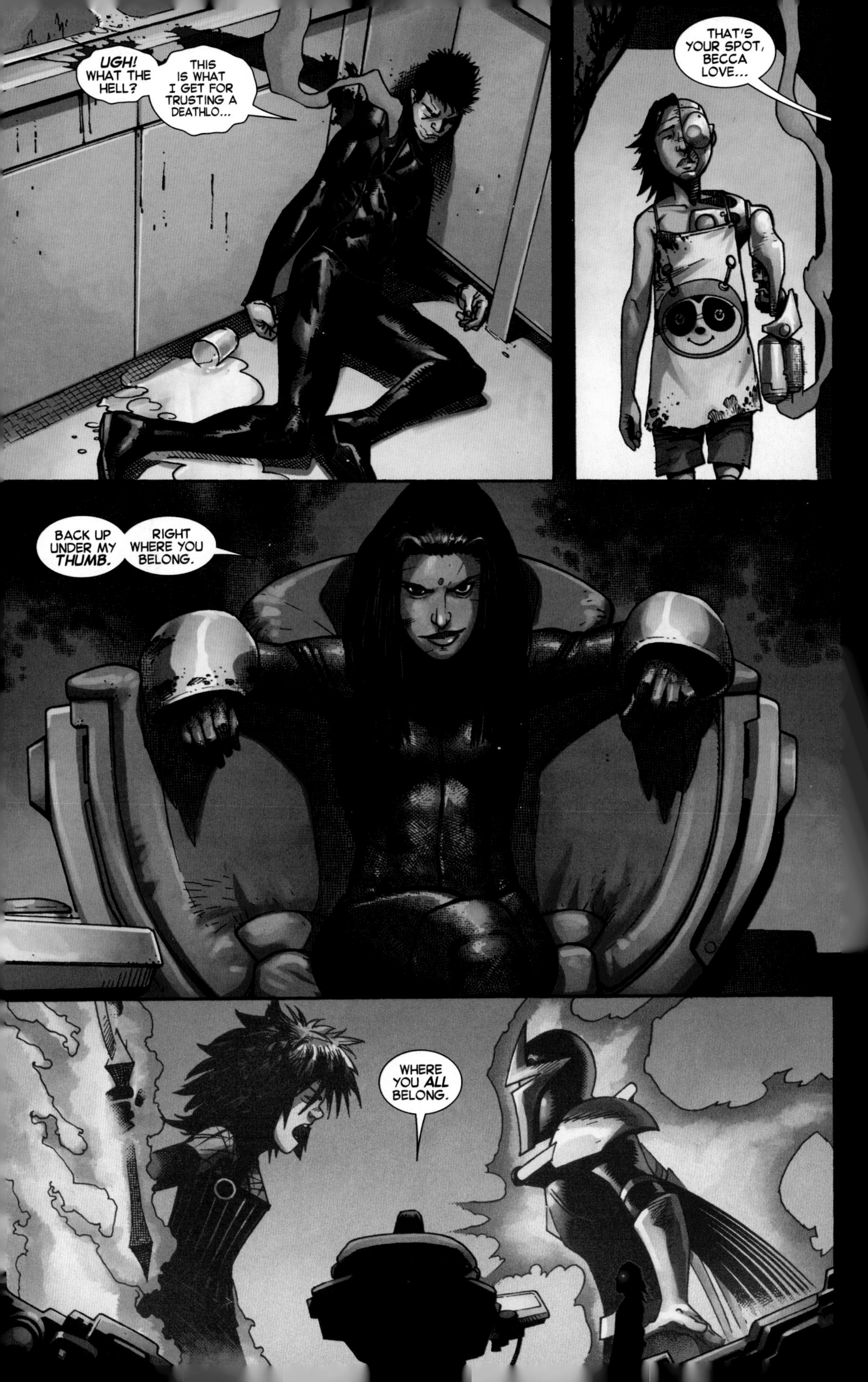
UGH! WHAT THE HELL?
THIS IS WHAT I GET FOR TRUSTING A DEATHLO...
THAT'S YOUR SPOT, BECCA LOVE...
BACK UP UNDER MY THUMB.
RIGHT WHERE YOU BELONG.
WHERE YOU ALL BELONG.

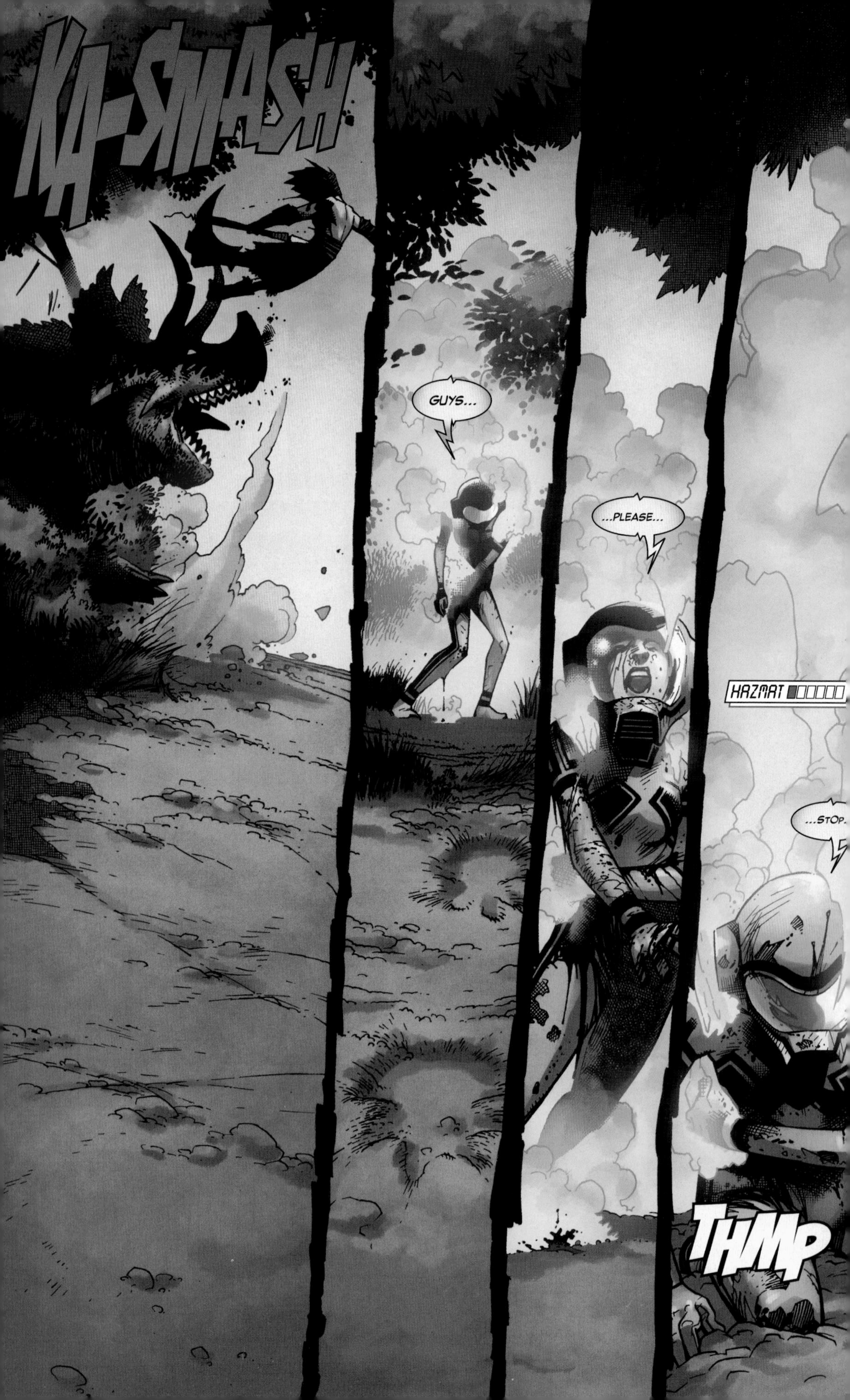
KA-SMASH
GUYS...
...PLEASE...
HAZMAT
...STOP...
THMP

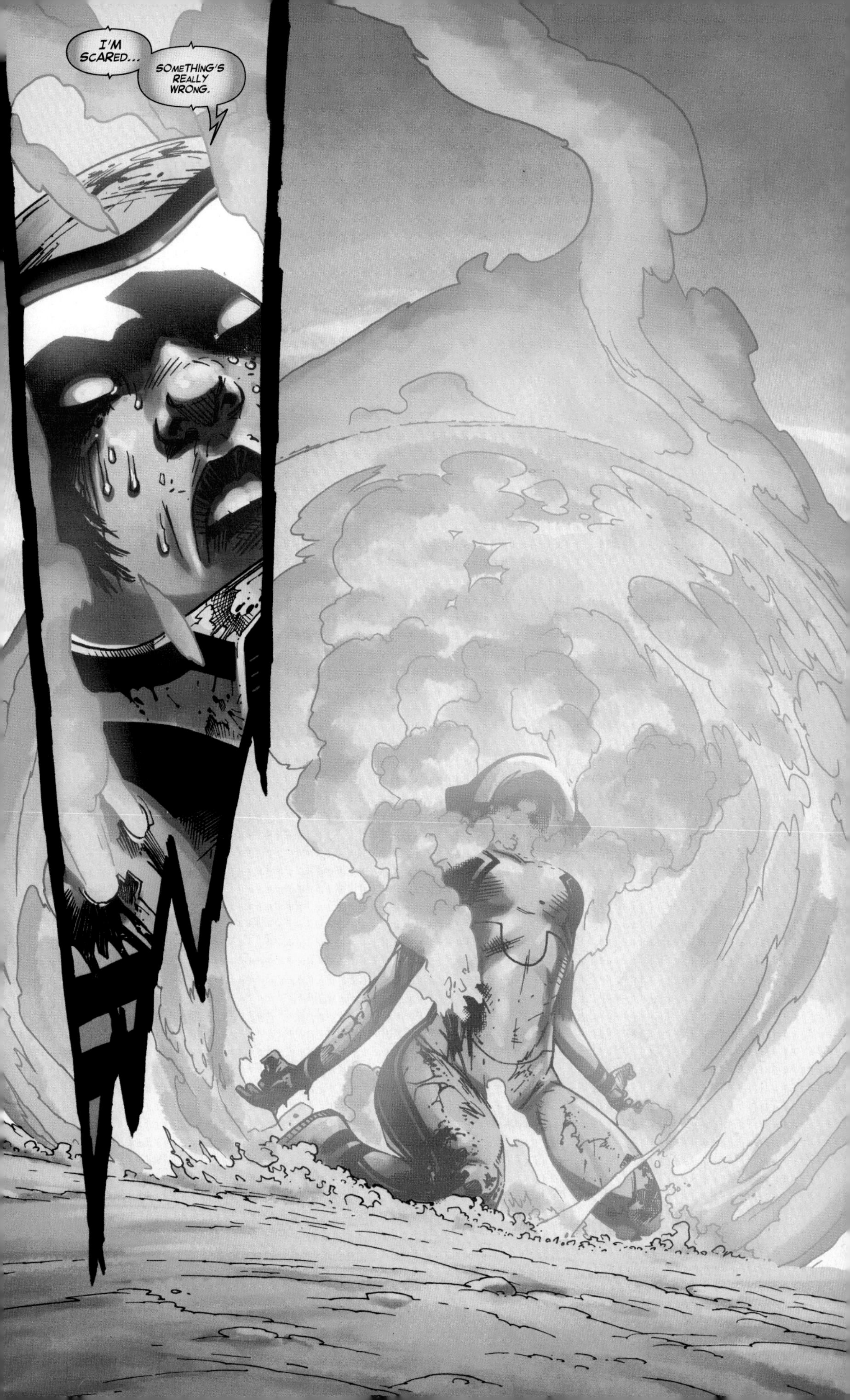
I'M SCARED...
SOMETHING'S REALLY WRONG.

GRADUATING CLASS OF 2013

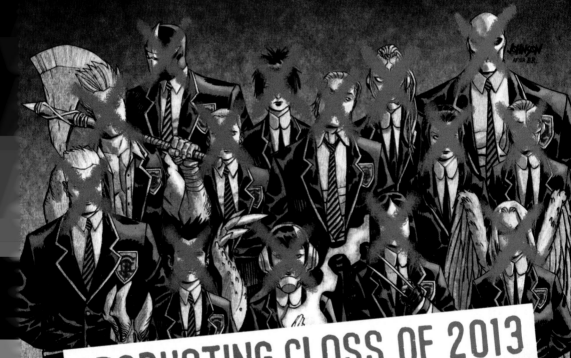

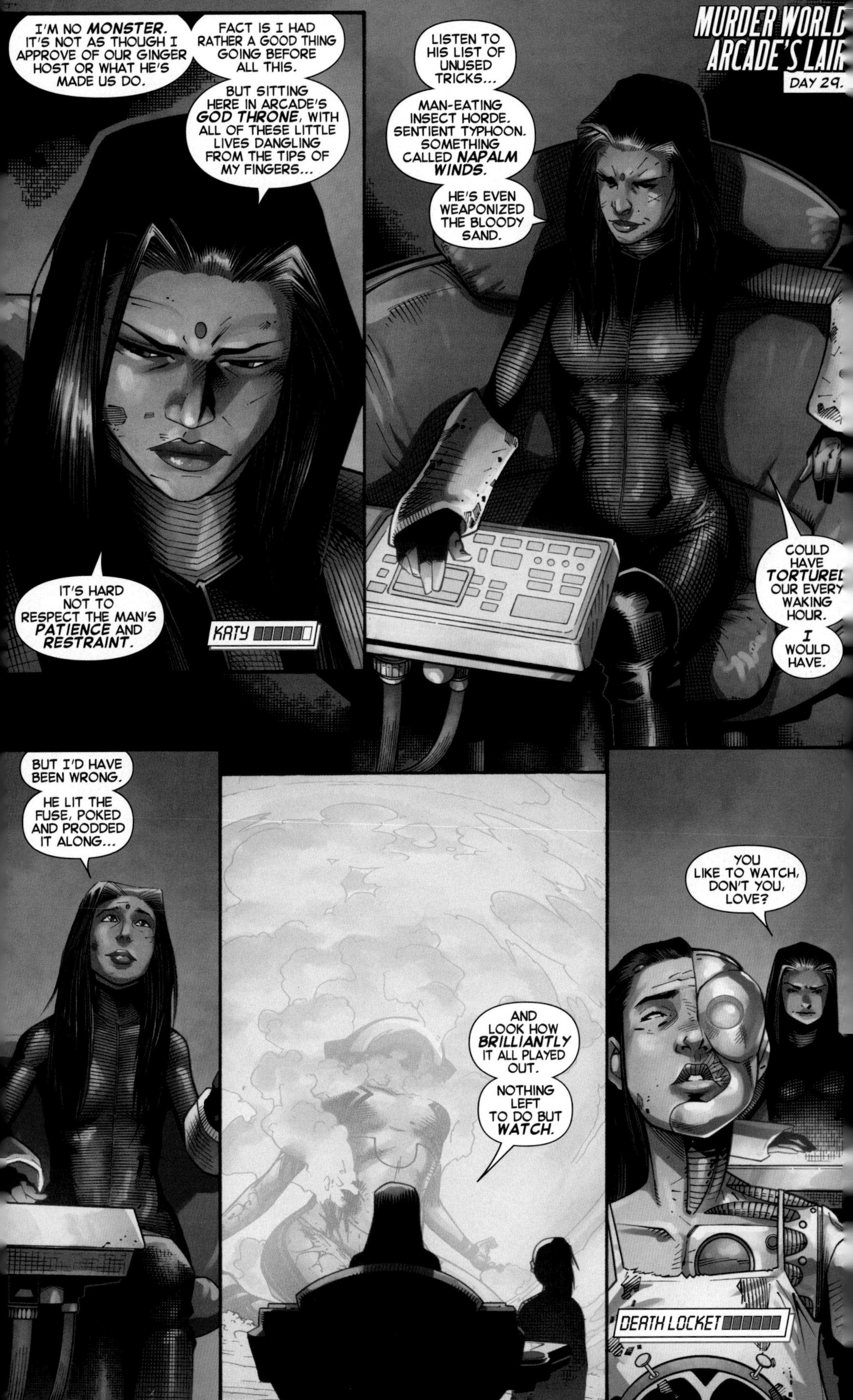

MURDER WORLD
ARCADE'S LAIR
DAY 29.
I'M NO MONSTER. IT'S NOT AS THOUGH I APPROVE OF OUR GINGER HOST OR WHAT HE'S MADE US DO.
FACT IS I HAD RATHER A GOOD THING GOING BEFORE ALL THIS.
BUT SITTING HERE IN ARCADE'S GOD THRONE, WITH ALL OF THESE LITTLE LIVES DANGLING FROM THE TIPS OF MY FINGERS...
IT'S HARD NOT TO RESPECT THE MAN'S PATIENCE AND RESTRAINT.
KATY
LISTEN TO HIS LIST OF UNUSED TRICKS...
MAN-EATING INSECT HORDE. SENTIENT TYPHOON. SOMETHING CALLED NAPALM WINDS.
HE'S EVEN WEAPONIZED THE BLOODY SAND.
COULD HAVE TORTURED OUR EVERY WAKING HOUR.
I WOULD HAVE.
BUT I'D HAVE BEEN WRONG.
HE LIT THE FUSE, POKED AND PRODDED IT ALONG...
AND LOOK HOW BRILLIANTLY IT ALL PLAYED OUT.
NOTHING LEFT TO DO BUT WATCH.
YOU LIKE TO WATCH, DON'T YOU, LOVE?
DEATH LOCKET

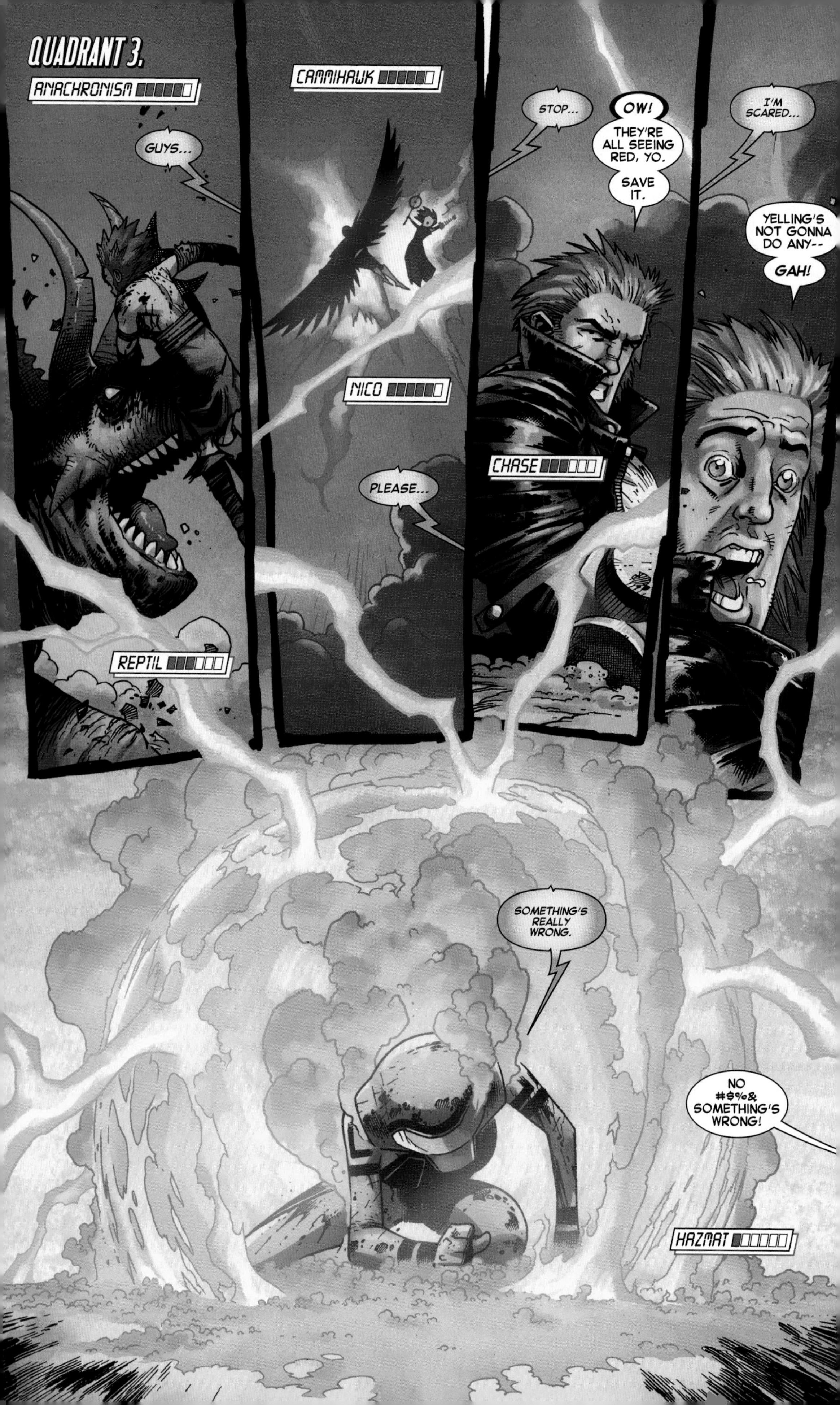
QUADRANT 3.
ANACHRONISM
GUYS...
REPTIL
CAMMIHAWK
NICO
PLEASE...
STOP...
OW!
THEY'RE ALL SEEING RED, YO.
SAVE IT.
CHASE
I'M SCARED...
YELLING'S NOT GONNA DO ANY--
GAH!
SOMETHING'S REALLY WRONG.
NO #$%& SOMETHING'S WRONG!
HAZMAT

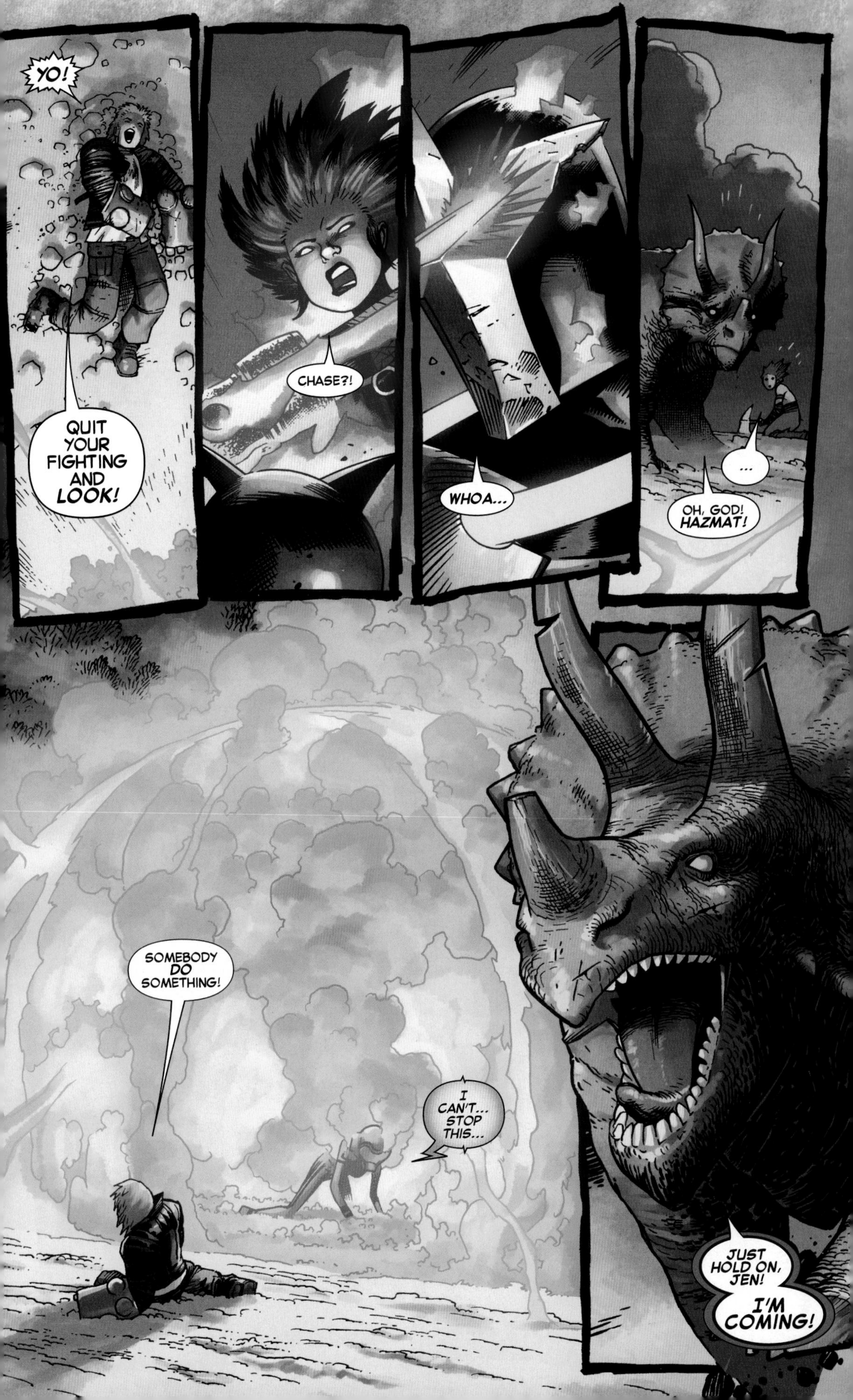
YO!
QUIT YOUR FIGHTING AND LOOK!
CHASE?!
WHOA...
...
OH, GOD! HAZMAT!
SOMEBODY DO SOMETHING!
I CAN'T... STOP THIS...
JUST HOLD ON, JEN!
I'M COMING!

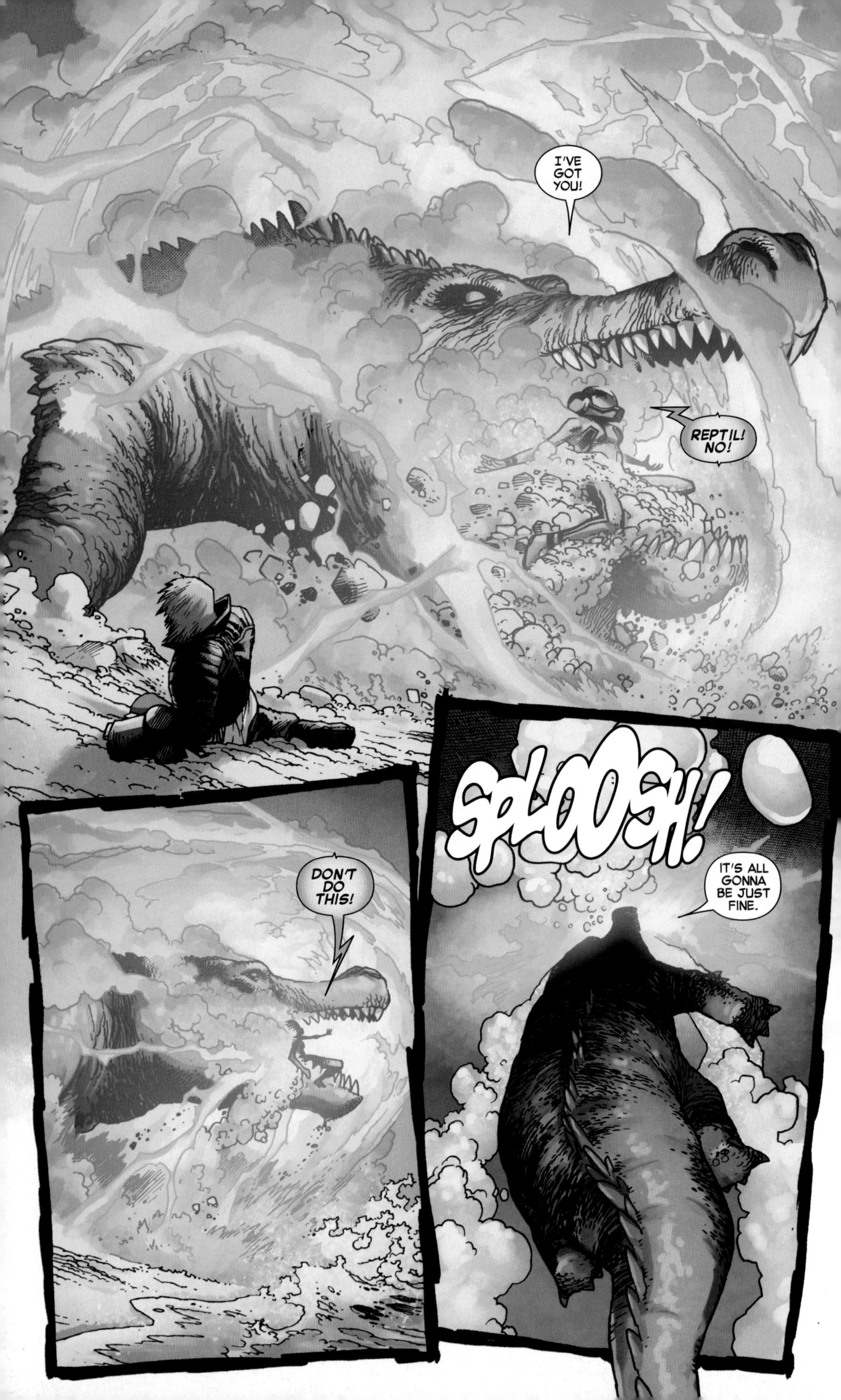
I'VE GOT YOU!
REPTIL! NO!
DON'T DO THIS!
SPLOOSH!
IT'S ALL GONNA BE JUST FINE.

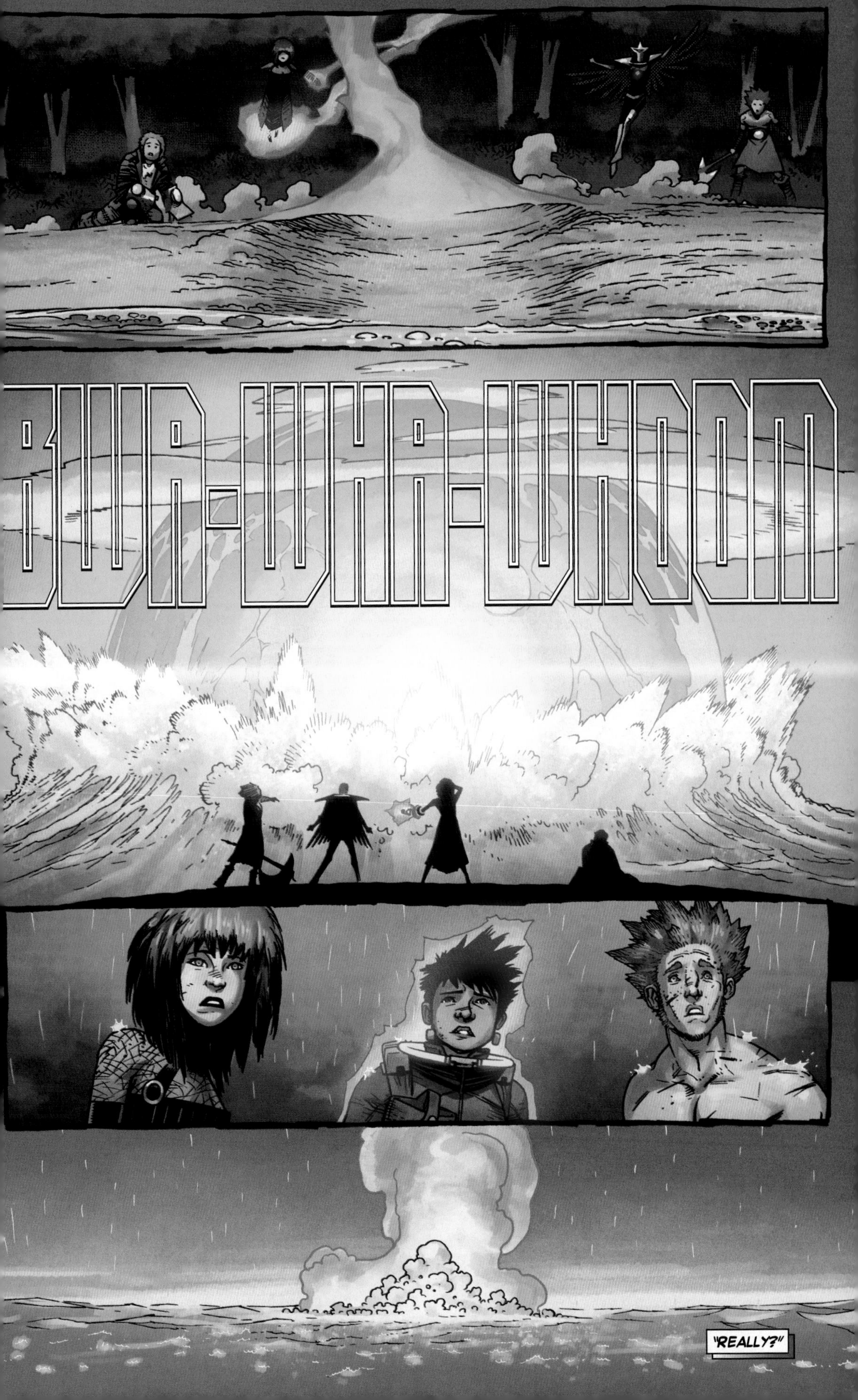
BWA-WHA-WHOOM
"REALLY?"

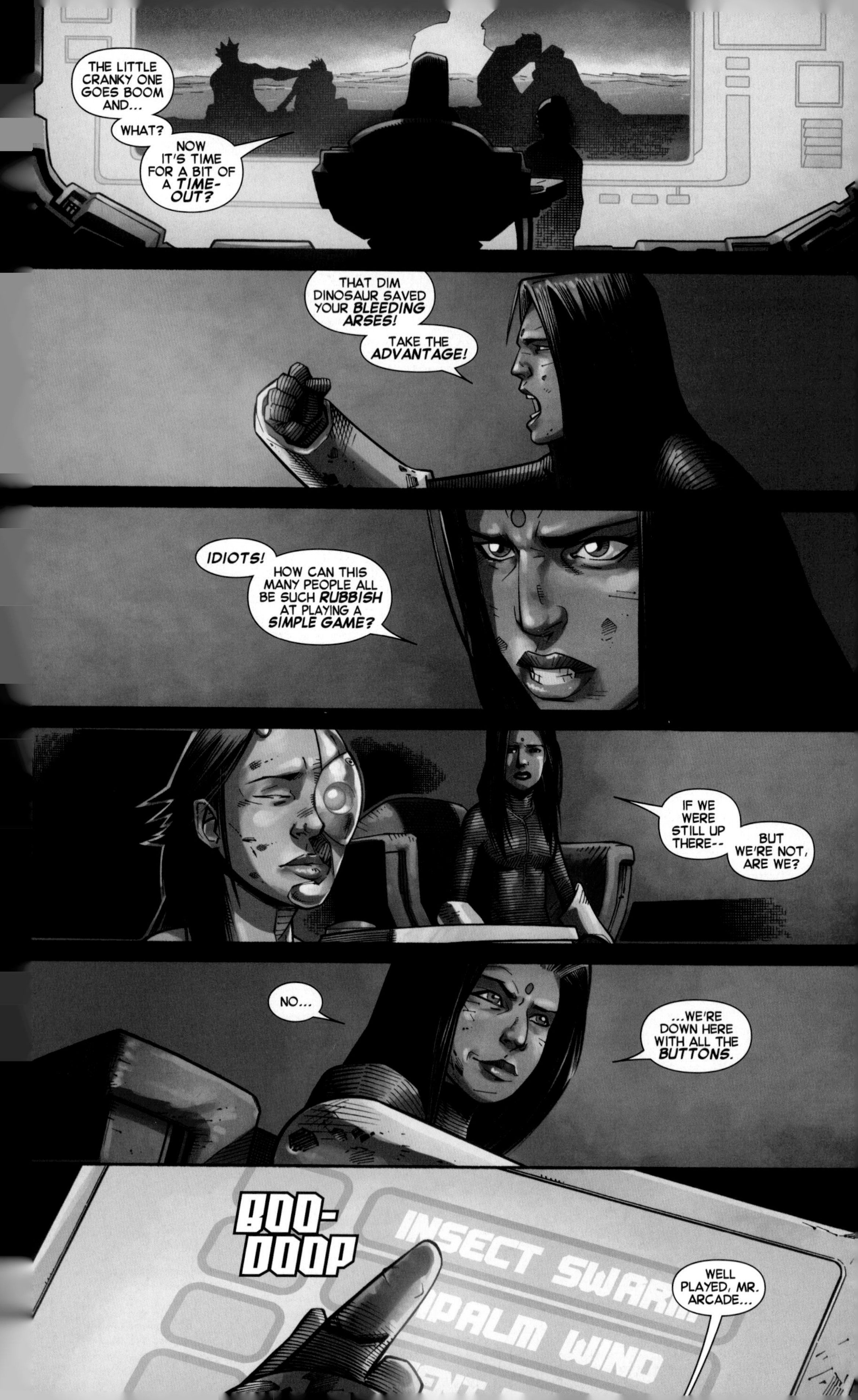
THE LITTLE CRANKY ONE GOES BOOM AND...
WHAT?
NOW IT'S TIME FOR A BIT OF A TIME-OUT?
THAT DIM DINOSAUR SAVED YOUR BLEEDING ARSES!
TAKE THE ADVANTAGE!
IDIOTS!
HOW CAN THIS MANY PEOPLE ALL BE SUCH RUBBISH AT PLAYING A SIMPLE GAME?
IF WE WERE STILL UP THERE--
BUT WE'RE NOT, ARE WE?
NO...
...WE'RE DOWN HERE WITH ALL THE BUTTONS.
BOO-DOOP
INSECT SWARM
NAPALM WIND
WELL PLAYED, MR. ARCADE...

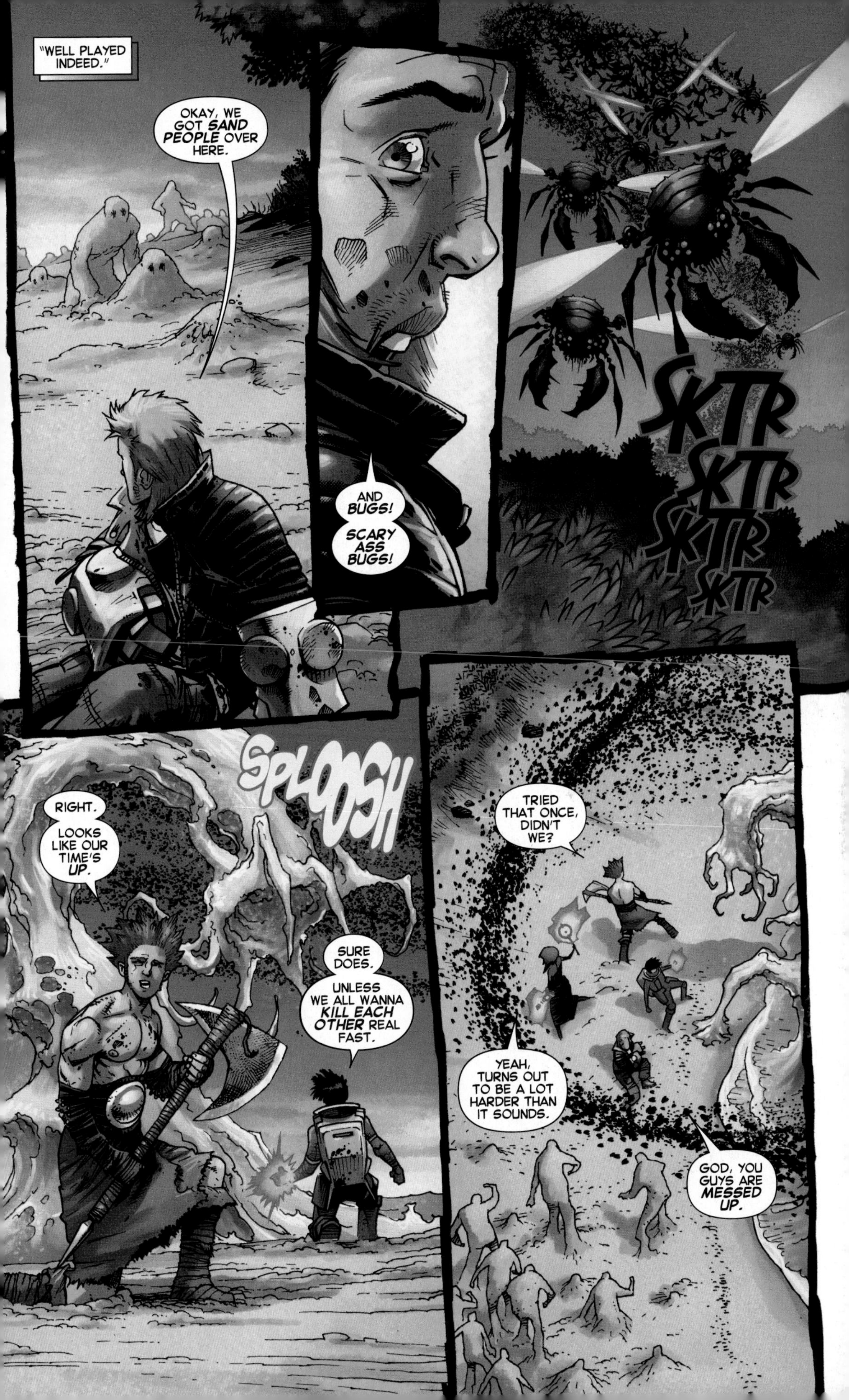
"WELL PLAYED INDEED."
OKAY, WE GOT SAND PEOPLE OVER HERE.
AND BUGS!
SCARY ASS BUGS!
SKTR SKTR SKTR SKTR
SPLOOSH
RIGHT.
LOOKS LIKE OUR TIME'S UP.
SURE DOES.
UNLESS WE ALL WANNA KILL EACH OTHER REAL FAST.
TRIED THAT ONCE, DIDN'T WE?
YEAH, TURNS OUT TO BE A LOT HARDER THAN IT SOUNDS.
GOD, YOU GUYS ARE MESSED UP.

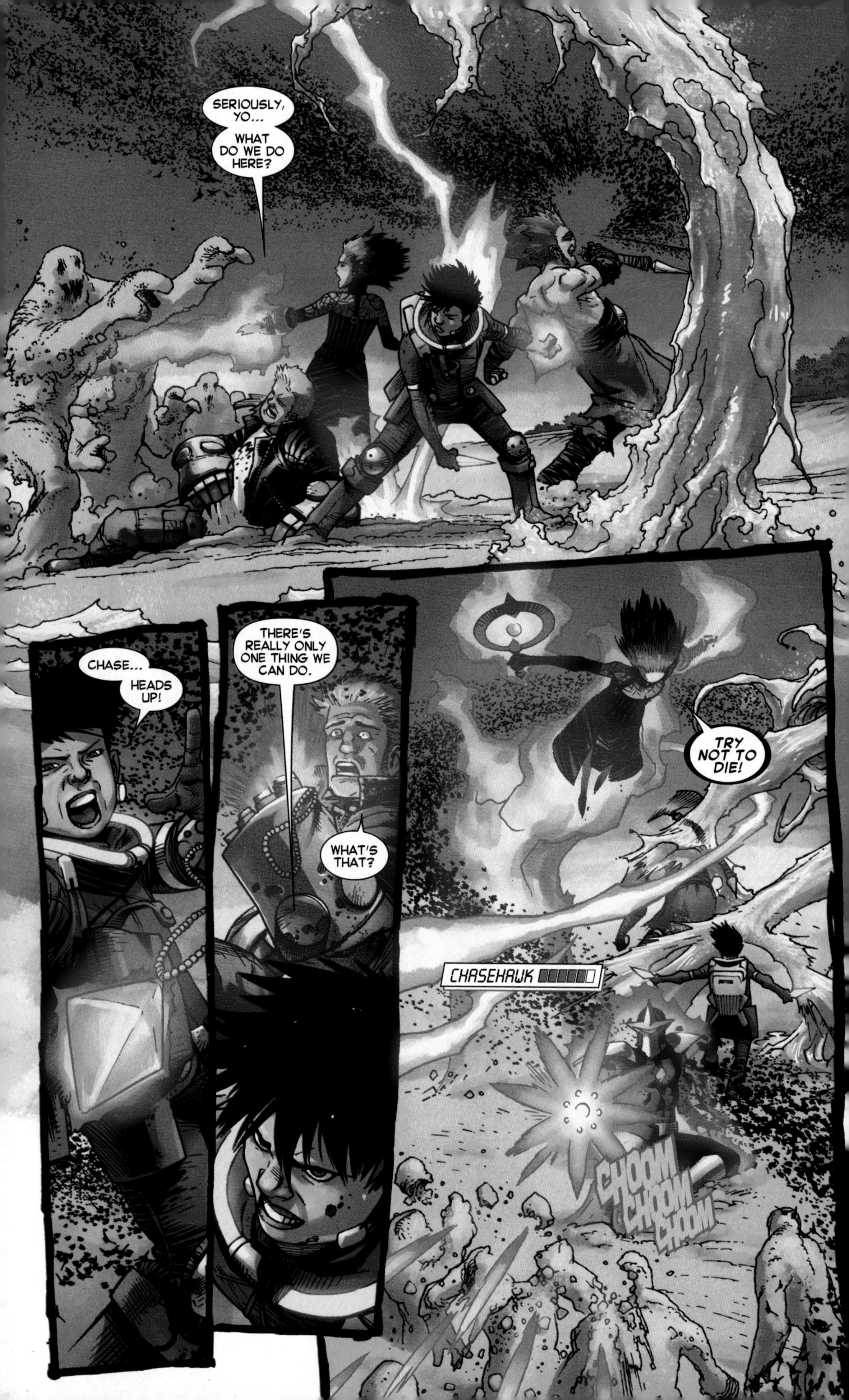
SERIOUSLY, YO...
WHAT DO WE DO HERE?
CHASE... HEADS UP!
THERE'S REALLY ONLY ONE THING WE CAN DO.
WHAT'S THAT?
TRY NOT TO DIE!
CHASEHAWK
CHOOM CHOOM CHOOM

THAT'S *BETTER*, ISN'T IT?

YOU KNOW, DEATH LOCKET...

...THE HARDEST PART OF ENDING ALL THIS IS GOING TO BE *YOU.*

FOR THIS SOLE SURVIVOR PLOY TO *WORK*...

FOR ME TO LEAVE HERE WITH MY GOOD NAME...

I'LL HAVE TO KILL *YOU* AS WELL.

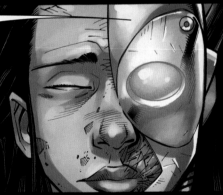

SHAME, THAT. WHO WANTS TO LOSE HER FAVORITE *TOY?*

I'M...

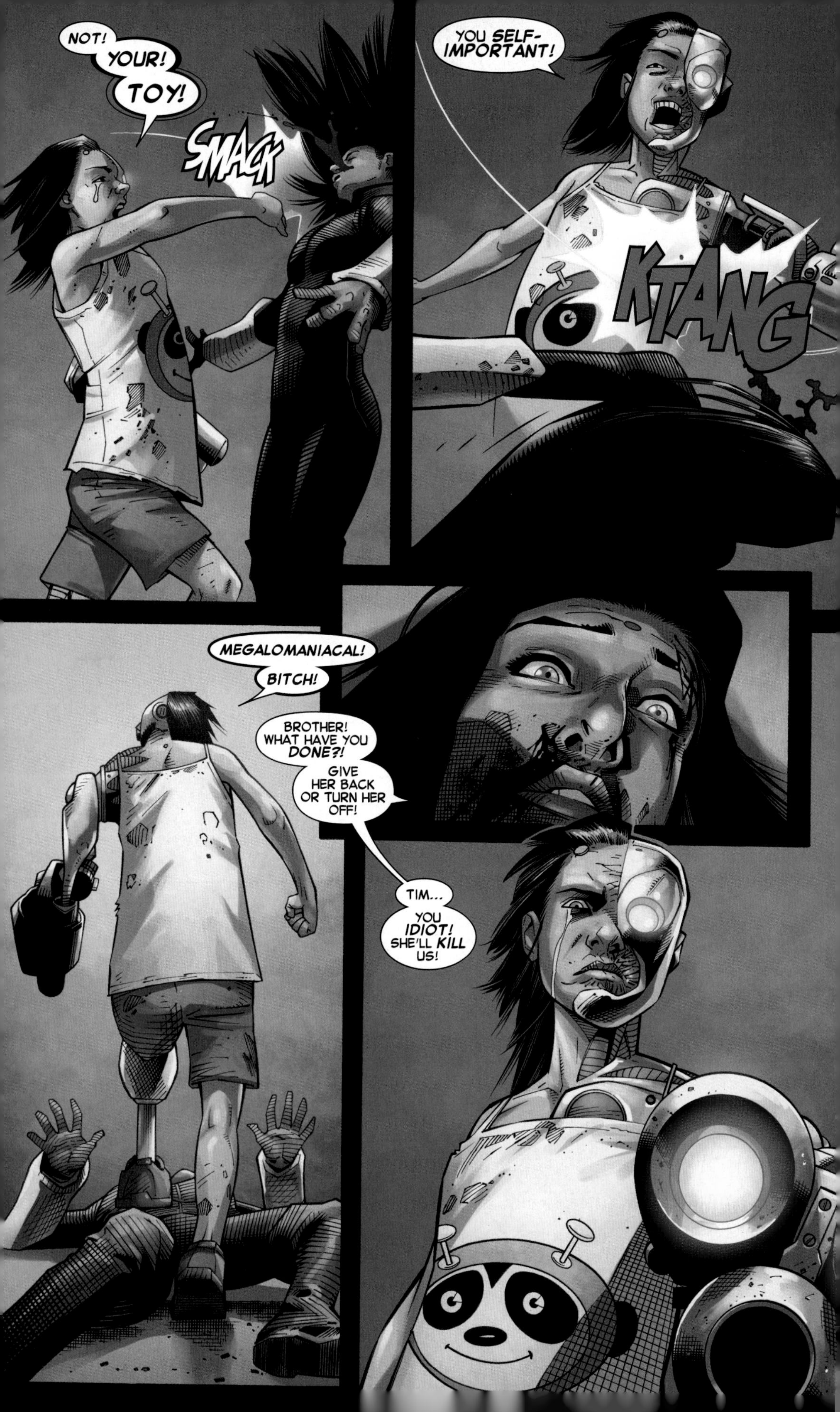
NOT!
YOUR!
TOY!
SMACK
YOU SELF-IMPORTANT!
KTANG
MEGALOMANIACAL!
BITCH!
BROTHER! WHAT HAVE YOU DONE?!
GIVE HER BACK OR TURN HER OFF!
TIM...
YOU IDIOT! SHE'LL KILL US!

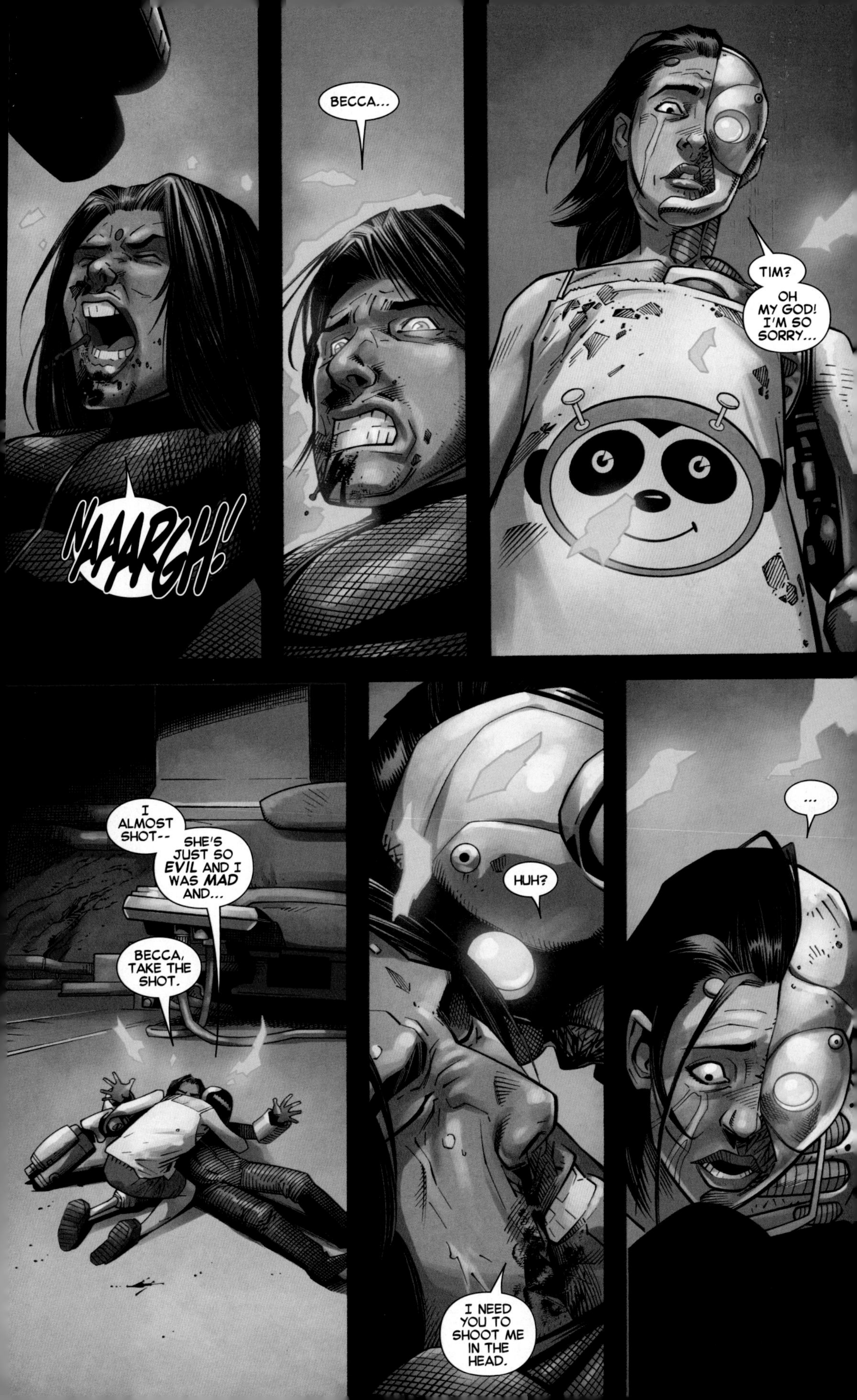
NAAAARGH!
BECCA...
TIM?
OH MY GOD! I'M SO SORRY...
I ALMOST SHOT--
SHE'S JUST SO EVIL AND I WAS MAD AND...
BECCA, TAKE THE SHOT.
HUH?
I NEED YOU TO SHOOT ME IN THE HEAD.
...

NO.

I'M AFRAID IT'S THE *ONLY* WAY.

NO IT'S *NOT*! WE CAN GO SHUT IT ALL DOWN AND THEN--

I CAN'T *MOVE*. I CAN'T *WALK*.

SHE'S SO MUCH *STRONGER* THAN I AM...IT'S TAKING *ALL* I HAVE TO HOLD HER DOWN.

I WOULD NEVER ASK...

BUT IF YOU DON'T END THIS RIGHT NOW-- MY SISTER *WILL*.

TIM. I CAN'T.

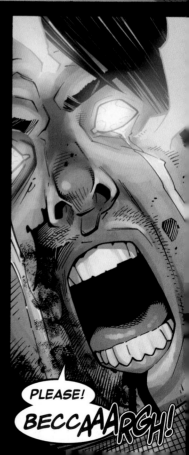

PLEASE! BECCAAAARGH!

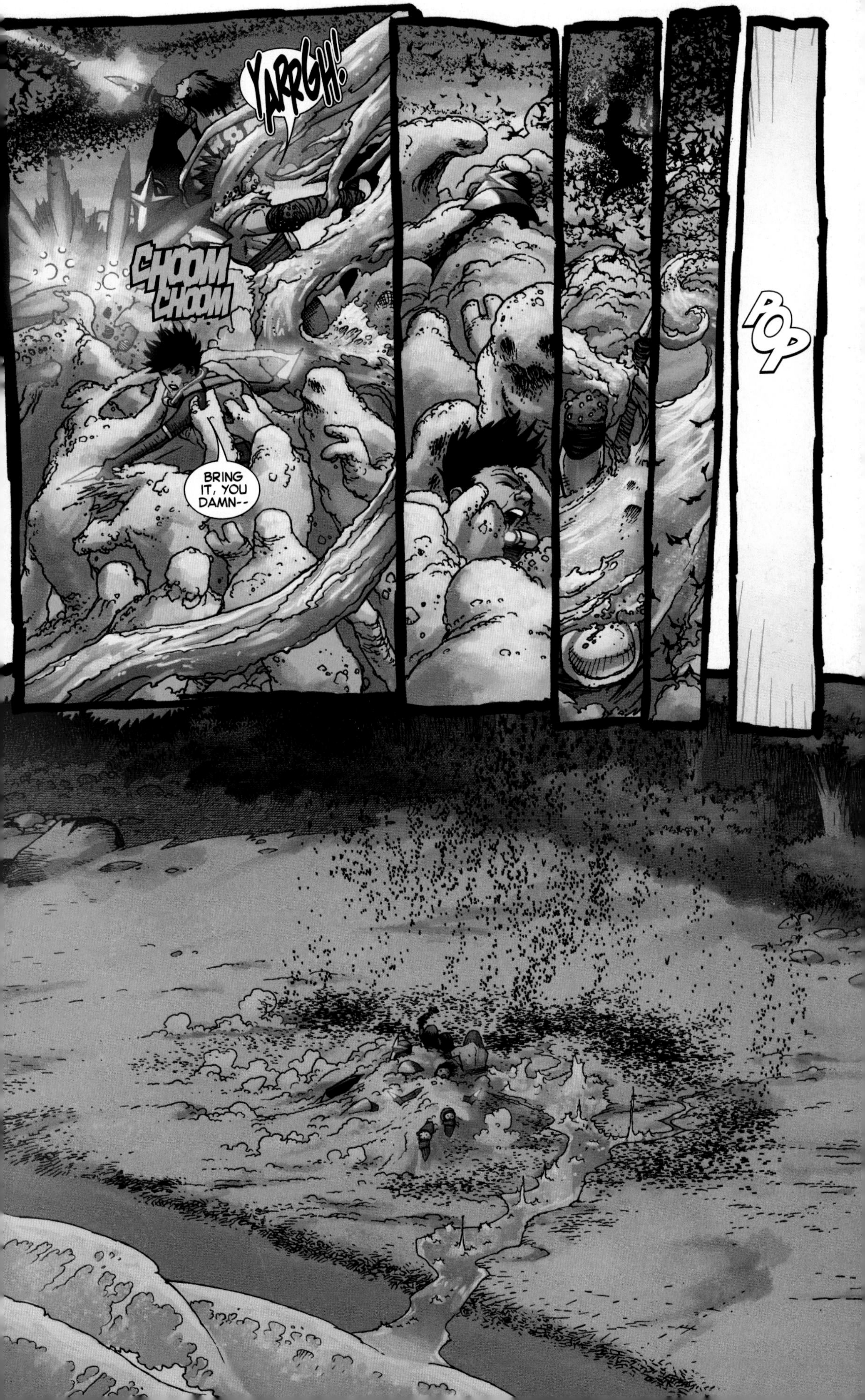

YARRGH!
CHOOM CHOOM
BRING IT, YOU DAMN--
POP

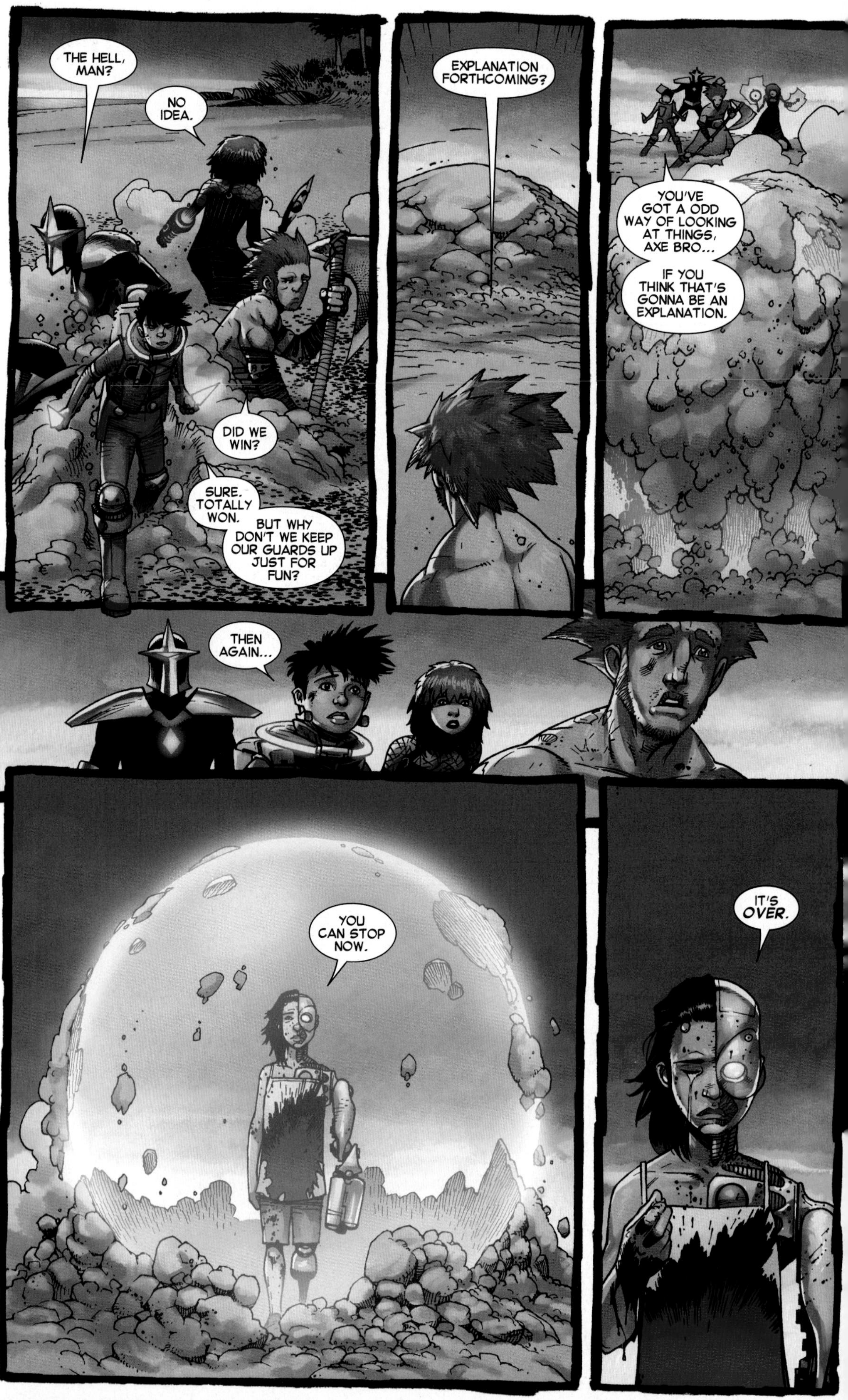
THE HELL, MAN?
NO IDEA.
DID WE WIN?
SURE. TOTALLY WON.
BUT WHY DON'T WE KEEP OUR GUARDS UP JUST FOR FUN?
EXPLANATION FORTHCOMING?
YOU'VE GOT A ODD WAY OF LOOKING AT THINGS, AXE BRO...
IF YOU THINK THAT'S GONNA BE AN EXPLANATION.
THEN AGAIN...
YOU CAN STOP NOW.
IT'S OVER.

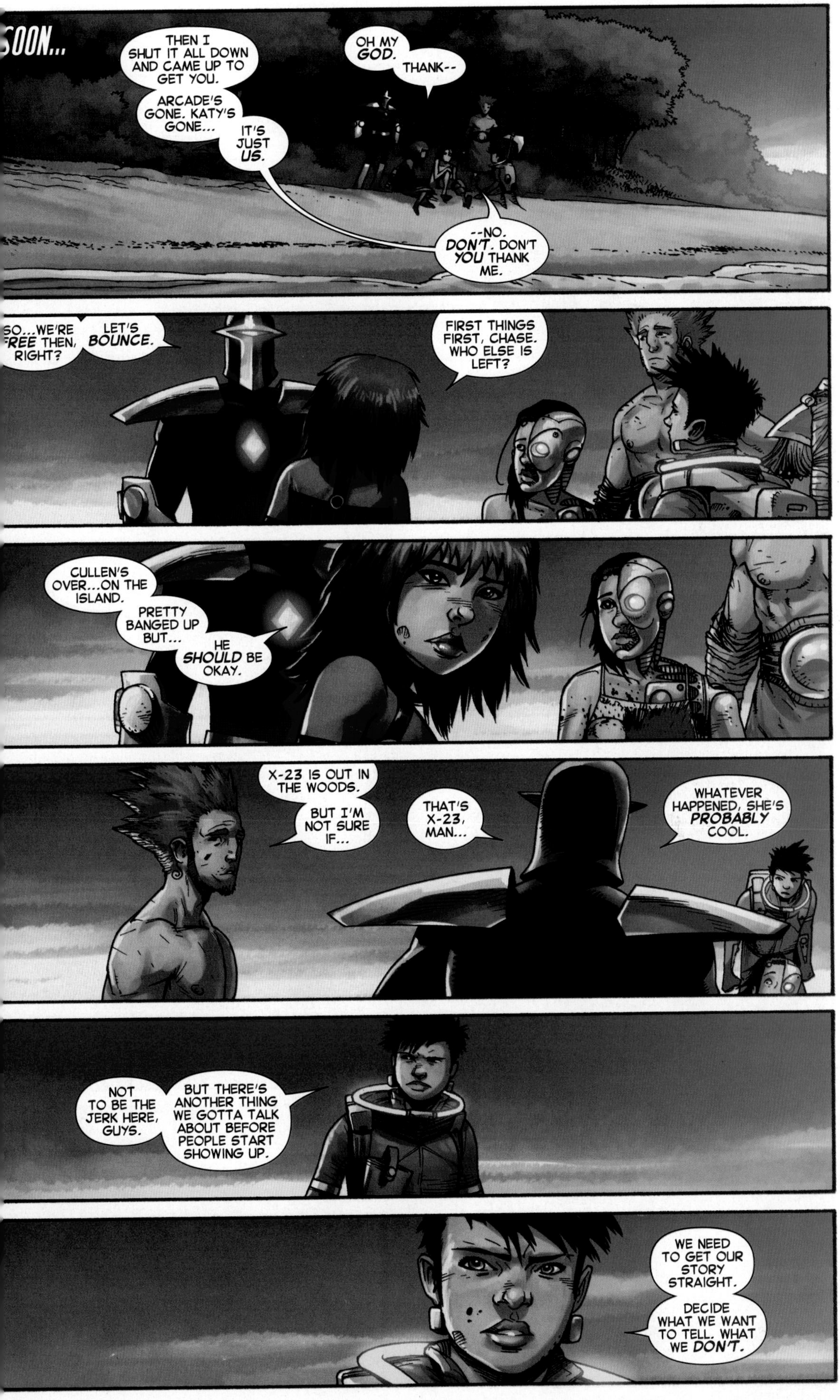
SOON...
THEN I SHUT IT ALL DOWN AND CAME UP TO GET YOU.
ARCADE'S GONE. KATY'S GONE...
IT'S JUST *US*.
OH MY *GOD*.
THANK--
--NO. *DON'T*. DON'T *YOU* THANK ME.
SO...WE'RE *FREE* THEN, RIGHT?
LET'S *BOUNCE*.
FIRST THINGS FIRST, CHASE. WHO ELSE IS LEFT?
CULLEN'S OVER...ON THE ISLAND.
PRETTY BANGED UP BUT...
HE *SHOULD* BE OKAY.
X-23 IS OUT IN THE WOODS.
BUT I'M NOT SURE IF...
THAT'S X-23, MAN...
WHATEVER HAPPENED, SHE'S *PROBABLY* COOL.
NOT TO BE THE JERK HERE, GUYS.
BUT THERE'S ANOTHER THING WE GOTTA TALK ABOUT BEFORE PEOPLE START SHOWING UP.
WE NEED TO GET OUR STORY STRAIGHT.
DECIDE WHAT WE WANT TO TELL. WHAT WE *DON'T*.

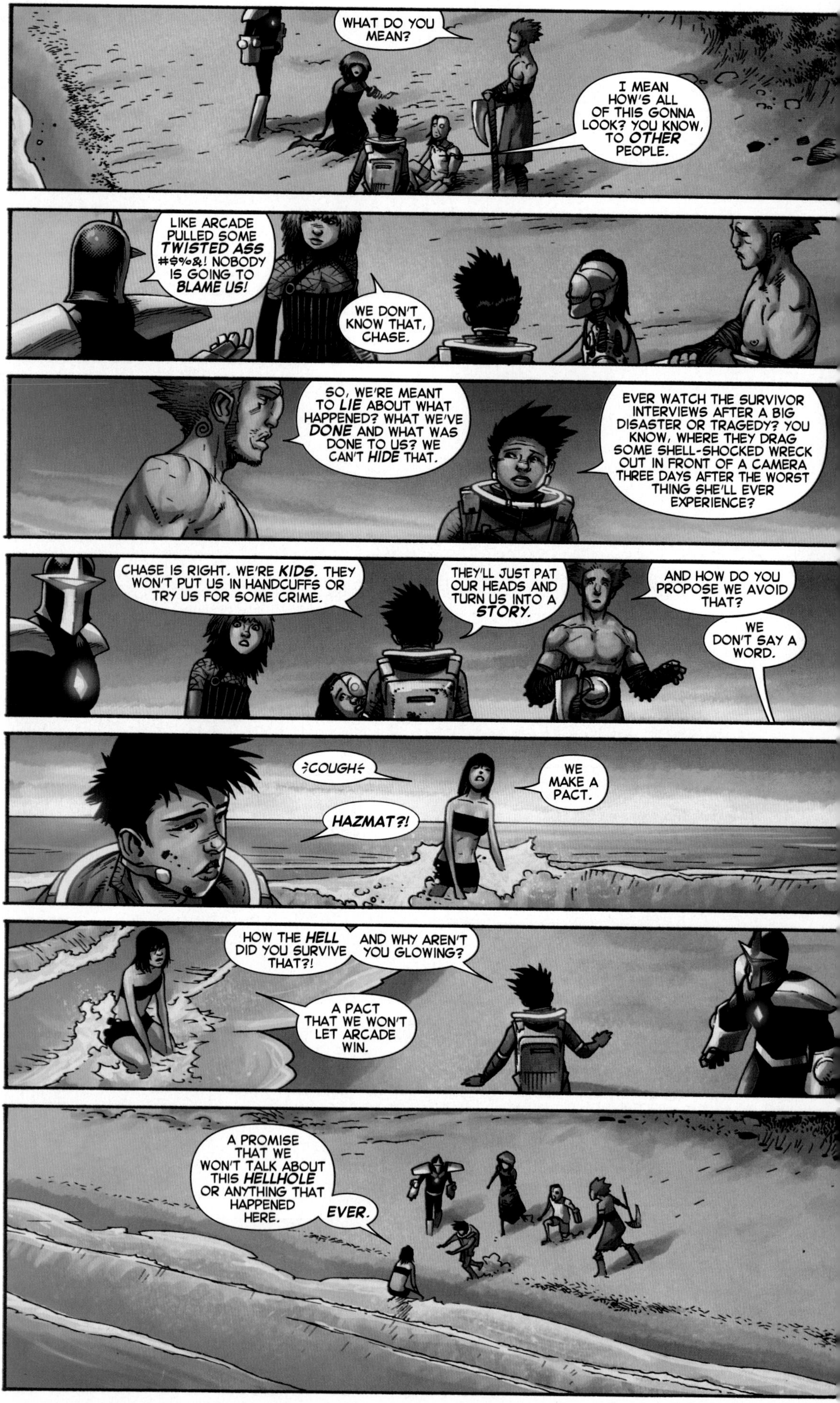

WHAT DO YOU MEAN?
I MEAN HOW'S ALL OF THIS GONNA LOOK? YOU KNOW, TO *OTHER* PEOPLE.
LIKE ARCADE PULLED SOME *TWISTED ASS* #$%&! NOBODY IS GOING TO *BLAME US!*
WE DON'T KNOW THAT, CHASE.
SO, WE'RE MEANT TO *LIE* ABOUT WHAT HAPPENED? WHAT WE'VE *DONE* AND WHAT WAS DONE TO US? WE CAN'T *HIDE* THAT.
EVER WATCH THE SURVIVOR INTERVIEWS AFTER A BIG DISASTER OR TRAGEDY? YOU KNOW, WHERE THEY DRAG SOME SHELL-SHOCKED WRECK OUT IN FRONT OF A CAMERA THREE DAYS AFTER THE WORST THING SHE'LL EVER EXPERIENCE?
CHASE IS RIGHT. WE'RE *KIDS.* THEY WON'T PUT US IN HANDCUFFS OR TRY US FOR SOME CRIME.
THEY'LL JUST PAT OUR HEADS AND TURN US INTO A *STORY.*
AND HOW DO YOU PROPOSE WE AVOID THAT?
WE DON'T SAY A WORD.
COUGH
WE MAKE A PACT.
HAZMAT?!
HOW THE *HELL* DID YOU SURVIVE THAT?!
AND WHY AREN'T YOU GLOWING?
A PACT THAT WE WON'T LET ARCADE WIN.
A PROMISE THAT WE WON'T TALK ABOUT THIS *HELLHOLE* OR ANYTHING THAT HAPPENED HERE.
EVER.

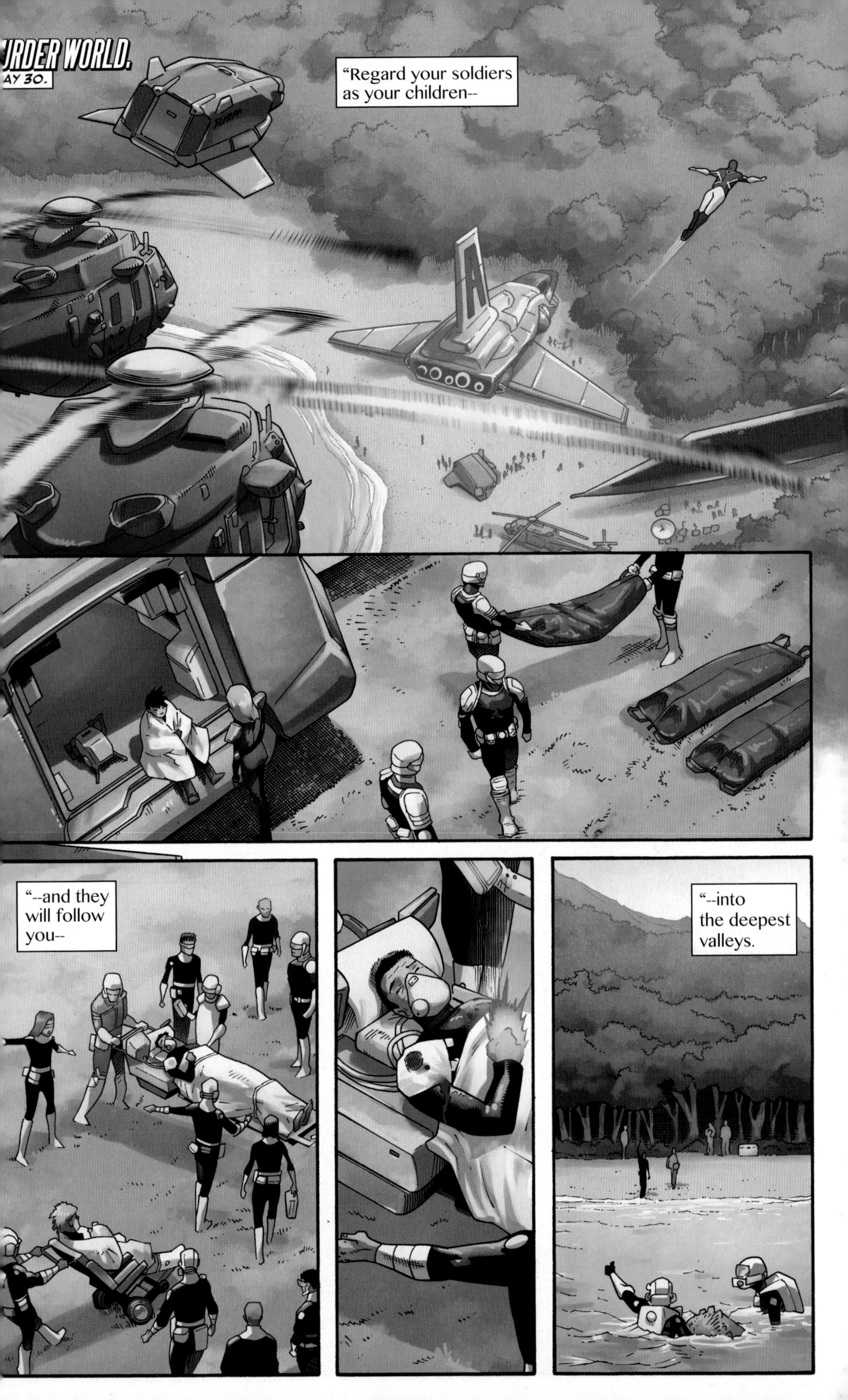
URDER WORLD.
AY 30.
"Regard your soldiers as your children--
"--and they will follow you--
"--into the deepest valleys.

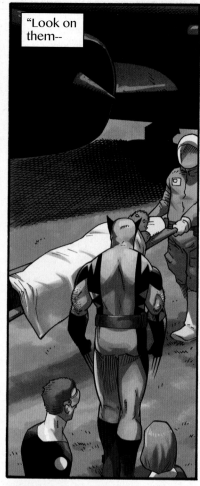

"Look on them--

"--as your own beloved sons--

"--and they will stand by you--

"--even unto death."
- *Sun Tzu, The Art of War*

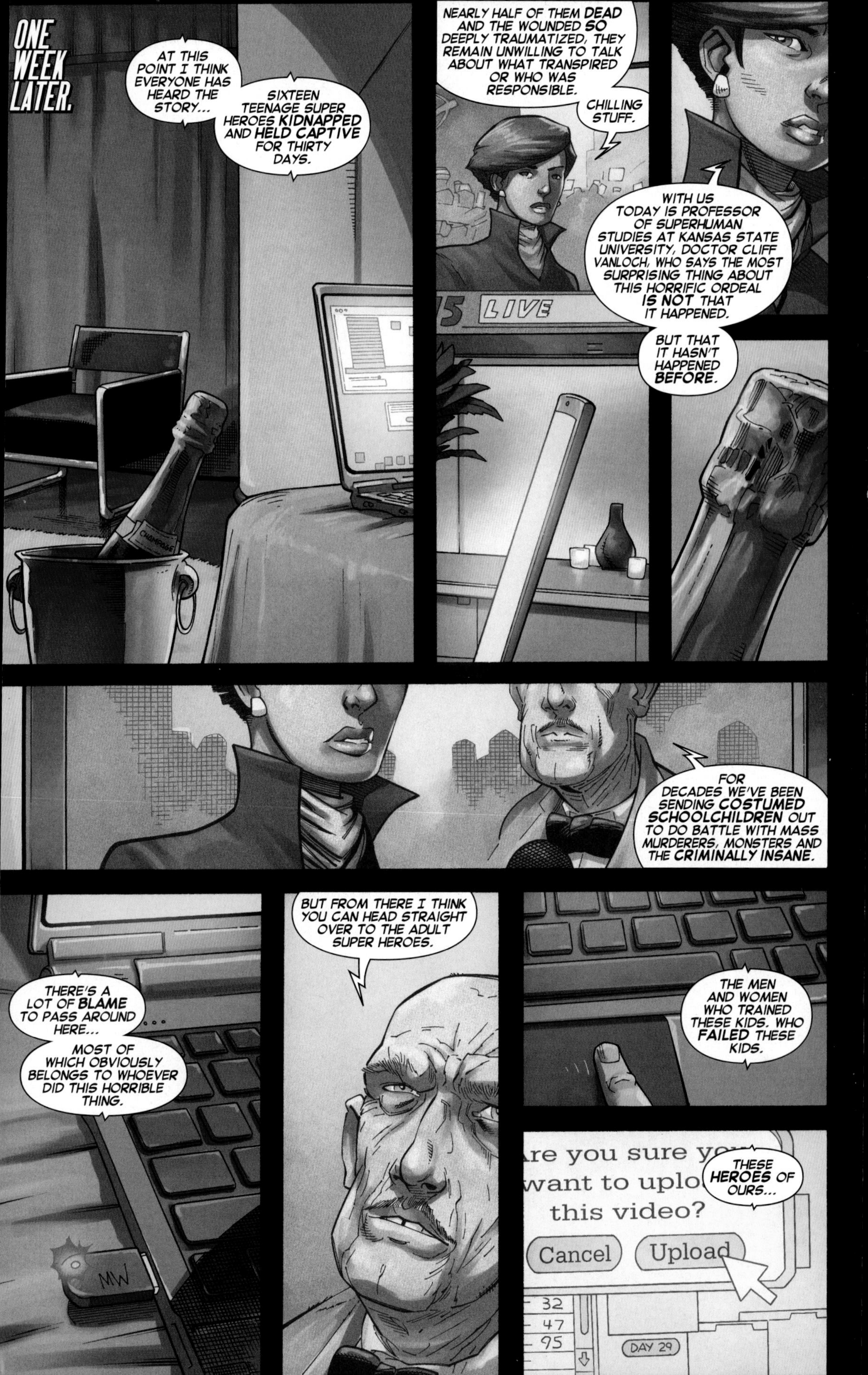
ONE WEEK LATER.
AT THIS POINT I THINK EVERYONE HAS HEARD THE STORY...
SIXTEEN TEENAGE SUPER HEROES KIDNAPPED AND HELD CAPTIVE FOR THIRTY DAYS.
NEARLY HALF OF THEM DEAD AND THE WOUNDED SO DEEPLY TRAUMATIZED, THEY REMAIN UNWILLING TO TALK ABOUT WHAT TRANSPIRED OR WHO WAS RESPONSIBLE.
CHILLING STUFF.
LIVE
WITH US TODAY IS PROFESSOR OF SUPERHUMAN STUDIES AT KANSAS STATE UNIVERSITY, DOCTOR CLIFF VANLOCH, WHO SAYS THE MOST SURPRISING THING ABOUT THIS HORRIFIC ORDEAL IS NOT THAT IT HAPPENED.
BUT THAT IT HASN'T HAPPENED BEFORE.
FOR DECADES WE'VE BEEN SENDING COSTUMED SCHOOLCHILDREN OUT TO DO BATTLE WITH MASS MURDERERS, MONSTERS AND THE CRIMINALLY INSANE.
THERE'S A LOT OF BLAME TO PASS AROUND HERE...
MOST OF WHICH OBVIOUSLY BELONGS TO WHOEVER DID THIS HORRIBLE THING.
BUT FROM THERE I THINK YOU CAN HEAD STRAIGHT OVER TO THE ADULT SUPER HEROES.
THE MEN AND WOMEN WHO TRAINED THESE KIDS. WHO FAILED THESE KIDS.
THESE HEROES OF OURS...
this video?
Cancel
Upload
32
47
95
DAY 29

THEY SHOULD BE ASHAMED OF THEMSELVES.

AND HOW.

BE-DOOP

POP

What Really Happened In Murder World? 1/30.

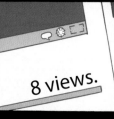

8 views.

16 views.

Full disclosure, AVENGERS ARENA isn't the book I wanted to write. Not at all. 18-issues later, that sounds unbelievably stupid to my ear. But it's the truth.

RUNAWAYS is my all time favorite Marvel comic. I'm an unabashed Veronica Mars super fan and I've seen every episode of Friday Night Lights four times. When editor Bill Rosemann asked me to pitch a teenage super hero book, my mind went to angsty relationships drama and mean girl bullying, not murder and fights to the death. And that's exactly what I pitched, straight teen drama set in a super hero school. It was my dream project.

That dream ended about two weeks later when Bill showed our pitch to Axel Alonso and Tom Brevoort. Instead of giving us notes or saying I could go to script, Tom and Axel pointed to a couple sentences near the end of the pitch that outlined what would have been our third arc. It was something about our kids competing in a tournament with other Marvel Universe schools that turns into a death match when a super villain takes control. The Triwizard Tournament meets The Hunger Games. Tom and Axel pointed to those two sentences and said, "There's your story. Just do that."

I never told this part of the story before, but I hated the idea. Instead of my dream project, they wanted me to do a Battle Royale homage? Were they serious? Could they really expect me to

stretch that half-baked notion into an ongoing series? And what about the teen drama I'd been so excited to write? Where was that going to fit? This was terrible and I didn't want to do it.

Turns out I've never been more wrong. Axel and Tom saw the potential in that seed of an idea. They understood the inherent drama and overwhelming stakes a story like this would provide. They knew the story we needed to tell, long before I did. I'll never thank them enough for pointing it out or Bill for talking me into giving it a shot.

The first thing I did after finishing the script for this final issue of ARENA was email Bill Rosemann to thank him. This book has been the highlight of my career. At times it was extremely taxing to write, but I've never been more proud to have my name on a cover. I'd like to thank Bill one last time for giving me the opportunity and sticking by me while I figured it all out. He's the straw that stirs the drink.

While I'm thanking people, no one has contributed more to this book than Kev Walker. From the pitch perfect drama in each facial expression to the fact that every action sequence looks better on the page than it did in my head, he made the book better with every stroke of his pencil. We straight up could not have done this without him.

But Kev didn't do it alone. We've been blessed with an incredible art and production

team since day one. Frank Martin, Rain Beredo and Jean-Francois Beaulieu made the book sing with their incredible colors. Alessandro Vitti, Riccardo Burchelli, Karl Moline, Jason Gorder, Mark Pennington and Rick Magyar brought their inimitable artistic talents to our insane 18 issues a year schedule. Christos Gage stepped in to give me a breather with his thoughtful look at the outside world in issue #13. Joe Caramagna both lettered the book beautifully and managed to go #18 issues without cursing my nitpicky post-lettering rewrites. And assistant editor Jon Moisan has helped keep all of our plates spinning at once.

Finally, I have to thank all of you, our readers. You guys are the reason the book made it to this conclusion. You took a chance on this series that everyone wanted to hate. You reached out and wrote us letters, expressing at first your fear and apprehension then later your appreciation. You let us change your minds and argued with those who refused to do the same. AVENGERS ARENA is your book. Thank you all so much for letting me write it.

Dennis Hopeless
Kansas City, MO
October 2013

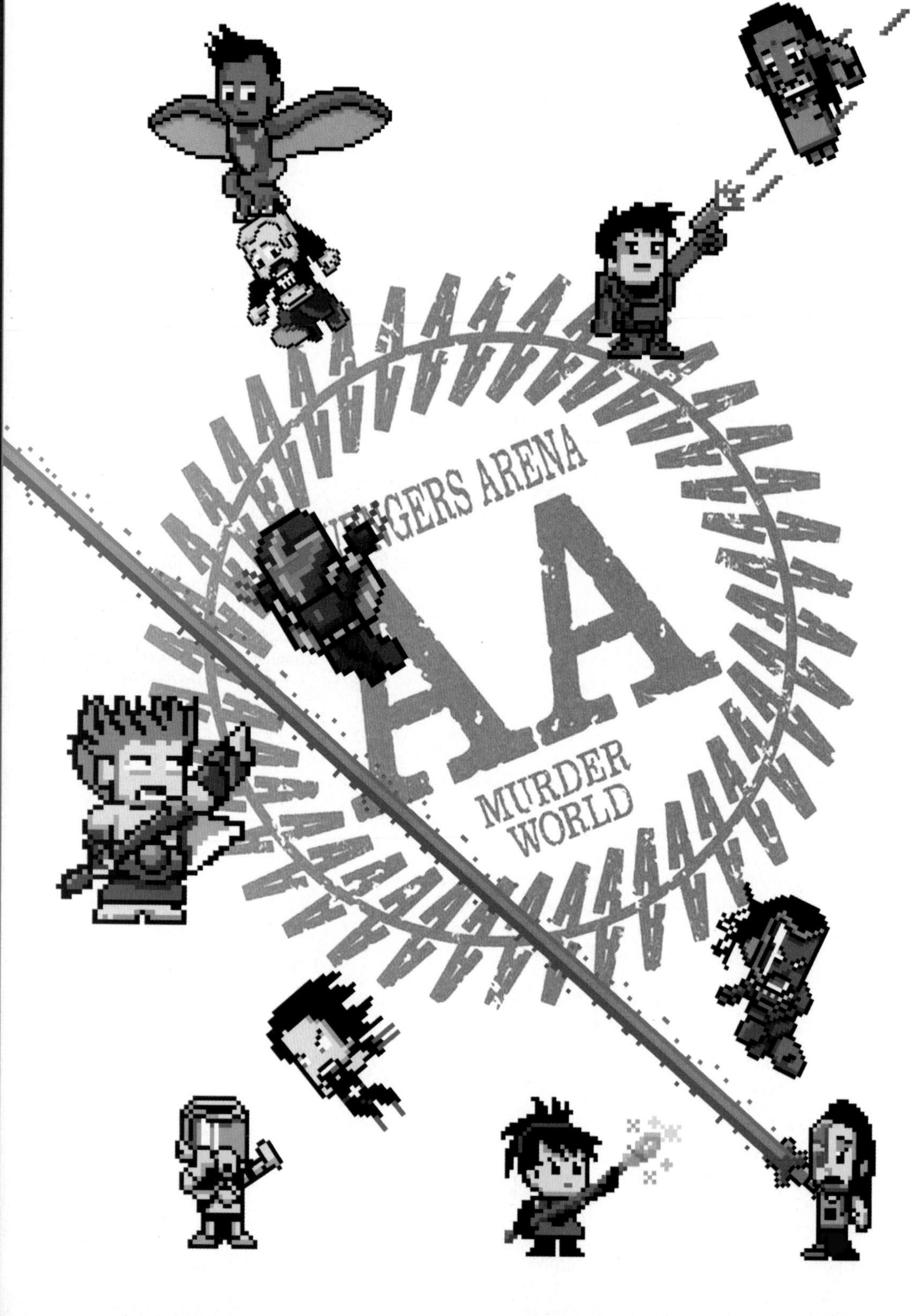
GERS ARENA
AA
MURDER
WORLD

COVER PROCESS BY MIKE DEODATO

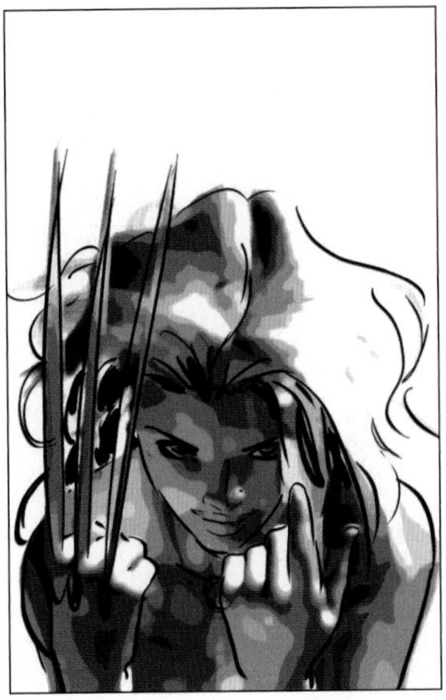

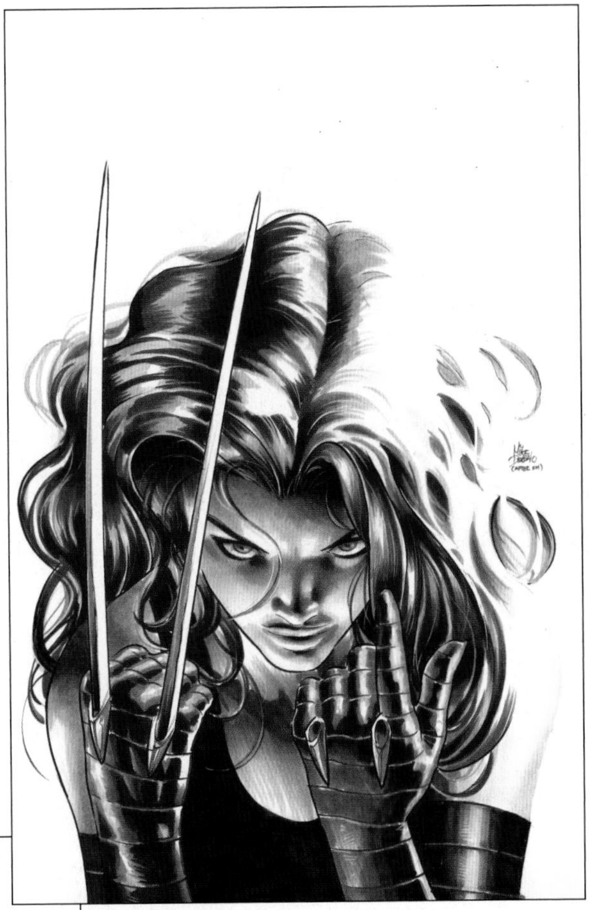

ISSUE #14, SKETCH & PENCILS

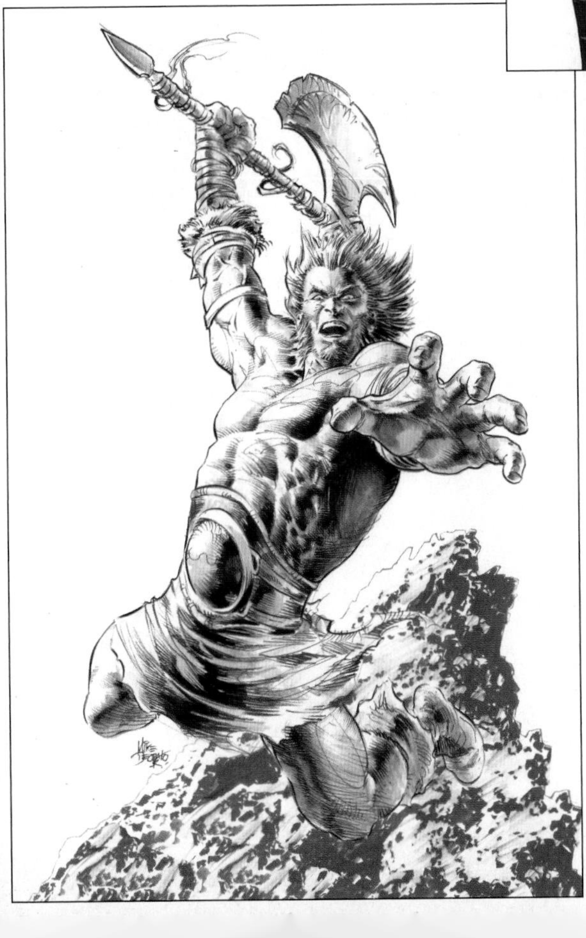

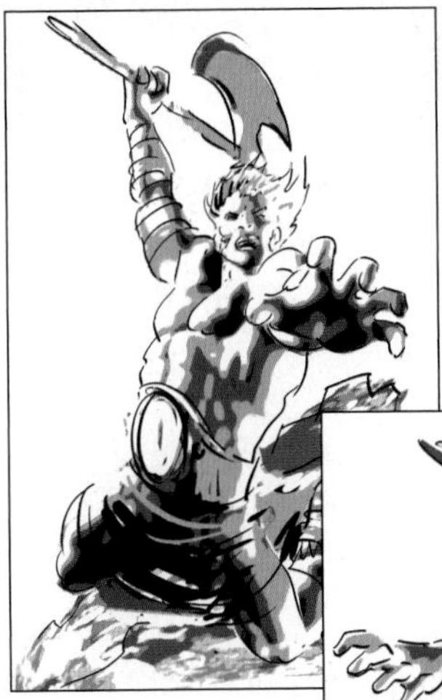

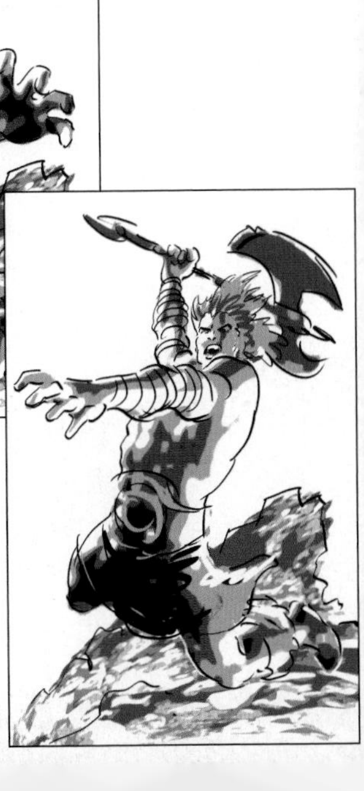

ISSUE #15, SKETCHES & PENCILS

COVER PROCESS BY FRANCESCO FRANCAVILLA

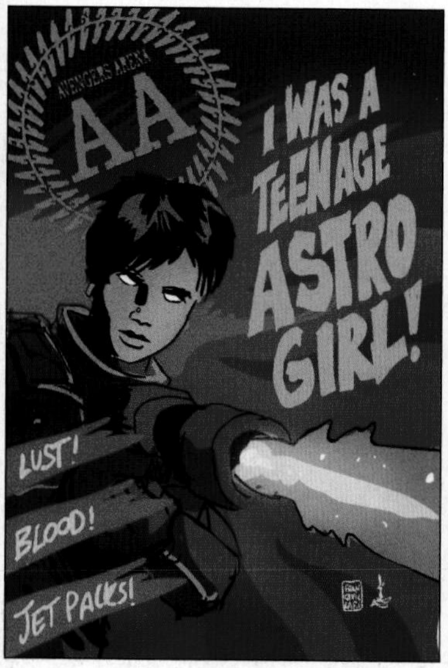
AVENGERS ARENA
AA
I WAS A TEENAGE ASTRO GIRL!
LUST!
BLOOD!
JET PACKS!

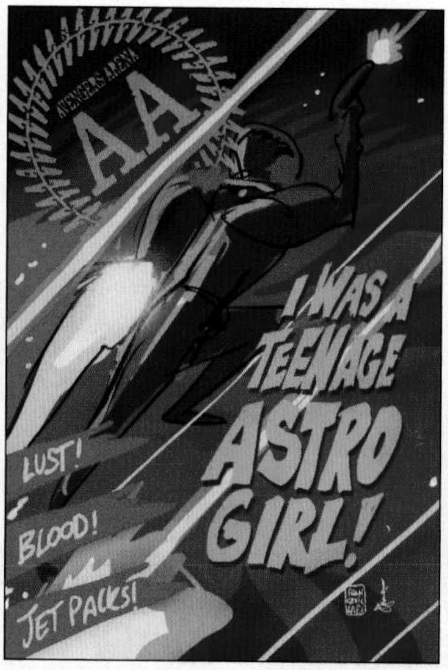
AVENGERS ARENA
AA
I WAS A TEENAGE ASTRO GIRL!
LUST!
BLOOD!
JET PACKS!

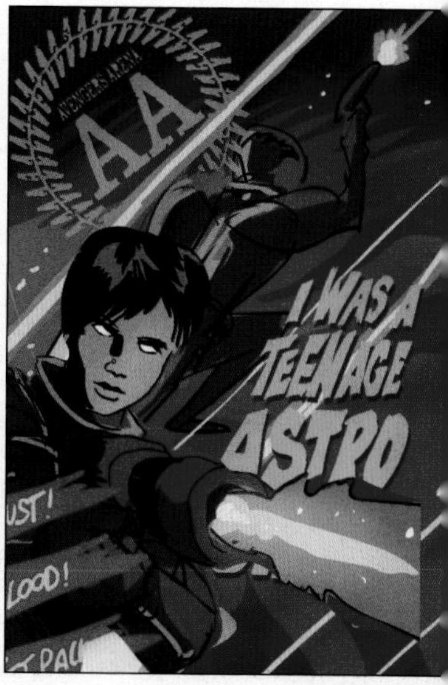
AVENGERS ARENA
AA
I WAS A TEENAGE ASTRO

ISSUE #16,
SKETCHES & FINAL

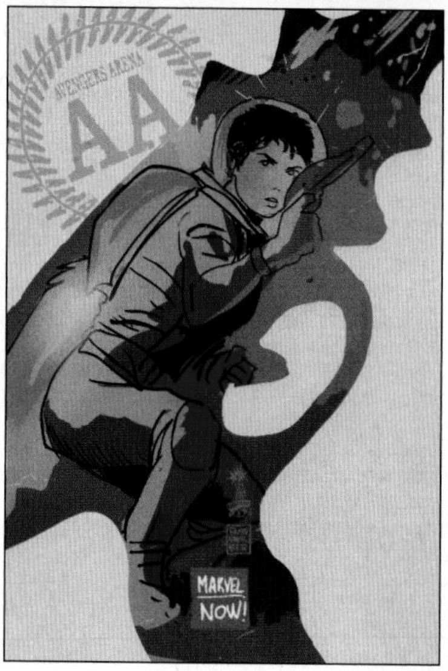
AVENGERS ARENA
AA
MARVEL NOW!

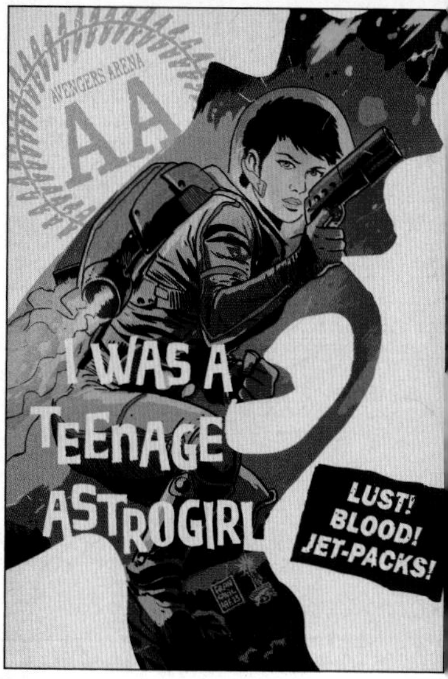
AVENGERS ARENA
AA
I WAS A TEENAGE ASTROGIRL
LUST! BLOOD! JET-PACKS!

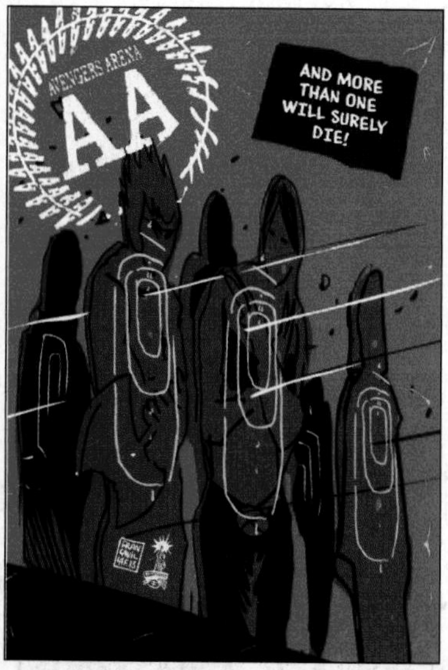
AVENGERS ARENA
AA
AND MORE THAN ONE WILL SURELY DIE!

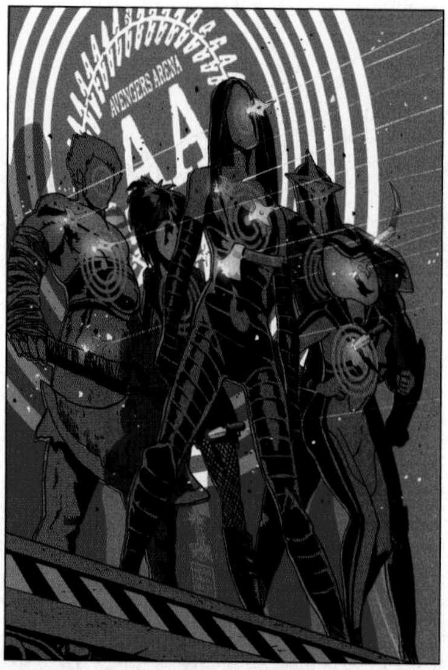
AVENGERS ARENA
AA

ISSUE #17,
SKETCHES & FINAL

ART PROCESS BY KEV WALKER & JASON GORDER

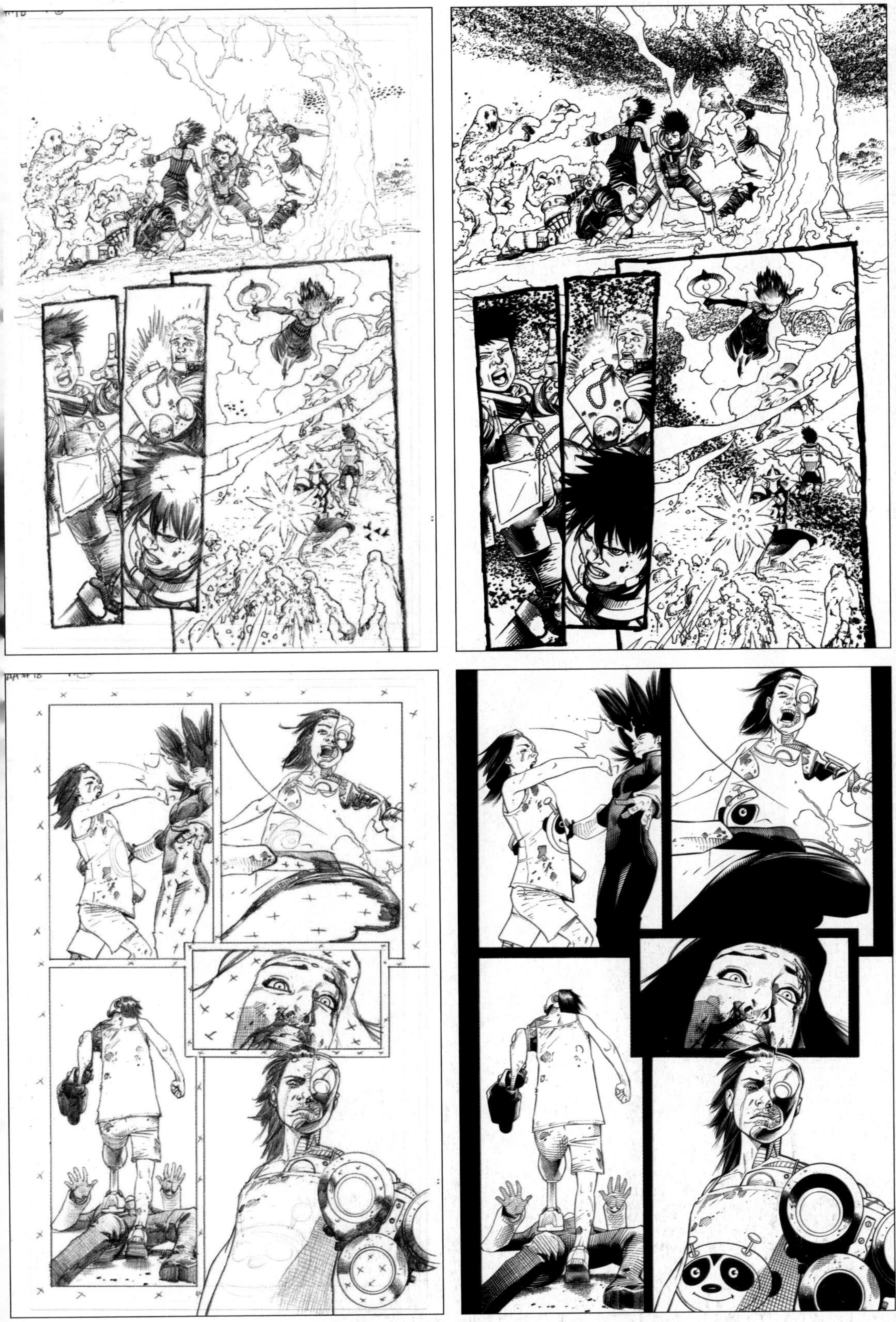

ISSUE #8, PAGES 8 & 10 PENCILS & INKS